ELEMENTARY LESSONS IN LOGIC.

ELEMENTARY LESSONS
IN LOGIC:

DEDUCTIVE AND INDUCTIVE.

WITH COPIOUS QUESTIONS AND EXAMPLES.

AND

A VOCABULARY OF LOGICAL TERMS.

BY

W. STANLEY JEVONS, M.A.

PROFESSOR OF LOGIC IN OWENS COLLEGE, MANCHESTER.

NEW EDITION.

London and New York:

MACMILLAN AND CO.

1888.

PREFACE.

IN preparing these Lessons I have attempted to show that Logic, even in its traditional form, can be made a highly useful subject of study, and a powerful means of mental exercise. With this view I have avoided the use of superfluous technical terms, and have abstained from entering into questions of a purely speculative or metaphysical character. For the puerile illustrations too often found in works on Logic I have generally substituted examples drawn from the distinct objects and ideas treated in the natural and experimental sciences; and in this and other respects have aimed at rendering these Lessons a suitable companion to a series of science school-books.

Logic is not only an exact science, but is the most simple and elementary of all sciences; it ought therefore undoubtedly to find some place in every course of education. The relations of propositions and the forms of argument present as precise a subject of instruction and as vigorous an exercise of thought, as the properties of geometrical figures, or the rules of Algebra. Yet every school-boy is made to learn mathematical problems which he will never employ in after life, and is left in total ignorance of those simple principles and forms of reasoning which will enter into the thoughts of every hour. Logic should no longer be considered an elegant and learned accomplishment; it should take its place as an indispensable study for every well-informed person. These Lessons I trust will introduce to the science many who have not leisure or inclination to read more elaborate treatises, and many who would not be attracted by the numerous but somewhat dry and brief compendiums published in past years.

It is desirable that Lessons in Logic should be made the basis of many exercises, and for this purpose I have supplied abundance of questions and examples at the end of the book, some of which are selected from the examination papers of the Oxford,

London, and Edinburgh Universities. In my own classes I have constantly found that the working and solution of logical questions, the examination of argu-ments and the detection of fallacies, is a not less practicable and useful exercise of mind than is the performance of calculations, and the solution of pro-blems in a mathematical class.

Except in a few places, where special notice is given, I have abstained from putting forward any views not commonly accepted by teachers of logic; and I have throughout devoted more attention to describing clearly and simply the doctrines in which logicians generally agree, than discussing the points in which there is a difference of opinion. The recent logical discoveries of Sir W. Hamilton, Archbishop Thomson, Prof. de Morgan, and especially the late Prof. Boole, cannot yet be fully adopted in an ele-mentary work, but I have attempted to give a clear notion of the results to which they inevitably lead.

In the latter Lessons which treat of Induction I have generally followed Sir John Herschel, Dr Whewell and Mr J. S. Mill, as the recognised authorities on the subject. These Lessons in fact may be regarded as an easy introduction to some of the most important parts of Mr Mill's treatise on Logic.

PREFACE.

At the end of almost every Lesson will be found references to the works in which the student will most profitably continue his reading of the subject treated, so that this little volume may serve as a guide to a more extended course of study.

TABLE OF CONTENTS.

SYLLOGISM.

FALLACIES.

RECENT LOGICAL VIEWS.

METHOD.

INDUCTION.

INTRODUCTION.

LESSON I.

DEFINITION AND SPHERE OF THE SCIENCE.

LOGIC may be most briefly defined as the **Science of Reasoning.** It is more commonly defined, however, as the **Science of the Laws of Thought,** and some logicians think it desirable to specify still more accurately that it is the Science of the Formal, or of the Necessary Laws of Thought. Before these definitions can be of any real use to us we must come to a clear understanding as to the meaning of the expressions; and it will probably appear that there is no great difference between them.

By a **Law of Thought** we mean a certain uniformity or agreement which exists and must exist in the modes in which all persons think and reason, so long as they do not make what we call mistakes, or fall into self-contradiction and fallacy. The laws of thought are natural laws with which we have no power to interfere, and which are of course not to be in any way confused with the artificial laws of a country, which are invented by men and can be altered by them. Every science is occupied in detecting and describing the natural laws which are inflexibly observed by the objects treated in the Science. The science of astronomy investigates the uniform or similar way in which the heavenly bodies, and in fact all material substances, tend to fall towards each other as a stone falls towards the earth, or to move round each other under the influence of this tendency. The universal law of gravitation is thus the natural law or uniformity treated in physical astronomy.

In chemistry the law of equivalent proportions describes the well ascertained fact that each chemical substance enters into combination with every other chemical substance only in certain definite proportions; as when exactly eight parts by weight of oxygen unite with one part of hydrogen to form water, or sixteen parts of oxygen and six parts of carbon unite to form carbonic acid in the ordinary burning of a flame or fire. Whenever we can detect uniformities or similarities we so far create science and arrive at natural laws. But there may be, and are, many things so fickle, complicated, and uncertain, that we can never be sure we have detected laws that they will uniformly obey; in such cases no science, in the proper sense of the word, is possible. There is no such thing, for instance, as a real science of human character, because the human mind is too variable and complicated a subject of investigation. There are no two persons so much alike that you may be sure of one acting in all circumstances as the other would; it thus becomes impossible to arrange persons in classes so that all who are in the same class shall act uniformly in the same manner in any given circumstances.

But there is a science of human reason or thought apart from the many other acts of mind which belong to human character, because there are modes in which all persons do uniformly think and reason, and must think and reason. Thus if two things are identical with a third common thing they are identical with each other. This is a law of thought of a very simple and obvious character, and we may observe concerning it,—

1. That all people think in accordance with it, and agree that they do so as soon as they understand its meaning.

2. That they think in accordance with it whatever may be the subject about which they are thinking.

Thus if the things considered are—

London,
The Metropolis,
The most populous city in Great Britain,

since "the Metropolis is identical with London," and "London is identical with the most populous city in Great Britain," it follows necessarily in all minds that "the metropolis is identical with the most populous city in Great Britain."

Again, if we compare the three following things—

Iron,
The most useful metal,
The cheapest metal,—

and it be allowed that " The most useful metal is Iron," and " Iron is the cheapest metal," it follows necessarily in all minds that "the most useful metal is the cheapest." We here have two examples of the general truth that things identical with the same thing are identical with each other; and this we may say is a general or necessary form of thought and reasoning.

Compare, again, the following three things,—

The earth,
Planets,
Bodies revolving in elliptic orbits.

We cannot say, as before, that "the earth is identical with the planets;" it is identical only with one of the planets, and we therefore say that "it is a planet." Similarly we may say that "the planets are bodies revolving in elliptic orbits," but only a part of the whole number so revolving. Nevertheless it follows that if the earth is among the planets, and the planets among bodies revolving in elliptic orbits, then the earth is among the latter.

A very elementary knowledge of chemistry enables us to argue similarly concerning the following ;—

> Iron,
> Metals,
> Elementary substances.

Iron is one of the metals, and metals are elements or simple undecomposable substances, in the sense of being among them or a part of them, but not as composing the whole. It follows necessarily that "Iron is one of the elementary substances." We have had then two examples of a fixed and necessary form of thought which is necessary and true whatever the things may be to which it is applied. The form of argument may be expressed in several different ways, and we shall have to consider it minutely in the lessons on the syllogism ; we may express it, for instance, by saying that "part of a part is part of the whole." Iron is part of the class of metals, which is part of the class of elements: hence iron is part of the class of elements.

If I now introduce another definition of Logic and say that it is "the science of the necessary forms of thought," the reader will I hope clearly apprehend the meaning of the expression "necessary forms of thought." A form is something which may remain uniform and unaltered, while the matter thrown into that form may be varied. Medals struck from the same dies have exactly the same form, but they may be of various matter, as bronze, copper, gold or silver. A building of exactly the same form might be constructed either of stone or bricks ; furniture of exactly similar shape may be made of oak, mahogany, walnut wood, etc. Just as we thus familiarly recognize the difference of form and substance in common tangible things, so we may observe in Logic, that the form of an argument is one thing, quite distinct from the various subjects or matter which may be treated in that form. We may almost exhibit to the eye the form of reasoning to which belong our two latter arguments, as follows :—

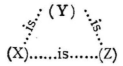

If within the three pairs of brackets, marked respectively X, Y and Z we place three names, such that the one in place of X may be said to come under that in Y, and that in Y under that in Z, then it necessarily follows that the first (X) comes under the last (Z).

Logic, then, is the science occupied in ascertaining and describing all the general forms of thought which we must employ so long as we reason validly. These forms are very numerous, although the principles on which they are constructed are few and simple. It will hence appear that logic is the most general of all the sciences. Its aid must be more often required than the aid of any other science, because all the particular sciences treat portions only of existing things, and create very different and often unconnected branches of knowledge. But logic treats of those principles and forms of thought which must be employed in every branch of knowledge. It treats of the very origin and foundations of knowledge itself ; and though it is true that the logical method employed in one science may differ somewhat from that em-

ployed in another science, yet whatever the particular
form may be, it must be logical, and must conform to the
laws of thought. There is in short something in which
all sciences must be similar; to which they must conform so long as they maintain what is true and self-
consistent; and the work of logic is to explain this
common basis of all science.

One name which has been given to Logic, namely the
Science of Sciences, very aptly describes the all extensive
power of logical principles. The cultivators of special
branches of knowledge appear to have been fully aware
of the allegiance they owe to the highest of the sciences,
for they have usually given names implying this allegiance. The very name of logic occurs as part of nearly
all the names recently adopted for the sciences, which are
often vulgarly called the " ologies," but are really the
"logics," the "o" being only a connecting vowel or part
of the previous word. Thus geology is logic applied to
explain the formation of the earth's crust; biology is logic
applied to the phenomena of life; psychology is logic
applied to the nature of the mind; and the same is the
case with physiology, entomology, zoology, teratology,
morphology, anthropology, theology, ecclesiology, thalat-
tology, and the rest*. Each science is thus distinctly
confessed to be a special logic. The name of logic itself
is derived from the common Greek word λόγος, which
usually means *word*, or the sign and outward manifesta-
tion of any inward thought. But the same word was also
used to denote the inward thought or reasoning of which
words are the expression, and it is thus probably that later
Greek writers on reasoning were led to call their science

---

* Except Philology, which is differently formed, and means
the love or study of words; the name of this science, if formed
upon the same plan, would be *logology*.

ἐπιστήμη λογική, or logical science ; also τέχνη λογική, or logical art. The adjective λογική, being used alone, soon came to be the name of the science, just as Mathematic, Rhetoric, and other names ending in " ic" were originally adjectives but have been converted into substantives.

Much discussion of a somewhat trifling character has arisen upon the question whether Logic should be considered a science only, an art only, or both at the same time. Sir W. Hamilton has even taken the trouble to classify almost all the writers on logic according as they held one opinion or the other. But it seems substantially correct and sufficient to say, that logic is a science in so far as it merely investigates the necessary principles and forms of thought, and thus teaches us to understand in what correct thinking consists; but that it becomes an art when it is occupied in framing rules to assist persons in detecting false reasoning. **A science teaches us to know and an art to do,** and all the more perfect sciences lead to the creation of corresponding useful arts. Astronomy is the foundation of the art of navigation on the ocean, as well as of the arrangement of the calendar and chronology. Physiology is the basis of the art of medicine, and chemistry is the basis of many useful arts. Logic has similarly been considered as the basis of an art of correct reasoning or investigation which should teach the true method to be observed in all sciences. The celebrated British logician Duns Scotus, who lived in the 13th century, and called logic the **Science of Sciences,** called it also the **Art of Arts,** expressing fully its preeminence. Others have thus defined it—" Logic is the art of directing the reason aright in acquiring the knowledge of things, for the instruction both of ourselves and others." Dr Isaac Watts, adopting this view of logic, called his well-known work " the Art of Thinking."

It may be fairly said however that Logic has more the form of a science than an art for this reason—all persons necessarily acquire the faculty and habit of reasoning long before they even know the name of logic. This they do by the natural exertion of the powers of mind, or by constant but unconscious imitation of others. They thus observe correctly but unconsciously the principles of the science in all very simple cases; but the contradictory opinions and absurd fallacies which are put forth by uneducated persons shew that this unaided exercise of mind is not to be trusted when the subject of discussion presents any difficulty or complexity. The study of logic then cannot be useless. It not only explains the principles on which every one has often reasoned correctly before, but points out the dangers which exist of erroneous argument. The reasoner thus becomes consciously a correct reasoner and learns consciously to avoid the snares of fallacy. To say that men can reason well without logical science is about as true as to say that they can live healthily without medicine. So they can—as long as they are healthy; and so can reasoners do without the science of reasoning—as long as they do reason correctly; but how many are there that can do so? As well might a man claim to be immortal in his body as infallible in his mind.

And if it be requisite to say a few words in defence of Logic as an art, because circumstances in the past history of the science have given rise to misapprehension, can it be necessary to say anything in its praise as a science? Whatever there is that is great in science or in art or in literature, it is the work of intellect. In bodily form man is kindred with the brutes, and in his perishable part he is but matter. It is the possession of conscious intellect, the power of reasoning by general notions that raises him above all else upon the earth; and who can say that the nature and procedure of this intellect is not almost the highest and most interesting subject of study in which we can engage? In vain would any one deny the truth of the favourite aphorism of Sir W. Hamilton—

IN THE WORLD THERE IS NOTHING GREAT BUT MAN.
IN MAN THERE IS NOTHING GREAT BUT MIND.

LESSON II.

THE THREE PARTS OF LOGICAL DOCTRINE.

IT has been explained in the previous lesson that Logic is the Science of Reasoning, or the Science of those Necessary Laws of Thought which must be observed if we are to argue consistently with ourselves and avoid self-contradiction. Argument or reasoning therefore is the strictly proper subject before us. But the most convenient and usual mode of studying logic is to consider first the component parts of which any argument must be made up. Just as an architect must be acquainted with the materials of a building, or a mechanic with the materials of a machine, before he can pretend to be acquainted with its construction, so the materials and instruments with which we must operate in reasoning are suitably described before we proceed to the actual forms of argument.

If we examine a simple argument such as that given in the last lesson, thus—

Iron is a metal,
Every metal is an element,
Therefore Iron is an element,—

we see that it is made up of three statements or assertions, and that each of these contains, besides minor
words, two nouns substantive or names of things, and the
verb " is." In short, two names, or terms, when connected
by a verb, make up an assertion or proposition; and
three such propositions make up an argument, called in
this case a syllogism. Hence it is natural and convenient first to describe terms, as the simplest parts; next
to proceed to the nature and varieties of propositions
constructed out of them, and then we shall be in a position to treat of the syllogism as a whole. Such accordingly are the three parts of logical doctrine.

But though we may say that the three parts of logic
are concerned with terms, propositions, and syllogisms,
it may be said with equal or greater truth that the acts of
mind indicated by those forms of language are the real
subject of our consideration. The opinions, or rather
perhaps the expressions, of logicians have varied on this
point. Archbishop Whately says distinctly that logic is
entirely conversant about language; Sir W. Hamilton, Mr
Mansel, and most other logicians treat it as concerned
with the acts or states of mind indicated by the words;
while Mr J. S. Mill goes back to the things themselves
concerning which we argue. Is the subject of logic, then,
language, thought, or objects? The simplest and truest
answer is to say that it treats in a certain sense of all
three. Inasmuch as no reasoning process can be explained or communicated to another person without
words, we are practically limited to such reasoning as is
reduced to the form of language. Hence we shall always
be concerned with words, but only so far as they are the
instruments for recording and referring to our thoughts.
The grammarian also treats of language, but he treats it
as language merely, and his science terminates with the
description and explanation of the forms, varieties, and

relations of words. Logic also treats of language, but only as the necessary index to the action of mind.

Again, so long as we think correctly we must think of things as they are; the state of mind within us must correspond with the state of things without us whenever an opportunity arises for comparing them. It is impossible and inconceivable that iron should prove not to be an elementary substance, if it be a metal, and every metal be an element. We cannot suppose, and there is no reason to suppose, that by the constitution of the mind we are obliged to think of things differently from the manner in which they are. If then we may assume that things really agree or differ according as by correct logical thought we are induced to believe they will, it does not seem that the views of the logicians named are irreconcileable. We treat of things so far as they are the objects of thought, and we treat of language so far as it is the embodiment of thought. If the reader will bear this explanation in mind, he will be saved from some perplexity when he proceeds to read different works on logic, and finds them to vary exceedingly in the mode of treatment, or at least of expression.

If, when reduced to language, there be three parts of logic, terms, propositions, and syllogisms, there must be as many different kinds of thought or operations of mind. These are usually called—

1. Simple apprehension.
2. Judgment.
3. Reasoning or discourse.

The first of these, **Simple Apprehension**, is the act of mind by which we merely become aware of something, or have a notion, idea, or impression of it brought into the mind. The adjective *simple* means apart from other things, and *apprehension* the taking hold by the mind. Thus the name or term *Iron* instantaneously makes the mind think of a strong and very useful metal, but does not tell us anything about it, or compare it with any thing else. The words *sun, Jupiter, Sirius, St Paul's Cathedral*, are also terms which call up into the mind certain well-known objects, which dwell in our recollection even when they are not present to our senses. In fact, the use of a term, such as those given as examples, is merely as a substitute for the exhibition of the actual things named.

Judgment is a different action of mind, and consists in comparing together two notions or ideas of objects derived from simple apprehension, so as to ascertain whether they agree or differ. It is evident, therefore, that we cannot judge or compare unless we are conscious of two things or have the notions of two things in the mind at the same time. Thus if I compare Jupiter and Sirius I first simply apprehend each of them; but bringing them into comparison I observe that they agree in being small, bright, shining bodies, which rise and set and move round the heavens with apparently equal speed. By minute examination, however, I notice that Sirius gives a twinkling or intermittent light, whereas Jupiter shines steadily. More prolonged observation shews that Jupiter and Sirius do not really move with equal and regular speed, but that the former changes its position upon the heavens from night to night in no very simple manner. If the comparison be extended to others of the heavenly bodies which are apprehended or seen at the same time, I shall find that there are a multitude of stars which agree with Sirius in giving a twinkling light and in remaining perfectly fixed in relative position to each other, whereas two or three other bodies may be seen which resemble Jupiter in giving a steady light, and also in changing their place from night to night among the fixed stars. I have now by the action of judgment formed in my mind the general notion of *fixed stars*, by bringing together mentally a number of objects which agree ; while from several other objects I have formed the general notion of *planets.* Comparing the two general notions together, I find that they do not possess the same qualities or appearances, which I state in the proposition, " Planets are not fixed stars."

I have introduced the expression **"General Notion"** as if the reader were fully acquainted with it. But though philosophers have for more than two thousand years constantly used the expressions, general notion, idea, conception, concept, &c., they have never succeeded in agreeing exactly as to the meaning of the terms. One class of philosophers called **Nominalists** say that it is all a matter of names, and that when we join together Jupiter, Mars, Saturn, Venus, &c., and call them *planets,* the common name is the bond between them in our minds. Others, called **Realists,** have asserted that besides these particular planets there really is something which combines the properties common to them all without any of the differences of size, colour, or motion which distinguish them. Every one allows in the present day however that nothing can physically exist corresponding to a general notion, because it must exist here or there, of this size or of that size, and therefore it would be one particular planet, and not any planet whatever. The Nominalists, too, seem equally wrong, because language, to be of any use, must denote something, and must correspond, as we have seen, to acts of mind. If then proper names raise up in our minds the images of particular things, like the sun, Jupiter, &c., general names should raise up general notions.

The true opinion seems to be that of the philosophers called **Conceptualists,** who say that the general notion is the knowledge in the mind of the common properties or resemblances of the things embraced under the notion. Thus the notion planet really means the consciousness in anybody's mind that there are certain heavenly bodies which agree in giving a steady light and in moving about the heavens differently from the fixed stars. It should be added, however, that there are many, including Sir W. Hamilton, who would be counted as Nominalists and who yet hold that with the general name is associated a consciousness of the resemblance existing between the things denoted by it. Between this form of the doctrine and conceptualism it is not easy to draw a precise distinction, and the subject is of too debatable a character to be pursued in this work.

It will appear in the course of these lessons that the whole of logic and the whole of any science consists in so arranging the individual things we meet in general notions or classes, and in giving them appropriate general names or terms, that our knowledge of them may be made as simple and general as possible. Every general notion that is properly formed admits of the statement of general laws or truths ; thus of the planets we may affirm that they move in elliptic orbits round the sun from west to east ; that they shine with the reflected light of the sun ; and so on. Of the fixed stars we may affirm that they shine with their own proper light ; that they are incomparably more distant than the planets ; and so on. The whole of reasoning will be found to arise from this faculty of judgment, which enables us to discover and affirm that a large number of objects have similar properties, so that whatever is known of some may be inferred and asserted of others.

It is in the application of such knowledge that we employ the third act of mind called discourse or reasoning, by which from certain judgments we are enabled, without any new reference to the real objects, to form a new judgment. If we know that iron comes under the

general notion of metal, and that this notion comes under
the still wider notion of element, then without further
examination of iron we know that it is a simple undecomposable substance called by chemists an element. Or
if from one source of information we learn that Neptune
is a planet, and from another that planets move in elliptic orbits, we can join these two portions of knowledge
together in the mind, so as to elicit the truth that Neptune moves in an elliptic orbit.

Reasoning or **Discourse**, then, may be defined as the
progress of the mind from one or more given propositions
to a proposition different from those given. Those propositions from which we argue are called **Premises**, and
that which is drawn from them is called the **Conclusion**.
The latter is said to follow, to be concluded, inferred or col-
lected from them; and the premises are so called because
they are put forward or at the beginning (Latin *præ*, before, and *mitto*, I send or put). The essence of the process consists in gathering the truth that is contained in
the premises when joined together, and carrying it with
us into the conclusion, where it is embodied in a new
proposition or assertion. We extract out of the premises all the information which is useful for the purpose
in view—and this is the whole which reasoning accomplishes.

I have now pointed out the three parts of logical doctrine, Terms, Propositions, and Reasoning or Syllogism,
into which the subject is conveniently divided. To the
consideration of these parts we shall proceed. But it
may be mentioned that a fourth part has often been
added called **Method**, which is concerned with the arrangement of the parts of any composition.

It is sometimes said that what proposition is to term,
and what syllogism is to proposition, such is method to
syllogism, and that a fourth division is necessary to com-

plete the doctrine of Logic. It is at any rate certain
however that this fourth part is much inferior in import
ance and distinctness to the preceding three; and all tha'
will be said of it is to be found in Lesson XXIV.

LESSON III.

TERMS, AND THEIR VARIOUS KINDS.

IT has been explained in the preceding lesson that every
assertion or statement expresses the agreement or difference of two things, or of two general notions. In
putting the assertion or statement into words, we must
accordingly have words suitable for drawing the attention
of the mind to the things which are compared, as well as
words indicating the result of the comparison, that is to
say, the fact whether they agree or differ. The words by
which we point out the things or classes of things in
question are called **Terms,** and the words denoting the
comparison are said to form the **Copula.** Hence a complete assertion or statement consists of two terms and a
copula, and when thus expressed it forms a **Proposition.**
Thus in the proposition " Dictionaries are useful books,"
the two terms are *dictionaries* and *useful books;* the copula is the verb *are*, and expresses a certain agreement of
the class dictionaries with the class of useful books consisting in the fact that the class of dictionaries forms part
of the class of useful books. In this case each term consists of only one or two words, but any number of words
may be required to describe the notions or classes com-

pared together. In the proposition "the angles at the base of an isosceles triangle are equal to each other," the first term requires nine words for its expression, and the second term, four words (equal to each other); and there is no limit to the number of words which may be employed in the formation of a term.

A term is so called because it forms one end (Latin, *terminus*) of a proposition, and strictly speaking it is a term only so long as it stands in the proposition. But we commonly speak of a term or a name meaning any noun, substantive or adjective, or any combination of words denoting an object of thought, whether that be, as we shall shortly see, an individual thing, a group of things, a quality of things, or a group of qualities. It would be impossible to define a name or term better than has been done by Hobbes: "A name is a word taken at pleasure to serve for a mark, which may raise in our mind a thought like to some thought which we had before, and which, being pronounced to others, may be to them a sign of what thought the speaker had before in his mind."

Though every term or name consists of words it is not every word which can form a name by itself. We cannot properly say "Not is agreeable" or "Probably is not true;" nothing can be asserted of a preposition, an adverb, and certain other parts of speech, except indeed that they are prepositions, adverbs, &c. No part of speech except a noun substantive, or a group of words used as a noun substantive, can form the subject or first term of a proposition, and nothing but a noun substantive, an adjective, the equivalent of an adjective, or a verb, can form the second term or predicate of a proposition. It may indeed be questioned whether an adjective can ever form a term alone; thus in "Dictionaries are useful," it may be said that the substantive *things* or *books* is understood in the predicate, the complete sen-

2

tence being "Dictionaries are useful *books*," but as this is a disputed point we will assume that words are divided into two kinds in the following manner :—

Words which stand, or appear to stand alone as complete terms, namely the substantive and adjective, and certain parts of a verb, are called **categorematic** words, from the Greek word κατηγορέω, to assert or predicate.

Those parts of speech, on the other hand, such as prepositions, adverbs, conjunctions, &c., which can only form parts of names or terms are called **syncategorematic** words, because they must be used *with* other words in order to compose terms (Greek σύν, with, and κατηγορέω). Of syncategorematic words we need not take further notice except so far as they form part of categorematic terms.

We have now to consider the various kinds and peculiarities of terms, so as to gain a clear idea of what they mean. Terms are first of all distinguished into *singular* or individual, and *general* or common terms, this being a very obvious division, but one of much importance. A **Singular term** is one which can denote only a single object, so long at least as it is used in exactly the same meaning; thus the Emperor of the French, the Atlantic Ocean, St Paul's, William Shakspeare, the most precious of the metals, are singular terms. All proper names belong to this class; for though John Jones is the name of many men, yet it is used not as meaning *any* of these men, but some single man—it has, in short, a different meaning in each case, just as London, the name of our capital, has no connexion in meaning with London in Canada.

General terms, on the contrary, are applicable in the same sense equally to *any one* of an indefinite number of objects which resemble each other in certain qualities. Thus *metal* is a general name because it may be applied indifferently to gold, silver, copper, tin, aluminium, or any of about fifty known substances. It is not the name of any one of these more than any other, and it is in fact applied to any substance which possesses metallic lustre, which cannot be decomposed, and which has certain other qualities easily recognised by chemists. Nor is the number of substances in the class restricted; for as new kinds of metal are from time to time discovered they are added to the class. Again, while Mars, Jupiter, Saturn, &c., are singular terms, since each can denote only a single planet, the term planet is a general one, being applicable to as many bodies as may be discovered to revolve round the sun as the earth does.

We must carefully avoid any confusion between general and collective terms. By a **collective term** we mean the name of a number of things when all joined together as one whole ; like the soldiers of a regiment, the men of a jury, the crew of a vessel : thus a collective term is the name of all, but not of each. A general term, on the other hand, is the name of a number of things, but of each of them separately, or, to use the technical expression, **distributively.** Soldier, juryman, sailor, are the general names which may belong to John Jones. Thomas Brown, &c., but we cannot say that John Jones is a regiment, Thomas Brown a jury, and so on. The distinction is exceedingly obvious when thus pointed out, but it may present itself in more obscure forms, and is then likely to produce erroneous reasoning, as will be pointed out in Lesson XX. It is easy to see that we must not divide terms into those which are general and those which are collective, because it will often happen that the same term is both general and collective, according as it is regarded. Thus, library is collective as regards the books in it, but is general as regards the great number of different libraries, private or public, which exist.

Regiment is a collective term as regards the soldiers which compose it, but general as regards the hundred different regiments, the Coldstream Guards, the Highland regiment, the Welsh Fusiliers, and the rest, which compose the British standing army. Army, again, is a collective whole, as being composed of a number of regiments organized together. Year is collective as regards the months, weeks, or days of which it consists, but is general as being the name either of 1869 or 1870, or any period marked by a revolution of the earth round the sun.

We have not always in the English language sufficient means of distinguishing conveniently between the general and collective use of terms. In Latin this distinctive use was exactly expressed by *omnes*, meaning *all* distributively, and *cuncti* meaning all taken together, a contracted form of *conjuncti* (joined together). In English *all men* may mean *any man* or *all men together*. Even the more exact word *every* is sometimes misused, as in the old proverb, 'Every little makes a mickle,' where it is obvious that every little portion cannot by itself make much, but only when joined to other little portions.

A second important distinction between terms is that of **concrete** terms and **abstract** terms; and it cannot be better described than in the words of Mr Mill, by saying that a concrete name is the name of a thing, the abstract name is the name of a quality, attribute, or circumstance of a thing. Thus *red house* is the name of a physically-existing thing, and is concrete; *redness* is the name of one quality of the house, and is abstract. The word abstract means *drawn from* (Latin, abstractus, from *abstrahere*, to draw away from), and indicates that the quality redness is thought of in the mind apart from all the other qualities which belong to the red house, or other red object. But though we can think of a quality by itself, we cannot suppose that the quality can exist physically

apart from the matter in which it is manifest to us. Redness means either a notion in the mind, or it means that
in red objects which excites the notion.

The reader should carefully observe that **adjectives**
are concrete, not abstract. If we say that a book is useful, it is to the book we apply the adjective *useful,* and
usefulness is the abstract noun which denotes the quality;
similarly, the adjectives *equal, grateful, reverent, rational,* are the names of things, and the corresponding abstract nouns are *equality, gratitude, reverence, rationality.*
This distinction will become more apparent in reading
Lesson V.

It is a good exercise to try and discover pairs of corresponding concrete and abstract names; thus animal
has animality; miser, miserliness; old, agedness, or old
age; substance, substantiality; soap, soapiness; shrub,
shrubbiness; and so on. But it by no means follows that
an abstract word exists for each concrete; table hardly has
an abstract tabularity; and though ink has inkiness, we
should not find the abstract of pen. It is by the accidents
of the history of language that we do or do not possess
abstract names; and there is a constant tendency to invent new abstract words in the progress of time and
science.

Unfortunately concrete and abstract names are frequently confused, and it is by no means always easy to
distinguish the meanings. Thus **relation** properly is the
abstract name for the position of two people or things to
each other, and those people are properly called **relatives**
(Latin, *relativus,* one who is related). But we constantly
speak now of *relations,* meaning the persons themselves;
and when we want to indicate the abstract relation
they have to each other we have to invent a new abstract
name *relationship.* Nation has long been a concrete
term, though from its form it was probably abstract at

first ; but so far does the abuse of language now go especially in newspaper writing, that we hear of *a nation-ality* meaning a nation, although of course if nation is
· the concrete, nationality ought to be the abstract, mean-ing the quality of being a nation. Similarly, *action intention, extension, conception,* and a multitude of other properly abstract names, are used confusedly for the corre-sponding concrete, namely, *act, intent, extent, concept,* &c. Production is properly the condition or state of a person who is producing or drawing something forth ; but it has now become confused with that which is produced, so that we constantly talk of the productions of a country, meaning the products.   The logical terms, Proposition, Deduction, Induction, Syllogism, are all properly abstract words, but are used concretely for a Proposition, a De-duction, an Induction, a Syllogism ; and it must be al-lowed that logicians are nearly as bad as other people in confusing abstract and concrete terms.   Much injury is done to language by this abuse.

Another very obvious division of terms is between those which are **positive**, and those which are **negative**. The difference is usually described by saying that posi-tive terms signify the existence or possession of a quality, as in grateful, metallic, organic, etc., while the correspond-ing negatives signify the absence of the same qualities as in ungrateful, non-metallic, inorganic.   The negative terms may be adjectives as above, or substantives, con-crete or abstract ; thus ingratitude, inequality, incon-venience are abstract negative terms ; and individuals, unequals, &c. are concrete negatives.   We usually consider as negative terms any which have a negative prefix such as *not, non, un, in,* &c. ; but there are a great many terms which serve as negatives without possessing any mark of their negative character.   Darkness is the negative of light or lightness, since it means the absence of light,

compound is the negative of element, since we should
give the name of compound to whatever can be *decomposed*, and element is what cannot be decomposed ; theoretically speaking every term has its corresponding negative, but it by no means follows that language furnishes
the term ready-made. Thus table has the corresponding
adjective tabular, but there is no similar negative *untabu-
lar;* one man may be called a bookworm, but there is no
negative for those who are not bookworms, because no
need of the expression has been felt. A constant process
of invention of new negative terms goes on more rapidly
perhaps than is desirable, for when an idea is not often
referred to it is better to express it by a phrase than add
to the length of the dictionary by a new-created word.

It would seem that in many cases a negative term
implies the presence of some distinct quality or fact.
Thus *inconvenience* doubtless implies the absence of
convenience, but also the presence of positive trouble or
pain occasioned thereby. Unhappiness is a negative
term, but precisely the same notion is expressed by the
positive term *misery*. The negative of healthy is un-
healthy, but the positive term sickly serves equally well.
It thus appears to be more a matter of accident than
anything else whether a positive or negative term is used
to express any particular notion. All that we can really
say is that every positive term necessarily implies the
existence of a corresponding negative term, which may be
the name of all those things to which the positive name
cannot be applied. Whether this term has been invented
or not is an accident of language: its existence may be
assumed in logic.

The reader may be cautioned against supposing that
every term appearing to be of a negative character on
account of possessing a negative prefix is really so. The
participle *unloosed* certainly appears to be the negative of

loosed; but the two words mean exactly the same thing, the prefix *un* not being really the negative; *invaluable,* again, means not what is devoid of value, but what is so valuable that the value cannot be measured; and a *shameless* action can equally be called by the positive term, a *shameful* action. Other instances might no doubt be found.

Great care should be taken to avoid confusing terms which express the presence or absence of a quality with those which describe its degree. *Less* is not the negative of *greater* because there is a third alternative, *equal.* The true negative of *greater* is *not-greater,* and this is equivalent to *either equal* or *less.* So it may be said that *disagreeable* is not the simple negative of *agreeable,* because there may be things which are neither one nor the other, but are *indifferent* to us. It would not be easy to say offhand whether every action which is not honest is dishonest, or whether there may not be actions of an intermediate character. The rule is that wherever the question is one of degree or quantity a medium is possible, and the subject belongs rather to the science of quantity than to simple logic; where the question is one of the presence or absence of a quality, there cannot be more than two alternatives, according to one of the Primary Laws of Thought, which we will consider in Lesson XIV. In the case of quantity we may call the extreme terms **opposites**; thus less is the opposite of greater, disagreeable of agreeable; in the case of mere negation we may call the terms **negatives** or **contradictories**, and it is really indifferent in a logical point of view which of a pair of contradictory terms we regard as the positive and which as the negative. Each is the negative of the other.

Logicians have distinguished from simple negative terms a class of terms called **privative**, such as *blind,* *dead,* &c. Such terms express that a thing has been *deprived* of a quality which it before possessed, or was capable of possessing, or usually does possess. A man may be born blind, so that he never did see, but he possesses the organs which would have enabled him to see except for some accident. A stone or a tree could not have had the faculty of seeing under any circumstances. No mineral substance can properly be said to die or to be dead, because it was incapable of life; but it may be called uncrystallized because it might have been in the form of a crystal. Hence we apply a privative term to anything which has not a quality which it was capable of having; we apply a negative term to anything which has not and could not have the quality. It is doubtful however whether this distinction can be properly carried out, and it is not of very much importance.

It is further usual to divide terms according as they are **relative** or **absolute**, that is, non-relative. The adjective absolute means whatever is "loosed from connection with anything else" (Latin *ab*, from, and *solutus*, loosed); whereas relative means that which is carried in thought, at least, into connection with something else. Hence a relative term denotes an object which cannot be thought of without reference to some other object, or as part of a larger whole. A father cannot be thought of but in relation to a child, a monarch in relation to a subject, a shepherd in relation to a flock; thus father, monarch, and shepherd are relative terms, while child, subject, and flock are the **correlatives** (Latin *con*, with, and *relativus*), or those objects which are necessarily joined in thought with the original objects. The very meaning, in fact, of father is that he has a child, of monarch that he has subjects, and of shepherd that he has a flock. As examples of terms which have no apparent relation to anything else, I may mention water, gas, tree. There does not seem to me to be anything so habitually associated with water that we must think of it as part of the same idea, and gas, tree, and a multitude of other terms, also denote objects which have no remarkable or permanent relations such as would entitle the terms to be called relatives. They may therefore be considered absolute or non-relative terms.

The fact, however, is that everything must really have relations to something else, the water to the elements of which it is composed, the gas to the coal from which it is manufactured, the tree to the soil in which it is rooted. By the very laws of thought, again, no thing or class of things can be thought of but by separating them from other existing things from which they differ. I cannot use the term mortal without at once separating all existing or conceivable things into the two groups *mortal* and *immortal;* metal, element, organic substance, and every other term that could be mentioned, would necessarily imply the existence of a correlative negative term, non-metallic, compound, inorganic substance, and in this respect therefore every term is undoubtedly relative. Logicians, however, have been content to consider as relative terms those only which imply some peculiar and striking kind of relation arising from position in time or space, from connexion of cause and effect, &c.; and it is in this special sense therefore the student must use the distinction.

The most important varieties of terms having been explained, it is desirable that the reader should acquire a complete familiarity with them by employing the exercises at the end of the book. The reader is to determine concerning each of the terms there given:—

1. Whether it is a categorematic or syncategorematic term.
2. Whether it is a general or a singular term.
3. Whether it is collective or distributive.

4. Whether it is concrete or abstract.
5. Whether it is positive, or negative, or privative.
6. Whether it is relative or absolute.

It will be fully pointed out in the next lesson that most terms have more than one meaning; and as the one meaning may be general and the other singular, the one concrete and the other abstract, and so on, it is absolutely necessary that the reader should first of all choose one precise meaning of the term which he is examining. And in answering the questions proposed it is desirable he should specify the way in which he regards it. Taking the word *sovereign*, we may first select the meaning in which it is equivalent to monarch; this is a general term in so far as it is the name of any one of many monarchs living or dead, but it is singular as regards the inhabitants of any one country. It is clearly categorematic, concrete, and positive, and obviously relative to the subjects of the monarch.

Read Mr Mill's chapter on *Names, System of Logic* Book I. chap. 2.

LESSON IV.

OF THE AMBIGUITY OF TERMS.

THERE is no part of Logic which is more really useful than that which treats of the ambiguity of terms, that is of the uncertainty and variety of meanings belonging to words. Nothing indeed can be of more importance to the attainment of correct habits of thinking and reasoning than a thorough acquaintance with the great imperfections of language. Comparatively few terms have one single clear meaning and one meaning only, and when ever two or more meanings are unconsciously confused together, we inevitably commit a logical fallacy. If, for instance, a person should argue that "punishment is an evil," and according to the principles of morality "no evil is to be allowed even with the purpose of doing good," we might not at the first moment see how to avoid the conclusion that "no punishments should be allowed," because they cause evil. A little reflection will show that the word evil is here used in two totally different senses; in the first case it means physical evil or pain; in the second moral evil, and because moral evil is never to be committed, it does not follow that physical evils are never to be inflicted, for they are often the very means of preventing moral evil.

Another very plausible fallacy which has often been put forth in various forms is as follows: "A thoroughly benevolent man cannot possibly refuse to relieve the poor, and since a person who cannot possibly act otherwise than he does can claim no merit for his actions, it follows that a thoroughly benevolent man can claim no merit for his actions." According to this kind of argument a man would have less merit in proportion as he was more virtuous, so as to feel greater and greater difficulty in acting wrongly. That the conclusion is fallacious every one must feel certain, but the cause of the fallacy can only be detected by observing that the words *cannot possibly* have a double meaning, in the first case referring to the influence of moral motives or good character, and in the second to circumstances entirely beyond a person's control; as, for instance, the compulsion of the laws, the want of money, the absence of personal liberty. The more a person studies the subtle variations in the meaning of common words, the more he will be convinced of the dangerous nature of the tools he has to use in all communications and arguments. Hence I must ask much attention to the contents of this Lesson.

Terms are said to be **univocal** when they can suggest to the mind no more than one single definite meaning. They are called **equivocal** or **ambiguous** when they have two or more different meanings. It will be observed, however, that a term is not equivocal because it can be applied to many objects when it is applied in the same sense or meaning to those different objects. Thus cathedral is the name of St Paul's, the York Minster, and the principal churches of Salisbury, Wells, Lincoln and a number of other cities, but it is not ambiguous, because all these are only various instances of the same meaning; they are all objects of the same description or kind. The word cathedral is probably univocal or of one logical meaning only. The word church, on the other hand, is equivocal, because it sometimes means the building in which religious worship is performed, sometimes the body of persons who belong to one sect or persuasion, and assemble in churches. Sometimes also the church means the body of the clergy as distinguished from the laity; hence there is a clear difference in the sense or meaning with which the word is used at different times.

Instances of univocal terms are to be found chiefly in technical and scientific language. Steam-engine, gasometer, railway train, permanent way, and multitudes of such technical names denoting distinct common objects, are sufficiently univocal. In common life the names penny, mantelpiece, teacup, bread and butter, have a sufficiently definite and single meaning. So also in chemistry, oxygen, hydrogen, sulphate of copper, alumina, lithia, and thousands of other terms, are very precise, the words themselves having often been invented in very recent years, and the meanings exactly fixed and maintained invariable. Every science has or ought to have a series of terms equally precise and certain in meaning. (See Lesson XXXIII.) The names of individual objects, buildings, events, or persons, again, are usually quite certain and clear, as in Julius Cæsar, William the Conqueror, the first Napoleon, Saint Peter's, Westminster Abbey, the Great Exhibition of 1851, and so on.

But however numerous may be the univocal terms which can be adduced, still the equivocal terms are astonishingly common. They include most of the nouns and adjectives which are in habitual use in the ordinary intercourse of life. They are called ambiguous from the Latin verb *ambigo*, to wander, hesitate, or be in doubt; or again *homonymous*, from the Greek ὁμός, like, and ὄνομα, name. Whenever a person uses equivocal words in such a way as to confuse the different meanings and fall into error, he may be said to commit the fallacy of **Equivocation** in the logical meaning of the name (see Lesson XX.); but in common life a person is not said to equivocate unless he uses words consciously and deceitfully in a manner calculated to produce a confusion of the true and apparent meanings.

I will now describe the various kinds and causes of ambiguity of words, following to some extent the interesting chapters on the subject in Dr Watts' *Logic*. In the first place we may distinguish three classes of equivocal words, according as they are—

    1. Equivocal in sound only.
    2. Equivocal in spelling only.
    3. Equivocal both in sound and spelling.

The first two classes are comparatively speaking of very slight importance, and do not often give rise to serious error. They produce what we should call trivial mistakes. Thus we may confuse, when spoken only, the words right, wright and rite (ceremony); also the words rein, rain and reign, might and mite, &c. Owing partly to defects of pronunciation mistakes are not unknown between the four words *air*, *hair*, *hare* and *heir*.

Words equivocal in spelling but not in sound are such as tear (a drop), and tear pronounced tare, meaning a rent in cloth ; or lead, the metal, and lead, as in following the lead of another person. As little more than momentary misapprehension, however, can arise from such resemblance of words, we shall pass at once to the class of words equivocal both in sound and spelling. These I shall separate into three groups according as the equivocation arises—

1. From the accidental confusion of different words.
2. From the transfer of meaning by the association of ideas.
3. From the logical transfer of meaning to analogous objects.

1. Under the first class we place a certain number of curious but hardly important cases in which ambiguity has arisen from the **confusion** of entirely different words, derived from different languages or from different roots of the same language, but which have in the course of time assumed the same sound and spelling. Thus the word *mean* denotes either that which is *medium* or mediocre, from the French *moyen* and the Latin *medius*, connected with the Anglo-Saxon *mid*, or *middle;* or it denotes what is low-minded and base, being then derived from the Anglo-Saxon *Gemœne*, which means "that belonging to the mœne or many," whatever in short is vulgar. The verb to *mean* can hardly be confused with the adjective *mean*, but it comes from a third distinct root, probably connected with the Sanscrit verb, *to think*.

As other instances of this casual ambiguity, I may mention *rent*, a money payment, from the French *rente* (*rendre*, to return), or a tear, the result of the action of *rending*, this word being of Anglo-Saxon origin and one of the numerous class beginning in *r* or *wr*, which imitate more or less perfectly the sound of the action which they denote. *Pound*, from the Latin *pondus*, a weight, is confused with *pound*, in the sense of a village pinfold for cattle, derived from the Saxon *pyndan*, to pen up. *Fell*, a mountain, is a perfectly distinct word from *fell*, a skin or hide; and *pulse*, a throb or beating, and *pulse*, peas, beans, or potage, though both derived from the Greek or Latin, are probably quite unconnected words. It is curious that *gin*, in the meaning of trap or machine, is a contracted form of *engine*, and when denoting the spirituous liquor is a corruption of *Geneva*, the place where the spirit was first made.

Certain important cases of confusion have been detected in grammar, as between the numeral *one*, derived from an Aryan root, through the Latin *unus*, and the indeterminate pronoun, *one* (as in "*one* ought to do *one's* duty"), which is really a corrupt form of the French word *homme* or man. The Germans to the present day use *man* in this sense, as in *man sagt*, *i.e.* one says.

2. By far the largest part of equivocal words have become so by a **transfer of the meaning** from the thing originally denoted by the word to some other thing habitually connected with it so as to become closely associated in thought. Thus, in Parliamentary language, the House means either the chamber in which the members meet, or it means the body of members who happen to be assembled in it at any time. Similarly, the word *church* originally denoted the building (κυριακόν, the Lord's House) in which any religious worshippers assemble, but it has thence derived a variety of meanings; it may mean a particular body of worshippers accustomed to assemble in any one place, in which sense it is used in Acts xiv. 23; or it means any body of persons holding

the same opinions and connected in one organization, as in the Anglican, or Greek, or Roman Catholic Church; it is also sometimes used so as to include the laity as well as the clergy; but more generally perhaps the clergy and religious authorities of any sect or country are so strongly associated with the act of worship as to be often called the church *par excellence.* It is quite evident moreover that the word entirely differs in meaning according as it is used by a member of the Anglican, Greek, Roman Catholic, Scotch Presbyterian, or any other existing church.

The word *foot* has suffered several curious but very evident transfers of meaning. Originally it denoted the foot of a man or an animal, and is probably connected in a remote manner with the Latin *pes, pedis,* and the Greek πούς, ποδός; but since the length of the foot is naturally employed as a rude measure of length, it came to be applied to a fixed measure of length; and as the foot is at the bottom of the body the name was extended by analogy to the foot of a mountain, or the feet of a table; by a further extension, any position, plan, reason, or argument on which we place ourselves and rely, is called the foot or footing. The same word also denotes soldiers who fight upon their feet, or infantry, and the measured part of a verse having a definite length. That these very different meanings are naturally connected with the original meaning is evident from the fact that the Latin and Greek words for foot are subject to exactly similar series of ambiguities.

It would be a long task to trace out completely the various and often contradictory meanings of the word *fellow.* Originally a fellow was what *follows* another, that is a companion; thus it came to mean the other of a pair, as one shoe is the fellow of the other, or simply an equal, as when we say that Shakspeare "hath not a fellow."

From the simple meaning of companion again it comes to denote vaguely a person, as in the question "What fellow is that?" but then there is a curious confusion of depreciatory and endearing power in the word; when a man is called a *mere fellow*, or simply a *fellow* in a particular tone of voice, the name is one of severe contempt; alter the tone of voice or the connected words in the least degree, and it becomes one of the most sweet and endearing appellations, as when we speak of a dear or good fellow. We may still add the technical meanings of the name as applied in the case of a Fellow of a College, or of a learned society.

Another good instance of the growth of a number of different meanings from a single root is found in the word *post*. Originally a post was something *posited*, or placed firmly in the ground, such as an upright piece of wood or stone; such meaning still remains in the cases of a lamp-post, a gate-post, signal-post, &c. As a post would often be used to mark a fixed spot of ground, as in a mile-post, it came to mean the fixed or appointed place where the post was placed, as in a military post, the post of danger or honour, &c. The fixed places where horses were kept in readiness to facilitate rapid travelling during the times of the Roman empire were thus called posts, and thence the whole system of arrangement for the conveyance of persons or news came to be called *the posts*. The name has retained an exactly similar meaning to the present day in most parts of Europe, and we still use it in post-chaise, post-boy, post-horse and postillion. A system of post conveyance for letters having been organised for about two centuries in England and other countries, this is perhaps the meaning most closely associated with the word post at present, and a number of expressions have thus arisen, such as post-office, postage, postal-guide, postman, postmaster, postal-telegraph, &c. Curi-

ously enough we now have iron letter-posts, in which the
word post is restored exactly to its original meaning.

Although the words described above were selected on
account of the curious variety of their meanings, I do not
hesitate to assert that the majority of common nouns
possess various meanings in greater or less number. Dr
Watts, in his *Logic*, suggests that the words book, bible,
fish, house, and elephant, are univocal terms, but the
reader would easily detect ambiguities in each of them.
Thus fish bears a very different meaning in natural history from what it does in the mouths of unscientific persons, who include under it not only true fishes, but shell-
fish or mollusca, and the cetacea, such as whales and
seals, in short all swimming animals, whether they have
the character of true fish or not. Elephant, in a station-
er's or bookseller's shop, means a large kind of paper
instead of a large animal. Bible sometimes means any
particular copy of the Bible, sometimes the collection
of works constituting the Holy Scriptures. The word
man is singularly ambiguous ; sometimes it denotes man
as distinguished from woman; at other times it is certainly used to include both sexes ; and in certain recent
election cases lawyers were unable to decide whether the
word man as used in the Reform Act of 1867 ought or
ought not to be interpreted so as to include women. On
other occasions *man* is used to denote an adult male as
distinguished from a boy, and it also often denotes one
who is emphatically a *man* as possessing a masculine
character. Occasionally it is used in the same way as
groom, for a servant, as in the proverb, " Like master,
like man." At other times it stands specially for a hus-
band.

3. Among ambiguous words we must thirdly distinguish
those which derive their various meanings in a somewhat
different manner, namely by analogy or real resemblance

When we speak of a sweet taste, a sweet flower, a sweet tune, a sweet landscape, a sweet face, a sweet poem, it is evident that we apply one and the same word to very different things; such a concrete thing as lump-sugar can hardly be compared directly with such an intellectual existence as Tennyson's *May Queen.* Nevertheless if the word sweet is to be considered ambiguous, it is in a different way from those we have before considered, because all the things are called sweet on account of a peculiar pleasure which they yield, which cannot be described otherwise than by comparison with sugar. In a similar way, we describe a pain as sharp, a disappointment as bitter, a person's temper as sour, the future as bright or gloomy, an achievement as brilliant; all these adjectives implying comparison with bodily sensations of the simplest kind. The adjective *brilliant* is derived from the French *briller*, to glitter or sparkle; and this meaning it fully retains when we speak of a brilliant diamond, a brilliant star, &c. By what a subtle analogy is it that we speak of a brilliant position, a brilliant achievement, brilliant talents, brilliant style! We cannot speak of a clear explanation, indefatigable perseverance, perspicuous style, or sore calamity, without employing in each of these expressions a double analogy to physical impressions, actions, or events. It will be shewn in the sixth Lesson that to this process we owe the creation of all names connected with mental feelings or existences.

Read Watts' *Logic*, Chapter IV.
Locke's *Essay on the Human Understanding*, Book III.
Chapters IX. and X.

LESSON V.

OF THE TWOFOLD MEANING OF TERMS— IN EXTENSION AND INTENSION.

THERE is no part of the doctrines of Logic to which I would more urgently request the attention of the reader than to that which I will endeavour to explain clearly in the present Lesson. I speak of the double meaning which is possessed by most logical terms—the meaning in **extension**, and the meaning in **intension**. I believe that the reader who once acquires a thorough apprehension of the difference of these meanings, and learns to bear it always in mind, will experience but little further difficulty in the study of logic.

The meaning of a term in extension consists of the **objects to which the term may be applied**; its meaning in intension consists of **the qualities which are necessarily possessed by objects bearing that name.** A simple example will make this distinction most apparent. What is the meaning of the name "metal"? The first and most obvious answer is that metal means either gold, or silver, or iron, or copper, or aluminium, or some other of the 48 substances known to chemists, and considered to have a metallic nature. These substances then form the plain and common meaning of the name, which is the meaning in extension. But if it be asked why the name is applied to all these substances and these only, the answer must be—Because they possess certain qualities which belong to the nature of metal. We cannot, therefore, know to what substances we may apply the name, or to what we may not, unless we know the qualities which are indispensable to the character of a metal. Now chemists lay these down to be somewhat as follows:—(1) A metal must be an element or simple substance incapable of decomposition or separation into simpler substances by any known means. (2) It must be a good conductor of heat and electricity. (3) It must possess a great and peculiar reflective power known as metallic lustre*.

These properties are common to all metals, or nearly all metals, and are what mark out and distinguish a metal from other substances. Hence they form in a certain way the meaning of the name metal, the meaning in intension, as it is called, to distinguish it from the former kind of meaning.

In a similar manner almost any other common name has a double meaning. "Steamship" denotes in extension the Great Eastern, the Persia, the Himalaya, or any one of the thousands of steamships existing or which have existed; in intension it means "a vessel propelled by steam-power." Monarch is the name of Queen Victoria, Victor Emmanuel, Louis Napoleon, or any one of a considerable number of persons who rule singly over countries; the persons themselves form the meaning in extension; the quality of *ruling alone* forms the intensive meaning of the name. Animal is the name in extension of any one of billions of existing creatures and of indefinitely greater numbers of other creatures that have existed or will exist; in intension it implies in all those creatures the existence of a certain animal life and sense, or at least the power of digesting food and exerting force, which are the marks of animal nature.

---

* It is doubtfully true that all metals possess metallic lustre, and chemists would find it very difficult to give any consistent explanation of their use of the name; but the statements in the text are sufficiently true to furnish an example.

It is desirable to state here that this distinction of extension and intension has been explained by logicians under various forms of expression. It is the peculiar misfortune of the science of logic to have a superfluity of names or synonyms for the same idea. Thus the intension of a term is synonymous with its **comprehension**, or **connotation**, or **depth**; while the extension is synonymous with the **denotation** or **breadth**. This may be most clearly stated in the form of a scheme:—

The extension, extent, breadth, denotation, domain, sphere or application of a name consists of the individual things to which the name *applies*.	The intension, intent, depth, connotation, or implication of a name consists of the qualities the possession of which by those things is *implied*.

Of these words, **denotation** and **connotation** are employed chiefly by Mr J. S. Mill among modern logical writers, and are very apt for the purpose. To denote is to *mark down*, and the name marks the things to which it may be applied or affixed; thus metal denotes gold, silver, copper, &c. To connote is *to mark along with* (Latin *con*, together; *notare*, to mark), and the connotation accordingly consists of the qualities before described, the possession of which is implied by the use of the name metal.

When we compare different but related terms we may observe that they differ in the quantity of their extension and intension. Thus the term *element* has a greater extension of meaning than *metal*, because it includes in its meaning all metals and other substances as well. But it has at the same time less intension of meaning; for among the qualities of a metallic substance must be found the qualities of an element, besides the other qualities peculiar to a metal. If again we compare the terms *metal* and *malleable metal*, it is apparent that the latter term does not include the metals antimony, arsenic, and bismuth, which are brittle substances. Hence *malleable metal* is a term of narrower meaning in extension than metal; but it has also deeper meaning in intension, because it connotes or implies the quality of malleability . in addition to the general qualities of a metal. *White malleable metal* is again a narrower term in extension because it does not include gold and copper; and I can go on narrowing the meaning by the use of qualifying adjectives until only a single metal should be denoted by the term.

The reader will now see clearly that a general law of great importance connects the quantity of extension and the quantity of intension, viz.—**As the intension of a term is increased the extension is decreased.** It must not be supposed, indeed, that there is any exact proportion between the degree in which one meaning is increased and the other decreased. Thus if we join the adjective *red* to metal we narrow the meaning much more than if we join the adjective *white,* for there are at least twelve times as many white metals as red. Again, the term white man includes a considerable fraction of the meaning of the term man as regards extension, but the term blind man only a small fraction of the meaning. Thus it is obvious that in increasing the intension of a term we may decrease the extension in any degree.

In understanding this law we must carefully discriminate the cases where there is only an apparent increase of the intension of a term, from those where the increase is real. If I add the term *elementary* to *metal,* I shall not really alter the extension of meaning, for all the metals are elements; and the elementary metals are neither more nor less numerous than the metals. But then the intension of the term is really unaltered at the same time; for the quality of an element is really found among the qua_ities of metal, and it is superfluous to specify it ovei again. A quality which belongs invariably to the whole of a class of things is commonly called a **property** of the class (see Lesson XII.), and we cannot qualify or restrict a term by its own property.

This is a convenient place to notice a distinction between terms into those which are **connotative** and those which are **non-connotative**, the latter consisting of the terms which simply denote things without implying any knowledge of their qualities. As Mr Mill considers this distinction to be one of great importance, it will be well to quote his own words*:—

"A non-connotative term is one which signifies a subject only, or an attribute only. A connotative term is one which denotes a subject, and implies an attribute. By a subject is here meant anything which possesses attributes. Thus John, or London, or England, are names which signify a subject only. Whiteness, length, virtue, signify an attribute only. None of these names, therefore, are connotative. But *white, long, virtuous,* are connotative. The word white denotes all white things, as snow, paper, the foam of the sea, &c., and implies, or, as it was termed by the schoolmen, *connotes* the attribute *whiteness.* The word white is not predicated of the attribute, but of the subjects, snow, &c. ; but when we predicate it of them, we imply, or connote, that the attribute whiteness belongs to them......

"All concrete general names are connotative. The word *man,* for example, denotes Peter, James, John, and an indefinite number of other individuals, of whom, taken as a class, it is the name. But it is applied to them, because they possess, and to signify that they possess, cer-

---

* *System of Logic,* Vol. I. p. 31, 6th ed. Book I. Chap. II.

§ 5

tain attributes. . . . What we call men, are the subjects, the individual Styles and Nokes; not the qualities by which their humanity is constituted. The name therefore is said to signify the subjects **directly,** the attributes **indirectly;** it **denotes** the subjects, and implies, or involves, or indicates, or, as we shall say henceforth, **connotes,** the attributes. It is a connotative name. . . .

" Proper names are not connotative : they denote the individuals who are called by them ; but they do not indicate or imply any attributes as belonging to those individuals. When we name a child by the name Paul, or a dog by the name Cæsar, these names are simply marks used to enable those individuals to be made subjects of discourse. It may be said, indeed, that we must have had some reason for giving them those names rather than any others ; and this is true ; but the name, once given, is independent of the reason. A man may have been named John, because that was the name of his father ; a town may have been named Dartmouth, because it is situated at the mouth of the Dart. But it is no part of the signification of the word John, that the father of the person so called bore the same name ; nor even of the word Dartmouth to be situated at the mouth of the Dart. If sand should choke up the mouth of the river, or an earthquake change its course, and remove it to a distance from the town, the name of the town would not necessarily be changed."

I quote this in Mr Mill's own words, because though it expresses most clearly the view accepted by Mr Mill and many others, it is nevertheless probably erroneous. The connotation of a name is confused with the etymological meaning, or the circumstances which caused it to be affixed to a thing. Surely no one who uses the name England, and knows what it denotes, can be ignorant of the peculiar qualities and circumstances of the country, and these form the connotation of the term. To any one who knows the town Dartmouth the name must imply the possession of the circumstances by which that town is characterised at the present time. If the river Dart should be destroyed or removed, the town would so far be altered, and the signification of the name changed. The name would no longer denote a town situated on the Dart, but one which was *formerly* situated on the Dart, and it would be by a mere historical accident that the form of the name did not appear suitable to the town. So again any proper name such as John Smith, is almost without meaning until we know the John Smith in question. It is true that the name alone connotes the fact that he is **a Teuton**, and *is* a male; but, so soon as we know the exact individual it denotes, the name surely implies, also, the peculiar features, form, and character, of that individual. In fact, as it is only by the peculiar qualities, features, or circumstances of a thing, that we can ever recognise it, no name could have any fixed meaning unless we attached to it, mentally at least, such a definition of the kind of thing denoted by it, that we should know whether any given thing was denoted by it or not. If the name John Smith does not suggest to my mind the qualities of John Smith, how shall I know him when I meet him? for he certainly does not bear his name written upon his brow *.

This, however, is quite an undecided question; and as Mr Mill is generally considered the best authority upon the subject, it may be well for the reader provisionally to accept his opinion, that singular or proper names are non-connotative, and all concrete general names are connotative. **Abstract** names, on the other hand, can hardly

* Further objections to Mr Mill's views on this point will be found in Mr Shedden's *Elements of Logic.* London, 1864. pp. 14, &c.

possess connotation at all, for as they already *denote* the attributes or qualities of something, there is nothing left which can form the connotation of the name. Mr Mill, indeed, thinks that abstract names may often be considered connotative, as when the name *fault* connotes the attribute of hurtfulness as belonging to fault. But if fault is a true abstract word at all I should regard hurtfulness as a part of its denotation; I am inclined to think that *faultiness* is the abstract name, and that fault is generally used concretely as the name of a particular action or thing that is faulty, or possesses faultiness. But the subject cannot be properly discussed here, and the reader should note Mr Mill's opinion that abstract names are usually non-connotative, but may be connotative in some cases.

> The subject of Extension and Intension may be pursued in Hamilton's *Lectures on Logic*, Lect. VIII. ; or in Thomson's *Laws of Thought*, Sections 48 to 52. It is much noticed in Spalding's *Logic* (Encyclopædia Britannica, 8th ed.).

LESSON VI.

THE GROWTH OF LANGUAGE.

WORDS, we have seen, become equivocal in at least three different ways—by the accidental confusion of different words, by the change of meaning of a word by its habitual association with other things than its original meaning, and by analogical transfer to objects of a similar nature. We must however consider somewhat more closely certain changes in language which arise out of the last cause, and which are in constant progress. We can almost trace in fact the way in which language is created and extended, and the subject is to the logician one of a highly instructive and important character. There are two great and contrary processes which modify language as follows :—

1. **Generalization**, by which a name comes to be applied to a wider class of objects than before, so that the extension of its meaning is increased, and the intension diminished.

2. **Specialization**, by which a name comes to be restricted to a narrower class, the extension being decreaseu and the intension increased.

The first change arises in the most obvious manner, from our detecting a resemblance between a new object, which is without a name, and some well-known object. To express the resemblance we are instinctively led to apply the old name to the new object. Thus we are well acquainted with *glass*, and, if we meet any substance having the same glassy nature and appearance, we shall be apt at once to call it a kind of glass ; should we often meet with this new kind of glass it woula probably come to share the name equally with the old and original kind of glass. The word *coal* has undergone a change of this kind ; originally it was the name of charked or charred wood, which was the principal kind of fuel used five hundred years ago. As mineral coal came into use it took the name from the former fuel, which it resembled more nearly than anything else, but was at first distinguished as sea-coal or pit-coal. Being now far the more common of the two, it has taken the simple name, and we distinguish charred wood as charcoal. Paper has undergone a like change ; originally denoting the *papyrus* used in the Roman Empire, it was transferred to the new writing material made of cotton or linen rags, which was introduced at a quite uncertain period. The word *character* is interesting or account of its logical employment; the Greek χαρακτήρ denoted strictly a tool for engraving, but it became trans-ferred by association to the marks or letters engraved with it, and this meaning is still retained by the word when we speak of Greek *characters,* Arabic *characters,* i. e. figures or letters. But inasmuch as objects often have natural marks, signs, or tokens, which may indicate them as well as artificial characters, the name was generalized, and now means any peculiar or distinctive mark or quality by which an object is easily recognised.

Changes of this kind are usually effected by no parti-cular person and with no distinct purpose, but by a sort of unconscious instinct in a number of persons using the name. In the language of science, however, changes are often made purposely, and with a clear apprehension of the generalization implied. Thus *soap* in ordinary life is applied only to a compound of soda or potash with fat; but chemists have purposely extended the name so as to include any compound of a metallic salt with a fatty substance. Accordingly there are such things as *lime-soap* and *lead-soap*, which latter is employed in making common diachylon plaster. Alcohol at first de-noted the product of ordinary fermentation commonly called spirits of wine, but chemists having discovered that many other substances had a theoretical composition closely resembling spirits of wine, the name was adopted for the whole class, and a long enumeration of different kinds of alcohols will be found in Dr Roscoe's lessons on chemistry. The number of known alcohols is likewise subject to indefinite increase by the progress of discovery. Every one of the chemical terms acid, alkali, metal, alloy, earth, ether, oil, gas, salt, may be shown to have under-gone great generalizations.

In other sciences there is hardly a less supply of

instances.   A lens originally meant a lenticular shaped
or double convex piece of glass, that being the kind of
glass most frequently used by opticians.   But as glasses
of other shapes came to be used along with *lenses*, the
name was extended to concave or even to perfectly flat
pieces of glass.   The words lever, plane, cone, cylinder,
arc, conic section, curve, prism, magnet, pendulum, ray,
light, and many others, have been similarly generalized.

In common language we may observe that even
proper or singular names are often generalized, as when
in the time of Cicero a good actor was called a Roscius
after an actor of preeminent talent.   The name Cæsar
was adopted by the successor of Julius Cæsar as an official
name of the Emperor, with which it gradually became
synonymous, so that in the present day the Kaisers of
Austria and the Czars of Russia both take their title from
Cæsar.   Even the abstract name Cæsarism has been
formed to express a kind of imperial system as established
by Cæsar.   The celebrated tower built by a king of
Egypt on the island of Pharos, at the entrance of the
harbour of Alexandria, has caused lighthouses to be called
phares in French, and pharos in obsolete English.   From
the celebrated Roman General Quintus Fabius Maximus
any one who avoids bringing a contest to a crisis is said
to pursue a Fabian policy.

In science also singular names are often extended, as
when the fixed stars are called distant *suns*, or the companions of Jupiter are called his *moons*.   It is indeed one
theory, and a probable one, that all general names were
created by the process of generalization going on in the
early ages of human progress.   As the comprehension of
general notions requires higher intellect than the apprehension of singular and concrete things, it seems natural
that names should at first denote individual objects, and
should afterwards be extended to classes.   We have a

glimpse of this process in the case of the Australian natives who had been accustomed to call a large dog *Cadli*, but when horses were first introduced into the country they adopted this name as the nearest description of a horse. A very similar incident is related by Captain Cook of the natives of Otaheite. It may be objected, however, that a certain process of judgment must have been exerted before the suitability of a name to a particular thing could have been perceived, and it may be considered probable that specialization as well as generalization must have acted in the earliest origin of language much as it does at present.

Specialization is an exactly opposite process to generalization and is almost equally important. It consists in narrowing the extension of meaning of a general name, so that it comes to be the name only of an individual or a minor part of the original class. It is thus we are furnished with the requisite names for a multitude of new implements, occupations and ideas with which we deal in advancing civilization. The name physician is derived from the Greek φυσι·ός natural, and φύσις, nature, so that it properly means one who has studied nature, especially the nature of the human body. It has become restricted, however, to those who use this knowledge for medical purposes, and the investigators of natural science have been obliged to adopt the new name *physicist*. The name *naturalist* has been similarly restricted to those who study animated nature. The name *surgeon* originally meant handicraftsman, being a corruption of *chirurgeon*, derived from the Greek χειρουργός, hand-worker. It has long been specialized however to those who perform the mechanical parts of the sanatory art.

Language abounds with equally good examples. Minister originally meant a servant, or one who acted as a *minor* of another. Now it often means specially the most

mportant man in the kingdom. A chancellor was a clerk
or even a door-keeper who sat in a place separated by
bars or *cancelli* in the offices of the Roman Emperor's
palace; now it is always the name of a high or even the
highest dignitary. Peer was an equal (Latin, *Par*), and
we still speak of being tried by our peers; but now, by the
strange accidents of language, it means the few who are
superior to the rest of the Queen's subjects in rank.
Deacon, Bishop, Clerk, Queen, Captain, General, are all
words which have undergone a like process of specializa-
ion. In such words as telegraph, rail, signal, station,
and many words relating to new inventions, we may
trace the progress of change in a lifetime.

One effect of this process of specialization is very soon
to create a difference between any two words which happen
from some reason to be synonymous. Two or more words
are said to be synonymous (from the Greek σύν, with, and
νομα, name) when they have the same meaning, as in the
case, perhaps, of teacher and instructor, similarity and
resemblance, beginning and commencement, sameness
and identity, hypothesis and supposition, intension and
comprehension. But the fact is that words commonly
called synonymous are seldom perfectly so, and there are
almost always shades of difference in meaning or use,
which are explained in such works as Crabb's *English
Synonyms*. A process called by Coleridge **desynonymi-
ation**, and by Herbert Spencer **differentiation**, is always
going on, which tends to specialize one of a pair of
synonymous words to one meaning and the other to
another. Thus wave and billow originally meant exactly
the same physical effect, but poets have now appropriated
the word 'billow,' whereas wave is used chiefly in practical
and scientific matters. Undulation is a third synonym,
which will probably become the sole scientific term for
wave in course of time. Cab was originally a mere

abbreviation of cabriolet, and therefore of similar meaning
but it is now specialized to mean almost exclusively a
hackney cab. In America car is becoming restricted to
the meaning of a railway car.

It may be remarked that it is a logical defect in a
language to possess a great number of synonymous terms
since we acquire the habit of using them indifferently
without being sure that they are not subject to ambiguities
and obscure differences of meaning. The English lan
guage is especially subject to the inconvenience of having
a complete series of words derived from Greek or Latin
roots nearly synonymous with other words of Saxon or
French origin. The same statement may, in fact, be
put into Saxon or classical English; and we often, as
Whately has well remarked, seem to prove a state
ment by merely reproducing it in altered language. The
rhetorical power of the language may be increased by the
copiousness and variety of diction, but pitfalls are thus
prepared for all kinds of fallacies. (See Lessons XX
and XXI.)

In addition to the effects of generalization and speci
alization, vast additions and changes are made in lan
guage by the process of **analogous or metaphorical exten
sion** of the meaning of words. This change may be said
no doubt, to consist in generalization, since there mus
always be a resemblance between the new and old appli
cations of the term. But the resemblance is often one of
a most distant and obscure kind, such as we should cal
analogy rather than identity. All words used metapho
rically, or as similitudes, are cases of this process of ex
tension. The name **metaphor** is derived from the Greek
words μετά, over, and φέρειν, to carry; and expresses ap
parently the transference of a word from its ordinary to a
peculiar purpose. Thus the old similitude of a ruler to
the pilot of the vessel gives rise to many metaphors, a

in speaking of the Prime Minister being at the Helm of the State. The word governor, and all its derivatives, is, in fact, one result of this metaphor, being merely a corrupt form of *gubernator*, steersman. The words compass, polestar, ensign, anchor, and many others connected with navigation, are constantly used in a metaphorical manner. From the use of horses and hunting we derive another set of metaphors; as, in taking the reins of government, overturning the government, taking the bit between the teeth, the Government Whip, being heavily weighted, &c. No doubt it might be shewn that every other important occupation of life has furnished its corresponding stock of metaphors.

It is easy to shew, however, that this process, besides going on consciously at the present day, must have acted throughout the history of language, and that we owe to it almost all, or probably all, the words expressive of refined mental or spiritual ideas. The very word *spirit*, now the most refined and immaterial of ideas, is but the Latin *spiritus*, a gentle breeze or breathing; and inspiration, *esprit*, or wit, and many other words, are due to this metaphor. It is truly curious, however, that almost all the words in different languages denoting mind or soul imply the same analogy to breath. Thus, *soul* is from the Gothic root denoting a strong wind or storm; the Latin words *animus* and *anima* are supposed to be connected with the Greek ἄνεμος, wind; ψυχή is certainly derived from ψύχω, to blow; πνεῦμα, air or breath, is used in the New Testament for Spiritual Being; and our word ghost has been asserted to have a similar origin.

Almost all the terms employed in mental philosophy or metaphysics, to denote actions or phenomena of mind, are ultimately derived from metaphors. Apprehension is the putting forward of the hand to take anything; comprehension is the taking of things together in a handful;

extension is the spreading out; intention, the bending to; explication, the unfolding; application, the folding to; conception, the taking up together; relation, the carrying back; experience is the thoroughly going through a thing; difference is the carrying apart; deliberation, the weighing out; interruption, the breaking between; proposition, the placing before; intuition, the seeing into; and the list might be almost indefinitely extended. Our English name for reason, the understanding, obviously contains some physical metaphor which has not been fully explained; with the Latin *intellect* there is also a metaphor.

Every sense gives rise to words of refined meaning; sapience, taste, insipidity, goût, are derived from the sense of taste; sagacity, from the dog's extraordinary power of smell; but as the sense of sight is by far the most acute and intellectual, it gives rise to the larger part of language; clearness, lucidity, obscurity, haziness, perspicuity, and innumerable other expressions, are derived from this sense.

It is truly astonishing to notice the power which language possesses by the processes of generalization, specialization, and metaphor, to create many words from one single root. Prof. Max Müller has given a remarkable instance of this in the case of the root *spec*, which means *sight*, and appears in the Aryan languages, as in the Sanscrit *spas*, the Greek σκέπτομαι, with transposition of consonants, in the Latin *specio*, and even in the English *spy*. The following is an incomplete list of the words developed from this one root; species, special, especial, specimen, spice, spicy, specious, speciality, specific, specialization, specie (gold, or silver), spectre, specification, spectacle, spectator, spectral, spectrum, speculum, specular, speculation. The same root also enters into composition with various prefixes; and we thus obtain a series of words, suspect, aspect, circumspect, expect, inspect, prospect, respect, retrospect, introspection, conspicuous, perspicuity, perspective; with each of which, again, a number of derivatives is connected. Thus, from suspect, we derive suspicion, suspicable, suspicious, suspiciously, suspiciousness. I have estimated that there are in all at least 246 words, employed at some period or other in the English language which undoubtedly come from the one root *spec.*

> J. S. Mill's *Logic*, Book IV. Chap. V. 'On the Natural
> History of the Variations in the Meanings of Terms.'
> Archbishop Trench, *On the Study of Words.*
> Max Müller, *Lectures on the Science of Language.*

LESSON VII.

LEIBNITZ ON KNOWLEDGE.

IN treating of terms it is necessary that we should clearly understand what a perfect notion of the meaning of a term requires. When a name such as *monarch,* or *civilization,* or *autonomy* is used, it refers the mind to some thing or some idea, and we ought if possible to obtain a perfect knowledge of the thing or idea before we use the word. In what does this perfect knowledge consist? What are its necessary characters? This is a question which the celebrated mathematician and philosopher Leibnitz attempted to answer in a small treatise or tract first published in the year 1684. This tract has been the basis of what is given on the subject in several recent works on Logic, and a complete translation of the tract has been appended by Mr Baynes to his translation of the *Port Royal Logic.* As the remarks of Leibnitz himself are not always easy to understand, I will not confine myself to his exact words, but will endeavour to give the simplest possible statement of his views, according as they have been interpreted by Dr Thomson or Sir W. Hamilton.

Knowledge is either obscure or clear; either confused or distinct; either adequate or inadequate; and lastly either symbolical or intuitive. Perfect knowledge must be clear, distinct, adequate and intuitive; if it fails in any one of these respects it is more or less imperfect. We may, therefore, classify knowledge as in the following scheme :—

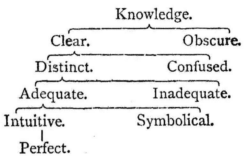

A notion, that is to say our knowledge of a thing, is obscure when it does not enable us to recognize the thing again and discriminate it from all other things. We have a clear notion of a rose and of most common flowers because we can recognise them with certainty, and do not confuse them with each other. Also we have a clear notion of any of our intimate friends or persons whom we habitually meet, because we recognise them whenever we see them with the utmost certainty and without hesitation. It is said that a shepherd acquires by practice a clear notion of each sheep of his flock, so as to enable him to single out any one separately, and a keeper of hounds learns the name and character of each hound, while other persons have only an obscure idea of the hounds generally, and could not discriminate one from the other. But the geologist cannot give a clear idea of what sandstone, conglomerate, or schist, or slate, or trap rock consists, because different rocks vary infinitely in degree and character, and it is often barely possible to say whether a rock is sandstone or conglomerate, schist or slate, and so on. In the lower forms of life the naturalist hardly has a clear notion of animal life, as distinguished from vegetable life; it is often difficult to decide whether a protophyte should be classed with animals or plants.

Clear knowledge, again, is **confused**, when we cannot distinguish the parts and qualities of the thing known, and can only recognise it as a whole. Though any one instantly knows a friend, and could discriminate him from all other persons, yet he would generally find it impossible to say how he knows him, or by what marks. He could not describe his figure or features, but in the very roughest manner. A person unpractised in drawing, who attempts to delineate even such a familiar object as a horse or cow, soon finds that he has but a confused notion of its form, while an artist has a distinct idea of the form of every limb. The chemist has a **distinct** as well as a clear notion of gold and silver, for he can not only tell with certainty whether any metal is really gold or silver, but he can specify and describe exactly the qualities by which he knows it; and could, if necessary, mention a great many other qualities as well. We have a very distinct notion of a chess-board, because we know it consists of 64 square spaces; and all our ideas of geometrical figures, such as triangles, circles, parallelograms, squares, pentagons, hexagons, &c. are or ought to be perfectly distinct. But when we talk of a *constitutional government* or a *civilized* nation, we have only the vaguest idea of what we mean. We cannot say exactly what is requisite to make a Government constitutional, without including also Governments which we do not intend to include; and so of civilized nations; these terms have neither distinct nor clear meanings.

It is to be remarked that no simple idea, such as that of *red colour*, can be distinct in the meaning here intended, because nobody can analyse red colour, or describe to another person what it is. A person who has been blind from birth cannot be made to conceive it; and it is only by bringing an actual red object before the eye that we can define its character. The same is generally true of all simple sensations, whether tastes, smells, colours, or sounds; these then may be clearly known, but not *distinctly*, in the meaning which Leibnitz gives to this word.

To explain the difference which Leibnitz intended to denote by the names **adequate** and **inadequate**, is not easy. He says, "When everything which enters into a distinct notion is distinctly known, or when the last analysis is reached, the knowledge is **adequate**, of which I scarcely know whether a perfect example can be offered —the knowledge of numbers, however, approaches near to it."

To have adequate knowledge of things, then, we must not only distinguish the parts which make up our notion of a thing, but the parts which make up those parts. For instance, we might be said to have an adequate notion of a chess-board, because we know it to be made up of 64 squares, and we know each of those squares distinctly, because each is made up of 4 equal right lines, joined at right angles. Nevertheless, we cannot be said to have a distinct notion of a straight line, because we cannot well define it, or resolve it into anything simpler. To be completely adequate, our knowledge ought to admit of analysis after analysis *ad infinitum*, so that adequate knowledge would be impossible. But, as Dr Thomson remarks, we may consider any knowledge adequate which carries the analysis sufficiently far for the purpose in view. A mechanist, for instance, has adequate knowledge of a machine, if he not only know its several wheels and parts, but the purposes, materials, forms, and actions of those parts; provided again that he knows all the mechanical properties of the materials, and the geometrical properties of the forms which may influence the working of the machine. But he is not expected to go on still further and explain why iron or wood of a particular quality is strong or brittle, why oil acts as a lubricator, or on what axioms the principles of mechanical forces are founded.

Lastly, we must notice the very important distinction of **symbolical** and **intuitive** knowledge. From the original meaning of the word, **intuitive** would denote that which we gain by *seeing* (Latin, *intueor*, to look at), and any knowledge which we have directly through the senses, or by immediate communication to the mind, is called *intuitive*. Thus we may learn intuitively what a square or a hexagon is, but hardly what a chiliagon, or figure of 1000 sides, is.

We could not tell the difference by sight of a figure of 1000 sides and a figure of 1001 sides. Nor can we imagine any such figure completely before the mind. It is known to us only by name or symbolically. All large numbers, such as those which state the velocity of light (186,000 miles per second), the distance of the sun (91,000,000 miles), and the like, are known to us only by symbols, and they are beyond our powers of imagination.

Infinity is known in a similar way, so that we can in an intellectual manner become acquainted with that of which our senses could never inform us. We speak also of *nothing*, of *zero*, of *that which is self-contradictory*, of the *non-existent*, or even of the *unthinkable* or *inconceivable*, although the words denote what can never be realized in the mind and still less be perceived through the senses intuitively, but can only be treated in a merely symbolical way.

In arithmetic and algebra we are chiefly occupied with symbolical knowledge only, since it is not necessary in working a long arithmetical question or an algebraical problem that we should realise to ourselves at each step the meaning of the numbers and symbols. We learn from algebra that if we multiply together the sum and difference of two quantities we get the difference of the squares; as, in symbols

$$(a + b)(a - b) = a^2 - b^2;$$

which is readily seen to be true, as follows ·

$$a + b$$
$$a - b$$
$$\overline{a^2 + ab}$$
$$\quad - ab - b^2$$
$$\overline{a^2 + 0 \ - b^2.}$$

In the above we act darkly or symbolically, using the letters *a* and *b* according to certain fixed rules, without knowing or caring what they mean; and whatever meaning we afterwards give to *a* and *b* we may be sure the process holds good, and that the conclusion is true without going over the steps again.

But in geometry, we argue by intuitive perception of the truth of each step, because we actually employ a representation in the mind of the figures in question, and satisfy ourselves that the requisite properties are really possessed by the figures. Thus the algebraical truth shown above in symbols may be easily proved to hold true of lines and rectangles contained under those lines, as a corollary of the 5th Prop. of Euclid's Second Book.

Much might be said concerning the comparative advantages of the intuitive and symbolical methods. The latter is usually much the less laborious, and gives the most widely applicable answers; but the symbolical seldom or never gives the same command and comprehension of the subject as the intuitive method. Hence the study of geometry is always indispensable in education, although the same truths are often more readily proved by algebra. It is the peculiar glory of Newton that he was able to explain the motions of the heavenly bodies by the geometric or intuitive method; whereas the greatest of his successors, such as Lagrange or Laplace, have treated these motions by the aid of symbols.

What is true of mathematical subjects may be applied to all kinds of reasoning; for words are symbols as much as A, B, C, or x, y, z, and it is possible to argue with words without any consciousness of their meaning. Thus if I say that " selenium is a dyad element, and a dyad element is one capable of replacing two equivalents of hydrogen," no one ignorant of chemistry will be able to attach any meaning to these terms, and yet any one will be able to conclude that " selenium is capable of replacing two equivalents of hydrogen." Such a person argues in a purely symbolical manner. Similarly, whenever in common life we use words, without having in mind at the moment the full and precise meaning of the words, we possess symbolical knowledge only.

There is no worse habit for a student or reader to acquire than that of accepting words instead of a knowledge of things. It is perhaps worse than useless to read a work on natural history about Infusoria, Foraminifera, Rotifera and the like, if these names do not convey clear images to the mind. Nor can a student who has not witnessed experiments, and examined the substances with his own eyes, derive any considerable advantage from works on chemistry and natural philosophy, where he will meet with hundreds of new terms which would be to him mere empty and confusing signs. On this account we should lose no opportunity of acquainting ourselves, by means of our senses, with the forms, properties and changes of things, in order that the language we employ may, as far as possible, be employed intuitively, and we may be saved from the absurdities and fallacies into which we might otherwise fall. We should observe, in short, the advice of Bacon—*ipsis consuescere rebus*—*to accustom ourselves to things themselves.*

Hamilton's *Lectures on Logic.* Lect. IX.
Baynes' *Port Royal Logic.* Part I. Chap. 9, and Appendix.

LESSON VIII.

KINDS OF PROPOSITIONS.

A TERM standing alone is not capable of expressing truth; it merely refers the mind to some object or class of objects, about which something may be affirmed or denied, but about which the term itself does not affirm or deny anything. "Sun," "air," "table," suggest to every mind objects of thought, but we cannot say that "sun is true," or "air is mistaken," or "table is false." We must join words or terms into sentences or propositions before they can express those reasoning actions of the mind to which truth or falsity may be attributed. "The sun is bright," "the air is fresh," "the table is unsteady," are statements which may be true or may be false, but we can certainly entertain the question of their truth in any circumstances. Now as the logical term was defined to be any combination of words expressing an act of simple apprehension, so a logical proposition is any combination of words expressing an act of judgment. The proposition is in short the result of an act of judgment reduced to the form of language.

What the logician calls a proposition the grammarian calls a **sentence.** But though every proposition is a sentence, it is not to be supposed that every sentence is a proposition. There are in fact several kinds of sentences more or less distinct from a proposition, such as a Sentence Interrogative or Question, a Sentence Imperative or a Command, a Sentence Optative, which expresses a wish, and an Exclamatory Sentence, which expresses an emotion of wonder or surprise. These kinds of sentence may possibly be reduced, by a more or less indirect mode of expression, to the form of a Sentence Indicative, which is the grammatical name for a proposition; but until this be done they have no proper place in Logic, or at least no place which logicians have hitherto sufficiently explained.

The name **proposition** is derived from the Latin words *pro*, before, and *pono*, I place, and means the laying or placing before any person the result of an act of judgment. Now every act of judgment or comparison must involve the two things brought into comparison, and every proposition will naturally consist of three parts— the two terms or names denoting the things compared, and the copula or verb indicating the connection between them, as it was ascertained in the act of judgment. Thus the proposition, "Gold is a yellow substance," expresses an agreement between gold and certain other substances previously called yellow in regard to their colour. Gold and yellow substance are evidently the two terms, and *is* the copula.

It is always usual to call the first term of a proposition the **subject**, since it denotes the *underlying* matter, as it were (Latin, *sub*, under, and *jactum*, laid) about which something is asserted. The second term is called the **predicate**, which simply means that which is affirmed or asserted. This name is derived from the Latin *prædĭcare*, to assert, whence comes the French name *prédicateur*, corrupted into our *preacher*. This Latin verb is not to be confused with the somewhat similar one *predīcere*, which has the entirely different meaning to *predict* or foretell. I much suspect that newspaper writers and others, who pedantically use the verb "to predi. cate," sometimes fall into this confusion, and really mean to *predict*, but it is in any case desirable that a purely technical term like *predicate* should not be needlessly introduced into common language, when there are so many other good words which might be used. This and all other technical scientific terms should be kept to their proper scientific use, and the neglect of this rule injures at once the language of common life and the language of science.

Propositions are distinguished into two kinds, according as they make a statement conditionally or unconditionally. Thus the proposition, "If metals are heated they are softened," is conditional, since it does not make an assertion concerning metals generally, but only in the circumstances when they become heated. Any circumstance which must be granted or supposed before the assertion becomes applicable is a *condition*. Conditional propositions are of two kinds, Hypothetical and Disjunctive, but their consideration will be best deferred to a subsequent Lesson (XIX). Unconditional propositions are those with which we shall for some time be solely concerned, and these are usually called **Categorical** Propositions, from the Greek verb κατηγορέω (*kategoreo*, to assert or affirm).

The following diagram will conveniently represent the classification of sentences and propositions as far as we have yet proceeded :—

$$\text{Sentence} \begin{cases} \text{Indicative} \\ \quad = \text{Proposition} \begin{cases} \text{Categorical} \\ \text{Conditional} \end{cases} \begin{cases} \text{Hypothetical.} \\ \text{Disjunctive.} \end{cases} \\ \text{Interrogative} \\ \text{Imperative} \\ \text{Optative} \\ \text{Exclamatory} \end{cases}$$

It is now necessary to consider carefully the several kinds of categorical propositions. They are classified according to **quality** and according to **quantity**. As regards quality they are either affirmative or negative ; as regards quantity they are either universal or particular.

An **affirmative** proposition is one which asserts a certain agreement between the subject and predicate, so that the qualities or attributes of the predicate belong to the subject. The proposition, "gold is a yellow substance," states such an agreement of gold with other yellow substances, that we know it to have the colour yellow, as well as whatever qualities are implied in the name *substance*. A **negative** proposition, on the other hand, asserts a difference or discrepancy, so that some at least of the qualities of the predicate do not belong to the subject. " Gold is not easily fusible" denies that the quality of being easily fused belongs to gold.

Propositions are again divided according to quantity into **universal** and **particular** propositions. If the proposition affirms the predicate to belong to the whole of the subject, it is an universal proposition, as in the example

" all metals are elements," which affirms that the quality of being undecomposable or of being simple in nature is true of all metals. But if we say " some metals are brit-tle," the quality of brittleness is affirmed only of some indefinite portion of the metals, and there is nothing in the proposition to make us sure that any certain metal is brittle. The name *particular* being derived from the diminutive of the Latin *pars* would naturally signify a small part, but in logic it must be carefully interpreted as signifying any part, from the smallest fraction up to nearly the whole. Particular propositions do not include cases where a predicate is affirmed of the whole or of none of the subject, but they include any between these limits. We may accordingly count among particular propositions all such as the following:—

A very few metals are less dense than water.

Most elements are metals.

Many of the planets are comparatively small bodies.

Not a few distinguished men have had distinguished sons.

The reader must carefully notice the somewhat subtle point explained further on, that the particular proposition though asserting the predicate only of a part of the sub-ject, does not deny it to be true of the whole.

Aristotle, indeed, considered that there were alto-gether four kinds of proposition as regards quantity, namely—

Proposition $\begin{cases} \text{Universal.} \\ \text{Particular.} \\ \text{Singular.} \\ \text{Indefinite.} \end{cases}$

The singular proposition is one which has a singular term for its subject, as in—

Socrates was very wise.

London is a vast city.

But we may fairly consider that a singular proposition is an universal one; for it clearly refers to the whole of the subject, which in this case is a single individual thing.

Indefinite or indesignate propositions are those which are devoid of any mark of quantity whatever, so that the form of words gives us no mode of judging whether the predicate is applicable to the whole or only part of the subject. *Metals are useful, Comets are subject to the law of gravitation,* are indefinite propositions. In reality, however, such propositions have no distinct place in logic at all, and the logician cannot properly treat them until the true and precise meaning is made apparent. The predicate must be true either of the whole or of part of the subject, so that the proposition, as it stands, is clearly incomplete; but if we attempt to remedy this and supply the marks of quantity, we overstep the proper boundaries of logic and assume ourselves to be acquainted with the subject matter or science of which the proposition treats. We may safely take the preceding examples to mean "*some metals* are useful" and "*all comets* are subject to the law of gravitation," but not on logical grounds. Hence we may strike out of logic altogether the class of indefinite propositions, on the understanding that they must be rendered definite before we treat them. I may observe, however, that in the following lessons I shall frequently use propositions in the indefinite form as examples, on the understanding that where no sign of quantity appears, the universal quantity is to be assumed. It is probable that wherever a term is used alone, it ought to be interpreted as meaning the whole of its class. But however this may be, we need not recognize the indefinite proposition as a distinct kind; and singular propositions having been resolved into universals, there remain only the two kinds, Universal and Particular.

Remembering now that there are two kinds of propo-

sition as regards quality, and two as regards quantity, we
shall be able to form altogether four varieties, thus :—

$$
\text{Proposition}
\begin{cases}
\text{Universal}
\begin{cases}
\text{Affirmative} & \textbf{A} \\
\text{Negative} & \textbf{E}
\end{cases} \\
\text{Particular}
\begin{cases}
\text{Affirmative} & \textbf{I} \\
\text{Negative} & \textbf{O}
\end{cases}
\end{cases}
$$

The vowel letters placed at the right hand are symbols or abbreviated names, which are always used to
denote the four kinds of proposition; and there will be
no difficulty in remembering their meaning if we observe
that **A** and **I** occur in the Latin verb *affirmo,* I affirm, and
E and **O** in *nego,* I deny.

There will not generally be any difficulty in referring
to its proper class any proposition that we meet with in
writings. The mark of universality usually consists of
some adjective of quantity, such as *all, every, each, any,*
the *whole;* but whenever the predicate is clearly intended
to apply to the whole of the subject we may treat the proposition as universal. The signs of a particular proposition are the adjectives of quantity, *some, certain, a few,*
many, most, or such others as clearly indicate *part at*
least.

The negative proposition is known by the adverbial
particle *not* being joined to the copula; but in the proposition **E**, that is the universal negative, we frequently use
the particle *no* or *none* prefixed to the subject. Thus,
" *no* metals are compound," " *none* of the ancients were
acquainted with the laws of motion," are familiar forms of
the universal negative.

The student must always be prepared too to meet with
misleading or ambiguous forms of expression. Thus the
proposition, " all the metals are not denser than water,"
might be taken as **E** or **O**, according as we interpret it to

mean "no metals are denser than water," or "not all the metals," &c., the last of course being the true sense. The little adjective *few* is very subject to a subtle ambiguity of this kind; for if I say "*few books* are at once learned and amusing," I may fairly be taken to assert that *a few books* certainly are so, but what I really mean to draw attention to is my belief that "*the greater number of books are not* at once learned and amusing." A proposition of this kind is generally to be classed rather as O than I. The word *some* is subject to an exactly similar ambiguity between *some but not all*, and *some at least, it may be all;* the latter appears to be the correct interpretation, as shewn in the following lesson (p 79).

As propositions are met with in ordinary language they are subject to various inversions and changes of the simple logical form.

(1) It is not uncommon, especially in poetry, to find the predicate placed first, for the sake of emphasis or variety ; as in " Blessed are the merciful ;" " Comes something down with eventide ;" " Great is Diana of the Ephesians." There is usually no difficulty in detecting such an inversion of the terms, and the sentence must then be reduced to the regular order before being treated in logic.

(2) The subject may sometimes be mistaken for the predicate when it is described by a relative clause, standing at the end of the sentence, as in "no one is free who is enslaved by his appetites." Here *free* is evidently the predicate, although it stands in the middle of the sentence, and "one who is enslaved by his appetites" is the real subject. This proposition is evidently of the form E.

Propositions are also expressed in various modes differing from the simple logical order, and some of the different kinds which arise must be noticed.

Exclusive propositions contain some words, such as *only, alone, none but,* which limit the predicate to the subject. Thus, in "elements alone are metals," we are informed that the predicate "metal" cannot be applied to anything except "elements," but we are not to understand that "all elements are metals." The same meaning is expressed by "none but elements are metals;" or, again, by "all that are not elements are not metals;" and this we shall see in the next lesson is really equivalent to "all metals are elements." Arguments which appear fallacious at first sight will often be found correct when they contain exclusive propositions and these are properly interpreted.

Exceptive propositions affirm a predicate of all the subject with the exception of certain defined cases, to which, as is implied, the predicate does not belong. Thus, "all the planets, except Venus and Mercury, are beyond the earth's orbit," is a proposition evidently equivalent to two, viz. that Venus and Mercury are not beyond the earth's orbit, but that the rest are. If the exceptions are not actually specified by name an exceptive proposition must often be treated as a particular one. For if I say "all the planets in our system except one agree with Bode's law," and do not give the name of that one exception, the reader cannot, on the ground of the proposition, assert of any planet positively that it does agree with Bode's law.

Some propositions are distinguished as **explicative** or **essential,** because they merely affirm of their subject a predicate which is known to belong to it by all who can define the subject. Such propositions merely unfold what is already contained in the subject. "A parallelogram has four sides and four angles," is an explicative or essential proposition. "London, which is the capital of England, is the largest city of Europe," contains two propositions; of which one merely directs our attention to a fact which all may be supposed to know, viz. that London is the capital of England.

Ampliative propositions, on the other hand, join a new predicate to the subject. Thus to those who do not know the comparative sizes of cities in Europe, the last example contains an ampliative proposition. The greater number of propositions are of this kind.

Tautologous or Truistic propositions are those which merely affirm the subject of itself, and give no information whatever; as in, "whatever is, is;" "what I have written, I have written."

It is no part of formal Logic to teach us how to interpret the meanings of sentences as we meet them in writings; this is rather the work of the grammarian and philologist. Logic treats of the relations of the different propositions, and the inferences which can be drawn from them; but it is nevertheless desirable that the reader should acquire some familiarity with the real logical meaning of conventional or peculiar forms of expression, and a number of examples will be found at the end of the book, which the reader is requested to classify and treat as directed.

In addition to the distinctions already noticed it has long been usual to distinguish propositions as they are pure or modal. The pure proposition simply asserts that the predicate does or does not belong to the subject, while the modal proposition states this *cum modo*, or with an intimation of the mode or manner in which the predicate belongs to the subject. The presence of any adverb of time, place, manner, degree, &c., or any expression equivalent to an adverb, confers modality on a proposition. "Error is always in haste;" "justice is ever equal;" "a perfect man ought always to be conquering himself," are examples of modal propositions in this acceptation of

the name. Other logicians, however, have adopted a
different view, and treat **modality** as consisting in the
degree of certainty or probability with which a judgment
is made and asserted. Thus, we may say, "an equilateral
triangle is *necessarily* equiangular;" "men are *generally*
trustworthy;" "a falling barometer *probably* indicates a
coming storm;" "Aristotle's lost treatises may *possibly* be
recovered;" and all these assertions are made with a different degree of certainty or modality. Dr Thomson is
no doubt right in holding that the modality does not
affect the copula of the proposition, and the subject could
only be properly treated in a work on Probable Reasoning.

Many logicians have also divided propositions according as they are **true** or **false**, and it might well seem
to be a distinction of importance. Nevertheless, it is
wholly beyond the province of the logician to consider
whether a proposition is true or not in itself; all that he
has to determine is the comparative truth of propositions
—that is, whether one proposition is true when another
is. Strictly speaking, logic has nothing to do with a proposition by itself; it is only in converting or transmuting
certain propositions into certain others that the work of
reasoning consists, and the truth of the conclusion is only
so far in question as it follows from the truth of what we
shall call the premises. It is the duty of the special sciences each in its own sphere to determine what are true
propositions and what are false, and logic would be but
another name for the whole of knowledge could it take
this duty on itself.

See Mr Mill's *System of Logic*, Book I. Chap. IV.
which generally agrees with what is given above. Chapters V. and VI. contain Mr Mill's views on the Nature
and Import of Propositions, which subject may be further

studied in Mr Mill's *Examination of Sir W. Hamilton's Philosophy,* Chap. XVIII.; Hamilton's *Lectures on Logic,* No. XIII.; and Mansel's *Prolegomena Logica,* Chap. II.; but the subject is too metaphysical in character to be treated in this work.

LESSON IX.

THE OPPOSITION OF PROPOSITIONS.

WE have ascertained that four distinct kinds of propositions are recognized by logicians,—the Universal affirmative, the Particular affirmative, the Universal negative, and the Particular negative, commonly indicated by the symbols A, I, E, O. It is now desirable to compare together somewhat minutely the meaning and use of propositions of these various kinds, so that we may clearly learn how the truth of one will affect the truth of others, or how the same truth may be thrown into various forms of expression.

The **proposition A** expresses the fact that the thing or class of things denoted by the subject is included in, and forms part of the class of things denoted by the predicate. Thus " all metals are elements" means that metals form a part of the class of *elements,* but not the whole. As there are altogether 63 known elements, of which 48 are metals, we cannot say that all elements are metals. The proposition itself does not tell us anything about *elements in general;* it is not in fact concerned with elements, metals being the subject about which it gives us information. This is best indicated by a kind of diagram, first used by the celebrated mathematician Euler, in his letters to a German princess. In Fig. 1, the metals are supposed to be enclosed in the small circle somewhat as sheep might be in a pinfold, this circle containing all the metals and nothing else. The greater circle is supposed to contain in a similar manner all the elements and nothing else. Now as the small circle is wholly within the larger one, it follows that all the metals must be counted as

Fig. 1.

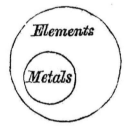

elements, but of the part of the elements outside the circle of metals we know nothing from the proposition.

The **particular affirmative** proposition I exactly resembles **A** in meaning, except that only part of the subject is brought into question. When I say that " some metals are brittle," I mean that of a collection of all the different metals a few at least might be picked out which would be found to be brittle ; but the word *some* is exceedingly indefinite, shewing neither the exact number of brittle metals, nor how we are to know them from the others, unless indeed by trying whether they are brittle. This proposition will be properly represented in Euler's mode by two intersecting circles, one supposed to enclose all metals, and the other all brittle substances. The mere fact of the two circles intersecting proves that some

Fig. 2.

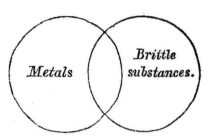

part of one class must coincide with some part of the other class, which is what the proposition is intended to express. Concerning the portions of the circles which do not overlap the proposition tells us nothing.

The **universal negative** proposition E denies the existence of any agreement or coincidence between the subject and predicate. Thus from "no metals are compound substances," we learn that no metal is to be found among compound substances, and it follows necessarily that no compound substance can be found among the metals. For were there a compound substance among the metals, there would evidently be one metal at least among the compound substances. This entire separation in thought of the two classes is well shewn in Euler's method by two disconnected circles.

Fig. 3.

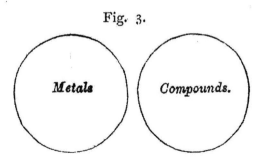

The reader will easily see that the proposition E is

distinguished from A and I, by the fact that it gives us some information concerning the *whole of the predicate,* because we learn that none of the objects included in the predicate can be found among those included in the sub-ject. The affirmative propositions, on the other hand, warranted us in holding that the objects denoted by the subject, or some particular part of them, were included in the predicate, but *they give us no warrant* for saying that any specified part of the predicate is in the subject. Because we merely know that a substance is an element, we do not learn from the proposition "all metals are ele-ments" whether it is a metal or not. And from the pro-position "some metals are brittle," we certainly cannot ascertain whether any particular brittle substance is a metal. We must seek the information from other sources. But from "no metals are compounds" we learn of any compour l substance that it is not a metal, as well as of a metal *t*hat it is not a compound substance.

The important difference above explained is expressed in technical language by saying that the proposition E *distributes its predicate,* whereas the affirmative proposi-tions A and I *do not distribute their predicates.* By dis-tribution of a term is simply meant *taking it universally,* or *referring to all parts of it;* and as the validity of any argument or syllogism will usually depend upon the suffi-cient distribution of the terms occurring in it, too much attention cannot be paid to this point.

Judging from the examples we have had, it will be seen that the universal affirmative distributes its subject, but not its predicate ; for it gives us some information concerning all metals, but not all elements. The parti-cular affirmative distributes neither subject nor predicate; for we do not learn anything from our example concern-ing all metals nor concerning all brittle substances. But the universal negative distributes both subject and predicate, for we learn something of *all metals* and also of *all compound substances.*

The particular negative proposition **O** will be found to distribute its predicate, but not its subject. When I say *some metals are not brittle*, I intentionally refer only to a part of the metals, and exclude them from the class of *brittle substances;* but I cannot help at the same time referring to the whole of the brittle substances. If the metals in question coincided with any part of the brittle substances they could not be said to be excluded from the class. To exclude a thing from any space, as from a particular chamber of a house, it must not merely be removed from some part, but from any part, or from the whole of that space or chamber. Euler's diagram for this proposition may be constructed in the same manner as for the proposition **I** as follows :—

Fig. 4.

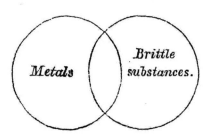

It is apparent that though part of the metals fall into the circle of brittle substances, yet the remaining portion are excluded from any part of the predicate.

We may state the result at which we have now arrived in the following form:—

				Subject.	Predicate.
Proposition	Universal	Affirmative	**A.**	Distributed.	Undistributed.
		Negative	**E.**	Distributed.	Distributed.
	Particular	Affirmative	**I.**	Undistributed.	Undistributed.
		Negative	**O.**	Undistributed.	Distributed.

We shall now discover with great ease the relations of the four propositions, each to each, that is to say, the way in which they are opposed to each other. It is obvious that the truth of one proposition interferes more or less completely with the truth of another proposition having the same subject and predicate. If "all metals are elements," it is impossible that "*some* metals are not elements," and still more palpably impossible, so to say, that "no metals should be elements." The proposition A, then, is **inconsistent** with both E and O; and, *vice versâ*, E and O are inconsistent with A. Similarly, E is inconsistent with A and I. But this important difference must be noted, that if A be false, O is necessarily true, but E may or may not be true. If it is not true that "all men are sincere," it follows that "some men are not sincere," but it does not in the least follow that "no men are sincere." This difference is expressed by saying that A and O are **contradictory** **propositions**, whereas A and E are called **contrary propositions**. It is plain that A and E, as in "all men are sincere" and "no men are sincere," represent the utmost possible contrariety of circumstances. In order to prove the falsity of A, it is sufficient to establish the truth of O, and it is superfluous, even if possible, to prove E; similarly E is disproved by proving I, and it is superfluous to prove A. Any person who asserts a universal proposition, either A or E, lays himself under the necessity of explaining away or disproving every' single exception brought against it. An opponent may always restrict himself to the much easier task of finding instances which apparently or truly contradict the universality of the statement, but if he takes upon himself to affirm the direct contrary, he is himself open to easy attack. Were it to be asserted, for instance, that "All Christians are more moral than Pagans," it would be easy to adduce examples showing that "Some Christians

are not more moral than Pagans," but it would be absurd
to suppose that it would be necessary to go to the contrary extreme, and shew that "No Christians are more
moral than Pagans." In short A is sufficiently and best
disproved by O, and E by I. It will be easily apparent
that, *vice versâ*, O is disproved by A, and I by E; nor is
there, indeed, any other mode at all of disproving these
particular propositions.

When we compare together the propositions I and O
we find that they are in a certain sense contrary in nature, one being affirmative and the other negative, but
that they are still consistent with each other. It is true
both that "Some metals are brittle," for instance Antimony, Bismuth and Arsenic; but it is also true that
"Some metals are not brittle." And the reader will observe that when I affirm "Some metals are elements,"
there is nothing in this to prevent the truth of "Some
metals are not elements," although on other grounds we
know that this is not true. The propositions I and O are
called subcontraries each of the other, the name con-
noting a less degree of contrariety than exists between A
and E.

As regards the relation of A to I and E to O, it is plain
that the truth of the universal includes and necessitates
the truth of the particular What may be affirmed or
denied of all parts of a class may certainly be affirmed or
denied similarly of some part of the class. From the
truth of the particular we have no right to infer either
the truth or falsity of the universal of the same quality.
These pairs of propositions are called subalterns, i. e.
one under the other (Latin *sub* under, and *alter* the other
of two), or we may say more exactly that I and O are
respectively the *subalternates* of A and E, each of which
is a *subalternans*.

The relations of the propositions just described are all clearly shown in the following scheme :—

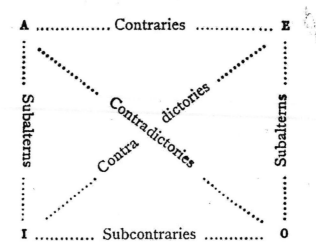

It is so highly important to apprehend completely and readily the **consistency** or **opposition** of propositions, that I will put the matter in another form.   Taking any two propositions having the same subject and predicate, they must come under one of the following statements :—

1.   Of contradictory propositions, one must be true and one false.

2.   Of contrary propositions, both cannot be true, and both may be false.

3.   Of subcontrary propositions, one only can be false, and both may be true.

4.   Of subalterns, the particular is true if the universal be true; but the universal may or may not be true when the particular is true.

I put the same matter in yet another form in the following table, which shows how the truth of each of A, E, I, and O, affects the truth of each of the others.

	A is	E is	I is	O is
f **A** be true	true	false	true	false.
„ **E** „ „	false	true	false	true.
„ **I** „ „	doubtful	false	true	doubtful.
„ **O** „ „	false	doubtful	doubtful	true.

It will be evident that from the affirmation of univer‹ ls more information is derived than from the affirmation ˙particulars. It follows that more information can be ːrived from the denial of particulars than from the ːnial of universals, that is to say, there are less cases left *ubtful*, as in the above table.

The reader may well be cautioned, however, against ι ambiguity which has misled some even of the most ɪinent logicians. In particular propositions the adjec ʀe *some* is to be carefully interpreted as *some, and there ay or may not be more or all.* Were we to interpret it *some, not more nor all*, then it would really give to the oposition the force of **I** and **O** combined. If I say " some en are sincere," I must not be taken as implying that ₕome men are not sincere;" I must be understood to edicate sincerity of some men, leaving the character of e remainder wholly unaffected. It follows from this at, when I deny the truth of a particular, I must not be ιderstood as implying the truth of the universal of the me quality. To deny the truth of " some men are mor- l" might seem very natural, on the ground that not *some* t *all men* are mortal; but then the proposition denied ʊuld really be *some men are not mortal*, i. e. **O** not **I**. ence when I deny that "some men are immortal" I ʒan that "no men are immortal;" and when I deny that ₗome men are not mortal," I mean that "all men are ɔrtal."

It has long been usual to compare propositions as

regards the quality of the subject matter to which th
refer, and what is technically called the **matter** was d
tinguished into three kinds, **necessary, contingent,** and i
possible. Necessary matter consists of any subject
which the proposition **A** may be affirmed; impossible
which **E** may be affirmed. Any subject or branch of knc
ledge in which universal statements cannot usually
made is called contingent matter, and it implies the tri
of **I** and **O.** Thus "comets are subject to gravitatio
though an indefinite or indesignate proposition (p. €
may be interpreted as **A,** because it refers to a part
natural science where such general laws obtain. I
"men are sincere" would be properly interpreted as p
ticular or **I,** because the matter is clearly contingent. 1
truth of the following statements is evident.

In necessary matter **A** and **I** are true; **E** and **O** false
In contingent matter **I** and **O** are true; **A** and **E** fals
In impossible matter **E** and **O** are true; **A** and **I** false

In reality, however, this part of logical doctrine
thoroughly illogical, because in treating a proposition
have no right, as already explained (p. 70), to assu
ourselves acquainted with the science to which it ref
Our duty is to elicit the exact consequences of any sta
ments given to us. We must learn in logic to transfc
information in every possible way, but not to add ex1
neous facts.

LESSON X.

CONVERSION OF PROPOSITIONS, AND IMMEDIATE INFERENCE.

WE are said to infer whenever we draw one truth from another truth, or pass from one proposition to another. As Sir W. Hamilton says, Inference is "the carrying out into the last proposition what was virtually contained in the antecedent judgments." The true sphere of the science of logic indeed is to teach the principles on which this act of inference must be performed, and all the previous consideration of terms and propositions is only useful or pertinent so far as it assists us to understand the processes of inference. We have to consider in succession all the modes in which the same information may be moulded into different forms of expression often implying results of an apparently different character. Logicians are not agreed exactly as to what we may include under the name Inference, and what we should not. All would allow that there is an act of inference when we see drops of water on the ground and believe that it has rained. This is a somewhat complicated act of inference, which we shall consider in later lessons under the subject of Induction. Few or none would say that there is an act of inference in passing from "The Duke of Cambridge is the Commander-in-chief," to "The Commander-in-chief is the Duke of Cambridge." But without paying much regard to the name of the process I shall in this

lesson point out all the ways in which we can from ;
single proposition of the forms A, E, I or O, pass to anothe
proposition.

We are said to **convert** a proposition when w‹
transpose its subject and predicate; but in order tha
the **converse** or converted proposition shall be inferre‹
from the **convertend**, or that which was to be converted
we must observe two rules (1) the quality of the pro
position (affirmative or negative) must be preserved, an‹
(2) *no term must be distributed in the Converse unless i
was distributed in the Convertend.*

If in "all metals are elements" we were simply t‹
transpose the terms, thus—"all elements are metals," w‹
imply a certain knowledge about *all elements,* wherea:
it has been clearly shewn that the predicate of A is un
distributed, and that the convertend does not really giv‹
us any information concerning *all elements.* All tha
we can infer is that "some elements are metals;" thi:
converse proposition agrees with the rule, and the pro
cess by which we thus pass from A to I is called **Con
version by Limitation, or Per accidens.**

When the converse is a proposition of exactly the
same form as the convertend the process is called **simpl‹
conversion.** Thus from "some metals are brittle sub
stances" I can infer "some brittle substances ar‹
metals," as all the terms are here undistributed. Thu:
I is simply converted into I.

Again, from "no metals are compounds," I can pas:
directly to "no compounds are metals," because thes‹
propositions are both in E, and all the terms are there
fore distributed. Euler's diagram (p. 73, Fig. 3) clearl}
shows, that if all the metals are separated from all th‹
compounds, all the compounds are necessarily separate‹
from all the metals. The proposition E is then simpl}
converted into E.

But in attempting to convert the proposition **O** we encounter a peculiar difficulty, because its subject is undistributed; and yet the subject should become by conversion the predicate of a negative proposition, which distributes its predicate. Take for example the proposition, "some existing things are not material substances." By direct conversion this would become "all material substances are not existing things;" which is evidently absurd. The fallacy arises from *existing things* being distributed in the converse, whereas it is particular in the convertend; and the rules of the Aristotelian logic prevent us from inserting the sign of particular quantity before the predicate. The converse would be equally untrue and fallacious were we to make the subject particular, as in "some material substances are not existing things." We must conclude, then, that the proposition **O** cannot be treated either by simple conversion or conversion by limitation. It is requisite to apply a new process, which may be called **Conversion by Negation,** and which consists in first changing the convertend into an affirmative proposition, and then converting it simply. If we attach the negation to the predicate instead of to the copula, the proposition becomes "some existing things are *immaterial* substances," and, converting simply, we have—"some immaterial substances are existing things," which may truly be inferred from the convertend. The proposition **O**, then, is only to be converted by this exceptional method of negation.

Another process of conversion can be applied to the proposition **A**, and is known as conversion by **contraposition.** From "all metals are elements," it necessarily follows that "all not-elements are not metals." If this be not at the first moment apparent, a little reflection will render it so, and from fig. 5 we see that if all the metals be among the elements, whatever is not element, or outside the circle of elements, must also be outside the circle of metals. We may also prove the truth

Fig. 5.

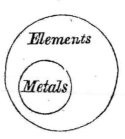

of the contrapositive proposition in this way, if we may anticipate the contents of Lesson XXIII.:—If what is not-element should be metal, then it must be an element by the original proposition, or it must be at once an element and not an element; which is impossible according to the Primary Laws of Thought (Lesson XIV.), since nothing can both have and not have the same property. It follows that what is not-element must be not-metal.

Mistakes may readily be committed in contrapositive conversion, from a cause which will be more apparent in Lesson XXII. We are very liable to infer from a proposition of the form "all metals are elements," that *all not-metals are not-elements*, which is not only a false statement in itself, but is not in the least warranted by the original proposition. In fig. 5, it is apparent that because a thing lies outside the circle of metals, it does not necessarily lie outside the circle of elements, which is wider than that of metals. Nevertheless the mistake is often made in common life, and the reader will do well to remember that the process of conversion by contraposition consists only in taking the negative of the predicate of the proposition A, as a new subject, and affirming of it universally the negative of the old subject.

Contrapositive conversion cannot be applied to the
particular propositions **I** and **O** at all, nor to the proposition **E**, in that form; but we may change **E** into **A** by
attaching the negation to the predicate, and then the
process can be applied. Thus "no men are perfect,"
may be changed into "all men are not-perfect," i.e.
"are imperfect," and then we infer by contraposition
"all not-imperfect beings are not-men." But *not-imperfect* is really the same as perfect, so that our new
proposition is really equivalent to "all perfect beings are
not men," or "no perfect beings are men," (**E**) the simple converse of the original proposition.

There remain to be described certain deductions
which may be drawn from a proposition without converting its terms. They may be called immediate inferences,
and have been very clearly described by Archbishop
Thomson in his "Outline of the Necessary Laws of
Thought" (pp. 156, &c.).

Immediate Inference by Privative Conception consists
in passing from any affirmative proposition to a negative
proposition implied in it, or equivalent to it, or *vice versa*,
in passing from a negative proposition to its corresponding affirmative.

The following table contains a proposition of each
kind changed by privative conception into an equivalent
proposition :

> **A** all metals are elements.
> **E** no metals are compounds.
>
> **E** no men are perfect.
> **A** all men are imperfect.
>
> **I** some men are trustworthy.
> **O** some men are not untrustworthy.
>
> **O** some men are not trustworthy.
> **I** some men are untrustworthy.

The truth of any of the above can be clearly illustrated

by diagrams; thus it will be apparent that if the whole circle of metals lies inside the circle of elements, no part can lie outside of that circle or among the compounds. Any of the above propositions may be converted, but the results will generally be such as we have already obtained. Thus the simple converse of "no metals are compounds" is "no compounds are metals," or "no not-elements are metals," the contrapositive of "all metals are elements." From the last example we get also by simple conversion "some untrustworthy beings are men," which is obviously the converse by negation, as before explained. Applying this kind of conversion to "some men are not untrustworthy," we have "some not-untrustworthy beings are men." Lastly, from "all men are imperfect" we may obtain through conversion by limitation, "some imperfect beings are men."

Immediate Inference by added determinants consists in joining some adjective or similar qualification both to the subject and predicate of a proposition, so as to render the meaning of each term narrower or better determined. Provided that no other alteration is made the truth of the new proposition necessarily follows from the truth of the original in almost all cases.

From "all metals are elements," we may thus infer that "all very heavy metals are very heavy elements." From "a comet is a material body" we infer "a visible comet is a visible material body." But if we apply this kind of inference too boldly we may meet with fallacious and absurd results. Thus, from "all kings are men," we might infer "all incompetent kings are incompetent men;" but it does not at all follow that those who are incompetent as kings would be incompetent in other positions. In this case and many others the qualifying adjective is liable to bear different meanings in the subject and predicate; but the inference will only be true of

necessity when the meaning is exactly the same in each
case. With comparative terms this kind of inference
will seldom be applicable; thus from "a cottage is a
building," we cannot infer "a huge cottage is a huge
building," since a cottage may be large when compared
with other cottages, but not with buildings generally.

Immediate Inference by Complex Conception is closely
similar to the last, and consists in employing the subject
and predicate of a proposition as parts of a more complex conception. From "all metals are elements," I can
pass to "a mixture of metals is a mixture of elements."
From "a horse is a quadruped" I infer "the skeleton of
a horse is the skeleton of a quadruped." But here again
the reader must beware of applying the process where
the new complex conception has a different meaning in
the subject and predicate. Thus, from "all Protestants
are Christians," it does not follow that "a majority of
Protestants are a majority of Christians," nor that "the
most excellent of the Protestants is the most excellent of
the Christians."

The student is recommended to render himself familiar with all the transformations of propositions, or immediate inferences described in this lesson; and copious
examples are furnished for the purpose. It is a good
exercise to throw the same proposition through a series
of changes, so that it comes out in its original form at
last, and thus proves the truth of all the intermediate
changes; but should conversion by limitation have been
used, the original universal proposition cannot be regained, but only the particular proposition corresponding
to it.

On Immediate Inference, Archbishop Thomson,
Outline of the Laws of Thought, §§ 85—92.

LESSON XI.

LOGICAL ANALYSIS OF SENTENCES.

PROPOSITIONS as they are usually to be found in written or spoken compositions seldom exhibit the simple
form, the conjunction of a subject, copula, and predicate,
which we have seen to be the proper logical construction.
Not only is the copula often confused with the predicate,
but several propositions may be combined into one grammatical sentence. For a full account of the analysis
of sentences I shall refer to several excellent little works
devoted to the subject; but I will here attempt to give a
sketch of the various ways in which a sentence may be
constructed.

So often is the copula united to the predicate in
ordinary language, that the grammarian treats the proposition as composed of only two parts, the subject and
predicate, or verb. Thus the proposition, "The sun
rises," apparently contains nothing but a subject "the
sun," and a predicate "rises;" but the proposition is
really equivalent to "the sun is rising," in which the
copula is distinctly shown. We shall, therefore, consider the verb or grammatical predicate as containing both
copula and logical predicate. In Latin one single word
may combine all the three parts of the proposition, as in
sum, "I am;" and the celebrated exclamation of Cæsar
Veni, vidi, vici, "I came, I saw, I conquered," contains
three distinct and complete propositions in three words.
These peculiar cases only arise, however, from the parts
of the proposition having been blended together and dis-

guised in one word ; and in the Latin *sum*, the letter *m* is a relic of the pronoun *me*, which is the real subject of the proposition. If we had a perfect acquaintance with the Grammar of any language it would probably not contradict the logical view of a sentence, but would perhaps explain how the several parts of the complete proposition had become blended and apparently lost, just as the words *will* and *not* are blended in the colloquial " I wont."

A **grammatical sentence** may contain any number of distinct propositions, which admit of being separated but which are combined together for the sake of brevity. In the sentence,

"Art is long and Time is fleeting,"

there are two distinct subjects, Art and Time, and two predicates, "long" and "fleeting," so that we have simply two propositions connected by the conjunction *and*. We may have however several distinct subjects with one and the same predicate ; as in

" Thirty days hath September,
April, June, and November. "

In this well-known couplet the predicate " having thirty days " is placed first for the sake of emphasis, and there are four subjects, September, April, &c., of each of which it is affirmed. Hence these lines really contain four distinct propositions.

Again, there may be one subject with a plurality of predicates, so that several different propositions are asserted without the repetition of the subject and copula. Thus the sentence

"Nitrogen is a colourless, tasteless, inodorous gas, slightly lighter than air," contains one subject only, *Nitrogen*, but four or five predicates; it is plainly equivalent to "Nitrogen is colourless," "Nitrogen is tasteless," " Nitrogen is a gas," and so on.

Lastly, we may have several subjects and several

predicates all combined in the same sentence, and with only one copula, so that each predicate is asserted of each subject ; and a great number of distinct propositions are condensed into one brief sentence. Thus in the sentence, " Iron, Copper, Lead and Zinc are abundant, cheap and useful metals," we have evidently four subjects, and we may be said to have four predicates, "abundant," "cheap," "useful," and " metal." As there is nothing to prevent our applying each predicate to each subject the sentence really contains 16 distinct propositions in only 11 words ; thus " Iron is abundant," " Iron is cheap," " Copper is abundant," " Copper is cheap," and so on. In the curious sentence,—

" Hearts, tongues, figures, scribes, bards, poets, cannot think, speak, cast, write, sing, number, his love to Antony*," Shakspeare has united six subjects and six predicates, or verbs, so that there are, strictly speaking, six times six or thirty-six propositions.

In all the cases above noticed the sentence is said to be compound, and the distinct propositions combined together are said to be coordinate with each other, that is of the same order or kind, because they do not depend upon each other, or in any way affect each other's truth. The abundance, cheapness, or utility of iron need not be stated in the same sentence with the qualities of copper, lead or zinc ; but as the predicates happen to be the same, considerable trouble in speaking or writing is saved by putting as many subjects as possible to the same set of predicates. It is truly said that brevity is the soul of wit, and one of the great arts of composition consists in condensing as many statements as possible into the fewest words, so long as the meaning is not confused thereby.

* *Antony and Cleopatra,* Act III. Sc. 2.

Propositions are however combined in a totally different manner when one proposition forms a part of the subject or predicate of the other. Thus in the sentence, "The man who is upright need not fear accusation," there are two verbs, and two propositions, but one of these only describes the subject of the other; "who is upright" evidently restricts the application of the predicate "need not fear accusation" to a part of the class "man." The meaning of the whole sentence might be expressed in the form

"The upright man need not fear accusation."

And it is clearly seen that the clause or apparent proposition is substituted for an adjective. Such a clause or proposition is called **subordinate**, because it merely assists in the formation of the principal sentence, and has no meaning apart from it; and any sentence containing a subordinate clause is said to be **complex.** Almost any part of a sentence may thus be replaced by a subordinate clause. Thus in "Oxygen and Nitrogen are the gases which form the largest part of the atmosphere," there is a subordinate clause making part of the predicate, and the meaning might be expressed nearly as well in this way, "Oxygen and Nitrogen are the gases forming the largest part of the atmosphere."

In the case of a modal proposition (see p. 69), or one which states the manner in which the predicate belongs to the subject, the mode may be expressed either by an adverb, or by a subordinate clause. "As a man lives so he dies" is such a proposition; for it means, "a man dies as he lives," and "as he lives" is equivalent to an adverb; if he lives well, he dies well; if he lives badly, he dies badly. Adverbs or adverbial clauses may also specify the time, place, or any other circumstance concerned in the truth of the main proposition.

Assuming the reader to be acquainted with the grammatical terms used, we may thus state the parts of which the most complex sentence must consist.

The **subject** may consist of—

1. A noun; as in "The *Queen* reigns."
2. A pronoun; as in "*She* reigns."
3. An adjective converted into a noun; as in "*Whites* are civilized."
4. A gerund; as "*Seeing* is believing."
5. An infinitive; as "*To see* is to believe."
6. A subordinate clause; as "*Who falls from virtue* is lost."

The subject may be qualified or restricted by combining with it an **attribute** which may be expressed in any of the following ways :

1. An adjective; as, "*Fresh* air is wholesome."
2. A participle; as "*Falling* stars are often seen."
3. A noun used as an adjective; as "*Iron* ships are now much employed."
4. A noun and preposition; as "ships *of iron* are now much employed."
5. A possessive case; as "*Chatham's* son was the great minister Pitt."
6. A noun in apposition; as "The Metropolis *London* is the most populous of cities."
7. A gerund or dative infinitive; as, "The desire *to go abroad* is common in Englishmen."

The **predicate** consists almost always of a verb, which often has some object or qualifying words; thus it may be—

1. A simple tense of a complete verb; as "The sun *rises*."
2. A compound tense; as "The sun *has risen*."
3. An incomplete verb and complement; as "The sea *appears rough*."

4. The verb "to be" and an adjective: as "Time *is fleeting.*"

5. A verb with an object; as "Warmth *melts ice.*"

6. A verb with an adverbial; as "The snow falls *thickly.*"

The **object** of a verb is usually a noun or pronoun, but any other of the six kinds of expressions which may serve as a subject may also serve as an object.

The **adverbial** qualifying a verb and expressing the manner, time, place, or other circumstance affecting the proposition may be—

1. An adverb; as "The days pass *slowly.*"

2. A noun and preposition; as "The resolution was passed *by a large majority.*"

3. An absolute phrase; as "The snow melts, *the sun having risen.*"

4. A dative infinitive; as "She stoops *to conquer.*"

5. Any phrase equivalent to an adverb; as "The dividends are paid *twice a year.*"

Various modes of exhibiting the construction of sentences by symbols and names for the several parts have been invented; but I believe that by far the simplest and most efficient mode is to exhibit the construction in the form of a diagram. Any two or more parts of a sentence which are co-ordinate with each other, or bear the same relation to any other part, are written alongside each other, and coupled together by a bracket; thus the diagram,—

Iron			abundant,
Copper	}	are {	cheap,
Lead			useful
Zinc			metals,

clearly shows that there are four co-ordinate subjects,

and four co-ordinate predicates in the example previously taken.

Whenever one part of a sentence is subordinate tᴄ another part it may be connected with it by a line drawn in any convenient direction. Thus the analysis of the following sentence is readily shown by the diagram below it :—

" No one who is a lover of money, a lover of pleasure, and a lover of glory, is likewise a lover of mankind ; but only he who is a lover of virtue."

```
                 ⎛ a lover of money,
     who is      ⎨ a lover of pleasure,
       |         ⎝ a lover of glory.
   one is not ⎱
   he only is  ⎰  a lover of mankind,
       |
   who is a lover of virtue.
```

We see that the sentence is both compound and complex, that is to say it contains two principal coordinate propositions with a common predicate, "a lover of mankind." The first proposition is negative and its subject is described by three subordinate clauses, while the second proposition is affirmative and has one subordinate clause.

I conclude this somewhat lengthy lesson with the analysis of a few sentences, of which the first consists of some remarkably complex lines from a poem of Bur-bidge :

" He who metes, as we should mete,
Could we His insight use, shall most approve,
Not that which fills most space in earthly eyes,
But what—though Time scarce note it as he flies—
Fills, like this little daisy at my feet,
Its function best of diligence in love."

which fills most space in earthly eyes

He shall most approve { not that
                      { but what fills best

who metes   its function of   like this little
                     diligence in   daisy at my
as we should mete   love   feet,

could we His insight use.   though Time scarce note it

                              as he flies.

"Most sweet it is with unuplifted eyes
    To pace the ground, if path there be or none,
While a fair region round the traveller lies
    Which he forbears again to look upon ;
Pleased rather with some soft ideal scene,
    The work of fancy, or some happy tone
Of meditation slipping in between,
    The beauty coming, and the beauty gone."
                                    WORDSWORTH.

It is most sweet

To pace the ground

with unuplifted   if path   while a fair region
     eyes   there { be   round the
                         { or none   traveller lies

which (region) he (the traveller) forbears to look upon

                      { some soft ideal scene
        pleased   {
        rather with   {   the work of fancy
                      { or some happy tone of meditation

        slipping in between the beauty coming
                and the beauty gone.

In the above sentence there is evidently one subject

"to pace the ground," which by means of the pronoun *it*, is connected with the predicate *most sweet*. The main part of the sentence however consists of three adverbials, expressing the manner and surrounding circumstances, and the third adverbial is developed in a very complicated manner. The sentence is not compound, but is complex on account of four subordinate propositions.

In the following sentence there is strictly but one principal proposition, " We find," but this is only a mode of introducing the true purport of the sentence, " the two classes of intellectual operations have much that is different, much that is common."

" When the notions with which men are conversant in the common course of life, which give meaning to their familiar language and which give employment to their hourly thoughts, are compared with the ideas on which exact science is founded, we find, that the two classes of intellectual operations have much that is different, much that is common."

we find—that the two classes (* †)

| | of intellectual | { much that is different |
| | operations have | { much that is common |

When the notions * are compared ─────────┐

with which	which give	which give	with the ideas †
men are	meaning	employ-	
conversant	to their	ment to	on which
in the	familiar	their hourly	exact science is
common	language	thoughts	founded.
course			
of life			

Here the two classes form a collective term, and have two coordinate predicates rendering the sentence so far a compound one. The greater part of the sentence, however, consists of a complicated subordinate sentence of the nature of an adverbial, expressing the time or occasion when this is found to be the case.

As a last example we take the sentence given below:—

"The law of gravitation, the most universal truth at which human reason has yet arrived, expresses not merely the general fact of the mutual attraction of all matter; not merely the vague statement that its influence decreases as the distance increases, but the exact numerical rate at which that decrease takes place; so that when its amount is known at any one distance it may be exactly calculated for any other."

at which human reason has yet arrived
|
the most universal truth
|
The law of gravitation expresses

not merely the general fact	not merely the vague statement	but the exact numerical rate
of the mutual attraction of all matter	that its influence decreases	at which that decrease takes place
	as the distance increases	

so that its amount may be calculated for any other dis‹
| [tance
when it is known at any one distance.

W. S. Dalgleish's *Grammatical Analysis*, or
J. D. Morell's *Analysis of Sentences*.
Alex. Bain's *English Composition and Rhetoric*, pp. 91—117, treats of construction of sentences.

LESSON XII.

THE PREDICABLES, DIVISION, AND DEFINITION.

It is desirable that the reader, before proceeding further, should acquire an exact comprehension of the meaning of certain logical terms which are known as the Predicables, meaning the kinds of terms or attributes which can always be predicated of any subject. These terms are five in number; genus, species, difference, property, and accident; and when properly employed are of exceeding use and importance in logical science. It would neither be possible nor desirable in this work to attempt to give any idea of the various and subtle meanings which have been attributed to the predicables by ancient writers, and the most simple and useful view of the subject is what alone can be given here.

Any class of things may be called a **genus** (Greek γένος, race or kind), if it be regarded as made up of two or more species. " Element" is a genus when we consider it as divided into the two species "metallic and non-metallic." Triangle is a genus as regards the species acute-angled, right-angled, and obtuse-angled.

On the other hand, a **species** is any class which is regarded as forming part of the next larger class, so that the terms genus and species are relative to each other, the genus being the larger class which is divided, and the species the two or more smaller classes into which the genus is divided.

It is indispensable, however, to regard these expressions in the double meaning of extension and intension.

From the explanation of these different meanings in Lesson V. it will be apparent that the extent of a genus or species is simply the number of individuals included in it, and there will always be fewer individuals in the species than in the genus. In extent the genus *book* includes all books of whatever size, language, or contents; if divided in respect to size the species of book are folio, quarto, octavo, duodecimo, &c.; and, of course, each of these species contains much fewer individual books than the whole genus.

In **intension** the genus means, not the individual things contained in it, but the sum of the qualities common to all those things, and sufficient to mark them out clearly from other classes. The species similarly means the sum of the qualities common to all the individuals forming part of the genus, and sufficient to mark them out from the rest of the genus, as well as from all other things. It is evident, therefore, that there must be more qualities implied in the meaning of the species than of the genus, for the species must contain all the qualities of the genus, as well as a certain additional quality or qualities by which the several species are distinguished from each other. Now these additional qualities form the **difference**, which may be defined as the quality or sum of qualities which mark out one part of a genus from the other part or parts. The difference (Latin *differentia*, Greek διαφορά) cannot have any meaning except in intension; and when we use all the terms wholly in intension we may say that *the difference added to the genus makes the species.* Thus if "building" be the genus, and we add the difference "used for a dwelling," we get the species "house." If we take "triangle" as the genus, it means the sum of the qualities of "three-sided rectilineal figure;" if we add the quality of "having two sides equal," we obtain the species "isosceles triangle."

It will easily be seen that the same class of thing
may be both a genus and a species at the same time, a
cording as we regard it as divided into smaller classes
forming part of a larger class.   Thus triangle, which
a genus as regards isosceles triangle, is a species as r
gards right-lined geometrical figures.   House is a speci
of building, but a genus with respect to mansion, cottag
villa, or other kinds of houses.   We may, in fact, have a
almost interminable chain of genera and species, eac
class being a species of the class next above it, and
genus as regards that next below.   Thus the genus Br
tish subject has the species Born in the United Kingdor
Colonial-born, and Naturalised.   Each of these become
a genus as regards the species male and female; eac
species again may be divided into adult and minor, edi
cated, uneducated, employed in some occupation or ui
employed, self-maintaining, maintained by friends,
pauper; and so on.   The subdivision may thus procee
until we reach a class of so restricted extent, that
cannot be divided except into individuals; in this cas
the species is called the **lowest species** or **infima specie**
All the intermediate genera and species of the chain ai
called *subaltern* (Latin *sub*, under, and *alter*, the other
two), because they stand one under the other.   If there b
a genus which is not regarded as a species, that is a
part of any higher genus, it is called the **summum genu**
the highest genus, or *genus generalissimum*, the mo:
general genus.   It is questionable whether we can the
set any limit to the chain of classes.   The class *Britis*
subject is certainly not an absolute *summum* genu
since it is but a species of *man*, which is a species
animal, living being, inhabitant of the earth, substanc
and so on.   If there were any real *summum* genus
would probably be " Being," or " Thing," or " Object cor
ceivable;" but we may usefully employ the term to signil

the highest class of things comprehended in any science or classification. Thus "material substance" is the summum genus examined in the science of chemistry; "inhabitant of the United Kingdom" is the summum genus enumerated and classified in the British census. Logical terms are only a species of words or phrases, but they are the summum genus as regards logic, which has nothing to do with the various parts of speech and the relations of words, syllables, and letters, examined by grammarians.

Several very useful expressions have been derived from the words genus and species. When a thing is so peculiar and unlike other things that it cannot easily be brought into one class with them, it is said to be **sui generis**, or of its own genus; thus the rings of Saturn are so different from anything else among the heavenly bodies that they may fairly be called *sui generis*. In zoology, the Ornithorhynchus, or Australian Duck-bill, the Amphioxus, and some other animals, are so peculiar that they may be called *sui generis*. When a substance is the same in all its parts, or when a number of things are all alike, we say that they are *homogeneous* (Greek ὁμός, like, γένος, kind), that is of the same nature; otherwise they may be called *heterogeneous* (Greek ἕτερος, other).

It is necessary to distinguish carefully the purely logical use of the terms genus and species from their peculiar use in natural history. A species is there a class of plants and animals supposed to have descended from common parents, and to be the narrowest class possessing a fixed form; the genus is the next higher class. But if we accept Darwin's theory of the origin of species, this definition of species becomes entirely illusory, since different genera and species must have according to this theory descended from common parents. The species then denotes a merely arbitrary amount of resemblance which naturalists choose to fix upon, and which it is not possible to define more exactly. This use of the term, then, has no connection whatever with the logical use, according to which any class of things whatever is a species, provided it is regarded as part of a wider class or genus.

The fourth of the Predicables is **Property** (Latin *proprium*, Greek ἴδιον, own), which it is hardly possible to define in a manner free from objection and difficulty, but which may perhaps be best described as any quality which is common to the whole of a class, but is not necessary to mark out that class from other classes. Thus it is a property of the genus "triangle" to have the three internal angles equal to two right angles; this is a very remarkable circumstance, which is always true of triangles, but it is not made a part of the genus, or is not employed in defining a triangle, because the possession of three straight sides is a sufficient mark. The properties of geometrical figures are very numerous; the Second Book of Euclid is occupied in proving a few properties of rectangles; the Third Book similarly of circles. As we commonly use the term property it may or may not belong to other objects as well as those in question; some of the properties of the circle may belong also to the ellipse; some of the properties of man, as for instance the power of memory, or of anger, may belong to other animals.

Logicians have invented various subtle divisions of properties, but it will be sufficient to say that a *peculiar property* is one which belongs to the whole of a class, and to that class only, as *laughter* is supposed to belong only to mankind; the property of containing the greatest space in a line of given length is peculiar to circles. When a property is not peculiar, it may belong to other classes of objects as well as that of which it is called the property. We may further distinguish the **Generic Property**, or that which belongs to the whole of the genus, from the **Specific Property**, which belongs to the whole of a *lowest* species.

Lastly, an **accident** (Latin *accidens*, Greek συμβεβηκός) is any quality which may indifferently belong or not belong to a class, as the case may be, without affecting the other qualities of the class. The word means that which *falls* or happens by chance, and has no necessary connection with the nature of a thing. Thus the absolute size of a triangle is a pure accident as regards its geometrical properties; for whether the side of a triangle be $\frac{1}{10}$ of an inch or a million miles, whatever Euclid proves to be true of one is true of the other. The birthplace of a man is an accident concerning him, as are also the clothes in which he is dressed, the position in which he rests, and so on. Some writers distinguish separable and inseparable accidents. Thus the clothes in which a man is dressed is a **separable accident,** because they can be changed, as can also his position, and many other circumstances; but his birthplace, his height, his Christian name, &c., are **inseparable accidents,** because they can never be changed, although they have no necessary or important relation to his general character.

As an illustration of some part of the scheme of classification described under the name of Predicables, I may here give, as is usual in manuals of Logic, the **Tree of Porphyry,** a sort of example of classification invented by one of the earliest Greek logicians, named Porphyrius. I have simplified the common form in which it is given by translating the Latin names and omitting superfluous words.

In this Tree we observe a succession of genera and species—Substance, Body, Living Being, Animal and Man. Of these Substance is the *summum genus*, because it is not regarded as a species of any higher class; Man

is the *infima species*, because it is a class not divided into any lower class, but only into individuals, of whom it is

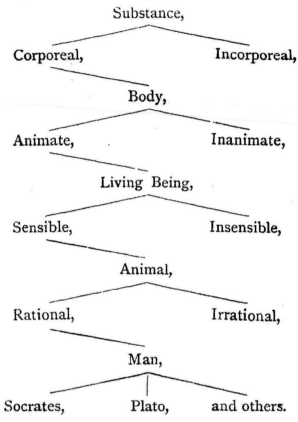

Substance,

Corporeal,   Incorporeal,

Body,

Animate,   Inanimate,

Living Being,

Sensible,   Insensible,

Animal,

Rational,   Irrational,

Man,

Socrates,   Plato,   and others.

usual to specify Socrates and Plato. Body, Living Being,
and Animal are called subaltern genera and species, because each is a species as regards the next higher genus,
and a genus as regards the next lower species. The
qualities implied in the adjectives Corporeal, Animate,
Sensible (*i.e.* capable of feeling) and Rational are the
successive differences which occasion a division of each
genus into species.   It will be evident that the negative
parts of the genera, namely Incorporeal Substance, In-

animate Body, &c., are capable of subdivision, which has not been carried out in order to avoid confusing the figure.

Logical division is the name of the process by which we distinguish the species of which a genus is composed. Thus we are said to divide the genus "book" when we consider it as made up of the groups folio, quarto, octavo, duodecimo books, &c., and the size of the books is in this case the ground, basis, or principle of division, commonly called the **Fundamentum Divisionis**. In order that a quality or circumstance may be taken as the basis of division, it must be present with some and absent with others, or must vary with the different species comprehended in the genus. A generic property of course, being present in the whole of the genus, cannot serve for the purpose of division. Three rules may be laid down to which a sound and useful division must conform :

1.   The constituent species must exclude each other.

2.   The constituent species must be equal when added together to the genus.

3.   The division must be founded upon one principle or basis.

It would be obviously absurd to divide books into folio, quarto, French, German and dictionaries, because these species overlap each other, and there may be French or German dictionaries which happen to be quarto or folio and belong to three different species at once. A division of this kind is said to be a **Cross Division**, because there is more than one principle of division, and the several species in consequence cross each other and produce confusion. If I were to divide rectilineal figures into triangles, parallelograms, rectangles and polygons of more than four sides, I should commit all the possible faults in one division. The species parallelogram and rectangle do not exclude each other, since all rectangles must be

parallelograms; the constituent species are not altogether
equal to the genus rectilineal figure, since irregular four-
sided figures which are not parallelograms have been
omitted; and there are three principles of division, namely
the number of sides, the directions of those sides, and the
angles contained. But when subdivision is employed,
and each of the species is considered as a genus which
may be subjected to a further separation, a new principle
of division may and in fact must be employed each time.
Thus I can divide rectilineal figures according to the three
principles mentioned above:

Rectilineal Figure

3 sides	4 sides	more than 4 sides
Triangle	Quadrilateral	Polygon

with parallel sides	without parallel sides
Parallelogram	Trapezium.

Here the principles of division are the number of their
sides, and in the case of four-sided figures their paral-
lelism. Triangles do not admit of division in this second
respect. We may make a new division of parallelograms,
adopting the equality of sides and the size of the angles
as the principles; thus:

Parallelogram

adjoining sides equal		adjoining sides not equal	
right-angled	not right-angled	right-angled	not right-angled
Square	Rhombus	Oblong	Rhomboid.

The most perfect divisions in a logical point of view
are produced by continually dividing each genus into two

species by a difference, of which an example has been given in the Tree of Porphyry. This process is called **Dichotomy** (Greek δίχα, in two; τέμνω, to cut); it is also called **Exhaustive Division** because it always of necessity obeys the second rule, and provides a place for every possible existing thing. By a Law of Thought to be considered in the next Lesson, every thing must either have a quality or not have it, so that it must fall into one or other division of the genus. This process of exhaustive division will be shewn to have considerable importance in Lesson XXIII., but in practice it is not by any means always necessary or convenient. It would, for instance, produce a needlessly long classification if we divided rectilineal figures thus :

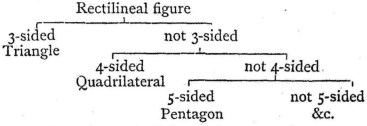

Rectilineal figure

   3-sided   not 3-sided
   Triangle
        4-sided   not 4-sided
        Quadrilateral
                5-sided   not 5-sided
                Pentagon   &c.

As we know beyond all doubt that every figure must have 3, 4, 5, 6, or more sides, and no figure can belong to more than one group, it is much better at once to enumerate the parts as Triangle, Quadrilateral, Pentagon, Hexagon, &c. Again, it would be very awkward if we divided the counties of England into Middlesex and not-Middlesex; the latter into Surrey and not-Surrey; the latter, again, into Kent and not-Kent. Dichotomy is useless, and even seems absurd in these cases, because we can observe the rules of division certainly in a much briefer division. But in less certain branches of knowledge our divisions can never be free from possible oversight unless they proceed by dichotomy. Thus, if we divide the population of the world into three branches, Aryan, Semitic, and

Turanian, some race might ultimately be discovered which is distinct from any of these, and for which no place has been provided; but had we proceeded thus—

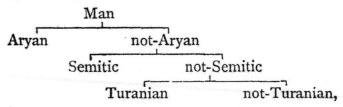

it is evident that the new race would fall into the last group, which is neither Aryan, Semitic, nor Turanian. All the divisions of naturalists are liable to this inconvenience. If we divide Vertebrate Animals into Mammalia, Birds, Reptiles, and Fish, it may any time happen that a new form is discovered which belongs to none of these, and therefore upsets the division.

A further precaution required in Division is not to proceed from a high or wide genus at once to a low or narrow species, or, as the phrase is, *divisio non faciat saltum* (the division should not make a leap). The species should always be those of the **proximate** or next higher genus; thus it would obviously be inconvenient to begin by dividing geometrical figures into those which have parallel sides and those which have not; but this principle of division is very proper when applied to the proximate genus.

Logical division must not be confused with physical division or **Partition**, by which an individual object, as a tree, is regarded as composed of its separate parts, root, trunk, branches, leaves, &c. There is even a third and distinct process, called **Metaphysical Division**, which consists in regarding a thing as an aggregate of qualities, and separating these in thought; as when we discriminate the form, colour, taste, and smell of an orange.

Closely connected with the subject of this Lesson is

the process of **Logical Definition**, by which we determine
the common qualities or marks of the objects belonging
to any given class of objects. We must give in a definition the briefest possible statement of such qualities as
are sufficient to distinguish the class from other classes,
and determine its position in the general classification of
conceptions. Now this will be fulfilled by regarding the
class as a species, and giving the proximate genus and
the difference. The word genus is here used in its intensive meaning, and denotes the qualities belonging to all
of the genus, and sufficient to mark them out; and as the
difference marks out the part of the genus in question,
we get a perfect definition of the species desired. But we
should be careful to give in a definition no superfluous
marks; if these are accidents and do not belong to the
whole, the definition will be improperly narrowed, as if
we were to define Quadrilateral Figures as figures with
four *equal* sides; if the superfluous marks belong to all
the things defined they are *Properties*, and have no effect
upon the definition whatever. Thus if I define parallelograms as " four-sided rectilineal figures, with the opposite
sides equal and parallel, and the opposite angles equal,"
I have added two properties, the equality of the opposite
sides and angles which necessarily follow from the paral-
lelism of the sides, and only add to the complexity of the
definition without rendering it more precise.

There are certain rules usually given in logical works
which express the precautions necessary in definition.

1. *A definition should state the essential attributes of
the species defined.* So far as any exact meaning can be
given to the expression "essential attributes," it means,
as explained above, the proximate genus and difference.

2. *A definition must not contain the name defined.*
For the purpose of the definition is to make the species
known, and as long as it is not known it cannot serve to

make itself known.   When this rule is not observed, there
is said to be '*circulus in definiendo*,' or 'a circle in defining,' because the definition brings us round again to the
very word from which we started.   This fault will usually
be committed by using a word in the definition which is
really a synonym of the name defined, as if I were to
define "Plant" as "an organized being possessing vegetable life," or elements as simple substances, vegetable
being really equivalent to plant, and simple to elementary.
If I were to define metals as "substances possessing metallic lustre," I should either commit this fault, or use the
term metallic lustre in a sense which would admit other
substances, and thus break the following rule.

3. *The definition must be exactly equivalent to the
species defined*, that is to say, it must be an expression the
denotation of which is neither narrower nor wider than
the species, so as to include exactly the same objects.
The definition, in short, must denote the species, the
whole species, and nothing but the species, and this may
really be considered a description of what a definition is.

4. *A definition must not be expressed in obscure, figura-
tive or ambiguous language.*   In other words, the terms
employed in the definition must be all exactly known,
otherwise the purpose of the definition, to make us acquainted with the sufficient marks of the species, is
obviously defeated.   There is no worse logical fault than
to define *ignotum per ignotius*, the unknown by the still
more unknown.   Aristotle's definition of the soul as 'The
Entelechy, or first form of an organized body which has
potential life,' certainly seems subject to this objection.

5. And lastly, *A definition must not be negative where
it can be affirmative.*   This rule however is often not
applicable, and is by no means always binding.

Read Mr Mill on the nature of Classification and the

five Predicables, *System of Logic*, Book I. Chap.
VII. For ancient Scholastic Views concerning De-
finition, see Mansel's *Artis Logicæ Rudimenta*
(Aldrich), App. Note C.

LESSON XIII.

PASCAL AND DESCARTES ON METHOD.

IT may be doubted whether any man ever possessed a
more acute and perfect intellect than that of Blaise
Pascal. He was born in 1623, at Clermont in Auvergne,
and from his earliest years displayed signs of a remarkable character. His father attempted at first to prevent
his studying geometry, but such was Pascal's genius and
love of this science, that, by the age of twelve, he had
found out many of the propositions of Euclid's first book
without the aid of any person or treatise. It is difficult
to say whether he is most to be admired for his mathematical discoveries, his invention of the first calculating
machine, his wonderful Provincial Letters written against
the Jesuits, or for his profound Pensées or Thoughts, a
collection of his reflections on scientific and religious
topics.

Among these Thoughts is to be found a remarkable
fragment upon Logical method, the substance of which is
also given in the *Port Royal Logic*. It forms the second
article of the *Pensées*, and is entitled *Réflexions sur la
Géométrie en général*. As I know no composition in
which perfection of truth and clearness of expression are
more nearly attained, I propose to give in this lesson a
free translation of the more important parts of this

fragment, appending to it rules of method from the *Port Royal Logic,* and from Descartes' celebrated *Essay on Method.* The words of Pascal are nearly as follows.

"The true method, which would furnish demonstrations of the highest excellence, if it were possible to employ the method fully, consists in observing two principal rules. The first rule is not to employ any term of which we have not clearly explained the meaning; the second rule is never to put forward any proposition which we cannot demonstrate by truths already known; that is to say, in a word, *to define all the terms,* and *to prove all the propositions.* But, in order that I may observe the rules of the method which I am explaining, it is necessary that I declare what is to be understood by **Definition.**

"We recognise in Geometry only those definitions which logicians call **Nominal Definitions,** that is to say, only those definitions which impose a name upon things clearly designated in terms perfectly known; and I speak only of those definitions."

Their value and use is to clear and abbreviate discourse by "expressing in the single name which we impose what could not be otherwise expressed but in several words; provided nevertheless that the name imposed remain divested of any other meaning which it might possess, so as to bear that alone for which we intend it to stand.

"For example, if we need to distinguish among numbers those which are divisible into two equal parts, from those which are not so divisible, in order to avoid the frequent repetition of this distinction, we give a name to it in this manner :—we call every number divisible into two equal parts an *Even Number.*

"This is a geometrical definition, because after having clearly designated a thing, namely any number divisible into two equal parts, we give it a name divested of every other meaning, which it might have, in order to bestow upon it the meaning designated.

"Hence it appears that definitions are very free, and that they can never be subject to contradiction, for there is nothing more allowable, than to give any name we wish to a thing which we have clearly pointed out. It is only necessary to take care that we do not abuse this liberty of imposing names, by giving the same name to two different things. Even that would be allowable, provided that we did not confuse the results, and extend them from one to the other. But if we fall into this vice, we have a very sure and infallible remedy;—it is, to substitute mentally the definition in place of the thing defined, and to hold the definition always so present in the mind, that every time we speak, for instance, of an even number, we may understand precisely that it is a number divisible into two equal parts, and so that these two things should be so combined and inseparable in thought, that as often as one is expressed in discourse, the mind may direct itself immediately to the other.

"For geometers and all who proceed methodically only impose names upon things in order to abbreviate discourse, and not to lessen or change the ideas of the things concerning which they discourse. They pretend that the mind always supplies the entire definition of the brief terms which they employ simply to avoid the confusion produced by a multitude of words.

"Nothing prevents more promptly and effectively the insidious fallacies of the sophists than this method, which we should always employ, and which alone suffices to banish all sorts of difficulties and equivocations.

"These things being well understood, I return to my explanation of the true method, which consists, as I said, in defining everything and proving everything.

"Certainly this method would be an excellent one,

were it not absolutely impossible. It is evident that the first terms we wished to define would require previous terms to serve for their explanation, and similarly the first propositions we wished to prove, would presuppose other propositions preceding them in our knowledge; and thus it is clear that we should never arrive at the first terms or first propositions.

"Accordingly in pushing our researches further and further, we arrive necessarily at primitive words which we cannot define, and at principles so clear, that we cannot find any principles more clear to prove them by. Thus it appears that men are naturally and inevitably incapable of treating any science whatever in a perfect method; but it does not thence follow that we ought to abandon every kind of method......The most perfect method available to men consists not in defining everything and demonstrating everything, nor in defining nothing and demonstrating nothing, but in pursuing the middle course of not defining things which are clear and understood by all persons, but of defining all others ; and of not proving truths known to all persons, but of proving all others. From this method they equally err who undertake to define and prove everything, and they who neglect to do it in things which are not self-evident."

It is made plain in this admirable passage that we can never by using words avoid an ultimate appeal to things, because each definition of a word must require one or more other words, which also will require definition, and so on *ad infinitum*. Nor must we ever return back upon the words already defined; for if we define *A* by *B*, and *B* by *C*, and *C* by *D*, and then *D* by *A*, we commit what may be called a *circulus in definiendo;* a most serious fallacy, which might lead us to suppose that we know the nature of *A*, *B*, *C*, and *D*, when we really know nothing about them.

XIII.]   ON METHOD.   115

Pascal's views of the geometrical method were clearly summed up in the following rules, inserted by him in the *Port Royal Logic**.

1. To admit no terms in the least obscure or equivocal without defining them.

2. To employ in the definitions only terms perfectly known or already explained.

3. To demand as axioms only truths perfectly evident.

4. To prove all propositions which are at all obscure, by employing in their proof only the definitions which have preceded, or the axioms which have been accorded, or the propositions which have been already demonstrated, or the construction of the thing itself which is in dispute, when there may be any operation to perform.

5. Never to abuse the equivocation of terms by failing to substitute for them, mentally, the definitions which restrict and explain them.

The reader will easily see that these rules are much more easy to lay down than to observe, since even geometers are not agreed as to the simplest axioms to assume, or the best definitions to make. There are many different opinions as to the true definition of parallel lines, and the simplest assumptions concerning their nature; and how much greater must be the difficulty of observing Pascal's rules with confidence in less certain branches of science. Next after Geometry, Mechanics is perhaps the most perfect science, yet the best authorities have been far from agreeing as to the exact definitions of such notions as *force, mass, moment, power, inertia,* and the most different opinions are still held as to the simplest axioms by which the law of the composition of forces may be proved. Nevertheless if we steadily bear in mind, in

---

* Mr Spencer Baynes' *Translation*, p. 317.

studying each science, the necessity of defining every term as far as possible, and proving each proposition which can be proved by a simpler one, we shall do much to clear away error and confusion.

I also wish to give here the rules proposed by the celebrated Descartes for guiding the reason in the attainment of truth. They are as follows :—

1. Never to accept anything as true, which we do not clearly know to be so ; that is to say, carefully to avoid haste or prejudice, and to comprise nothing more in our judgments than what presents itself so clearly and distinctly to the mind that we cannot have any room to doubt it.

2. To divide each difficulty we examine into as many parts as possible, or as may be required for resolving it.

3. To conduct our thoughts in an orderly manner, commencing with the most simple and easily known objects, in order to ascend by degrees to the knowledge of the most complex.

4. To make in every case enumerations so complete, and reviews so wide, that we may be sure of omitting nothing.

These rules were first stated by Descartes in his admirable *Discourse on Method*, in which he gives his reflections on the right mode of conducting the reason, and searching for truth in any of the sciences. This little treatise is easily to be obtained in the original French, and has also been translated into English by Mr Veitch*. The reader can be strongly advised to study it. Always to observe the rules of Descartes and Pascal, or to know whether we in every case observe them properly, is im-

* Published at Edinburgh in 1850.

possible, but it must nevertheless be valuable to know at what we ought to aim.

> Read Locke's brief *Essay on the Conduct of the Understanding*, which contains admirable remarks on the acquirement of exact and logical habits of thought.

LESSON XIV.

THE LAWS OF THOUGHT.

BEFORE the reader proceeds to the lessons which treat of the most common forms of reasoning, known as the syllogism, it is desirable that he should give a careful attention to the very simple laws of thought on which all reasoning must ultimately depend. These laws describe the very simplest truths, in which all people must agree, and which at the same time apply to all notions which we can conceive. It is impossible to think correctly and avoid evident self-contradiction unless we observe what are called the **Three Primary Laws of Thought**, which may be stated as follows:

1. The Law of Identity. **Whatever is, is.**
2. The Law of Contradiction **Nothing can both be and not be.**
3. The Law of Excluded Middle. **Everything must either be or not be.**

Though these laws when thus stated may seem absurdly obvious, and were ridiculed by Locke and others on that account, I have found that students are seldom able to see at first their full meaning and importance. It will be pointed out in Lesson XXIII. that logicians have overlooked until recent years the very simple way in which all arguments may be explained when these self-evident laws are granted; and it is not too much to say that the whole of logic will be plain to those who will constantly use these laws as the key.

The first of the laws may be regarded as the best definition we can give of identity or sameness. Could any one be ignorant of the meaning of the word **Identity**, it would be sufficient to inform him that **everything is identical with itself.**

The second law however is the one which requires more consideration. Its meaning is that nothing can have at the same time and at the same place contradictory and inconsistent qualities. A piece of paper may be blackened in one part, while it is white in other parts; or it may be white at one time, and afterwards become black; but we cannot conceive that it should be both white and black at the same place and time. A door after being open may be shut, but it cannot at once be shut and open. Water may feel warm to one hand and cold to another hand, but it cannot be both warm and cold to the same hand. No quality can both be present and **absent** at the same time; and this seems to be the most simple and general truth which we can assert of all things. It is the very nature of existence that a thing cannot be otherwise than it is; and it may be safely said that all fallacy and error arise from unwittingly reasoning in a way inconsistent with this law. All statements or inferences which imply a combination of contradictory qualities must be taken as impossible and false, and the breaking of this law is the mark of their being false. It can easily be shewn that if Iron be a metal, and every metal an element, Iron must be an element or it can be nothing at all, since it would combine qualities which are inconsistent (see **Lesson XXIII**).

The Law of Excluded Middle is much less self-evident than either of the two preceding ones, and the reader will not perhaps see at the first moment that it is equally important and necessary with them. Its meaning may be best explained by saying that it is impossible to mention any *thing* and any *quality* or circumstance, without allowing that the quality or circumstance either belongs to the thing or does not belong. The name of the law expresses the fact that there is no third or middle course; the answer must be Yes or No. Let the thing be *rock* and the quality *hard;* then rock must be either *hard* or *not-hard.* Gold must be either white or not white; a line must be either straight or not straight; an action must be either virtuous or not virtuous. Indeed when we know nothing of the terms used we may nevertheless make assertions concerning them in accordance with this law. The reader may not know and in fact chemists may not really know with certainty, whether *vanadium* is a metal or not a metal, but any one knows that it must be one or the other. Some readers may not know what a cycloid is or what an isochronous curve is; but they must know that a cycloid is either an isochronous curve or it is not an isochronous curve.

This law of excluded middle is not so evident but that plausible objections may be suggested to it. Rock, it may be urged, is not always either hard or soft, for it may be half way between, a little hard and a little soft at the same time. This objection points to a distinction which is of great logical importance, and when neglected often leads to fallacy. The law of excluded middle affirmed nothing about *hard* and *soft*, but only referred to *hard* and *not-hard;* if the reader chooses to substitute soft for not-hard he falls into a serious confusion between opposite terms and contradictory terms. It is quite possible that a thing may be neither hard nor soft, being half way between; but in that case it cannot be fairly called hard, so that the law holds true. Similarly water must be either warm or not-warm, but it does not follow .that it must be warm or cold. The alternative not-warm evidently includes all cases in which it is cold besides cases where it is of a medium temperature, so that we should call it neither warm nor cold. We must thus carefully distinguish questions of degree or quantity from those of simple logical fact. In cases where a thing or quality may exist to a greater or less extent there are many alternatives. Warm water, for, instance may have any temperature from 70° perhaps up to 120°. Exactly the same question occurs in cases of geometrical reasoning; for Euclid in his Elements frequently argues from the self-evident truth that any line must be either greater than, equal to, or less than any other line. While there are only two alternatives to choose from in logic there are three in Mathematics; thus one line, compared with another, may be—

$$\text{In Logic.} \begin{cases} \text{greater} \dots \dots \dots \text{greater} \\ \text{not-greater} \dots \begin{cases} \dots \dots \text{equal} \\ \dots \dots \text{less} \end{cases} \end{cases} \begin{matrix} \text{In} \\ \text{Mathematics.} \end{matrix}$$

. Another and even more plausible objection may be raised to the third law of thought in this way. *Virtue* being the thing proposed, and *triangular* the quality, the Law of Excluded Middle enables us at once to assert that virtue is either triangular or not-triangular. At first sight it might seem false and absurd to say that an immaterial notion such as virtue should be either triangular or not, because it has nothing in common with those material substances occupying space to which the notion of figure belongs. But the absurdity would arise, not from any falseness in the law, but from misinterpretation of the expression *not-triangular*. If in saying that a thing is "not triangular" we are taken to imply that it has some figure though not a triangular figure, then of course the expression cannot be applied to virtue or anything immaterial. In strict logic however no such implied meaning is to be allowed, and not-triangular will include both things which have figure other than triangular, as well as things which have not the properties of figure at all; and it is in the latter meaning that it is applicable to an immaterial thing.

These three laws then being universally and necessarily true to whatever things they are applied, become the foundation of reasoning. All acts of reasoning proceed from certain judgments, and the act of judgment consists in comparing two things or ideas together and discovering whether they agree or differ, that is to say whether they are identical in any qualities. The laws of thought inform us of the very nature of this identity with which all thought is concerned. But in the operation of discourse or reasoning we need certain additional laws, or axioms, or self-evident truths, which may be thus stated :

1. *Two terms agreeing with one and the same third term agree with each other.*

2. *Two terms of which one agrees and the other does not agree with one and the same third term, do not agree with each other.*

These self-evident truths are commonly called the Canons or Fundamental Principles of Syllogism, and they are true whatever may be the kind of agreement in question. The example we formerly used (p. 3) of the agreement of the terms "Most useful metal" and "cheapest metal" with the third common term " Iron," was but an instance of the first Canon, and the agreement consisted in complete identity. In the case of the " Earth," the " Planets," and " Bodies revolving in elliptic orbits," the agreement was less complete, because the Earth is only one of many Planets, and the Planets only a small portion of all the heavenly bodies, such as Satellites, Comets, Meteors, and Double-Stars which revolve in such orbits.

The second of the Canons applies to cases where there is disagreement or difference, as in the following example :

> Venus is a planet.
> Planets are not self-luminous.
> Therefore Venus is not self-luminous.

The first of these propositions states a certain agreement to exist between Venus and planet, just as in the previous case of the Earth, but the second proposition states a disagreement between Planet and self-luminous bodies; hence we infer a disagreement between Venus and self-luminous body. But the reader will carefully observe that *from two disagreements we can never infer anything*. If the following were put forth as an argument it would be evidently absurd :—

> Sirius is not a planet.
> Planets are not self-luminous.
> Therefore Sirius is not self-luminous.

Both the premises or propositions given are true, and yet the conclusion is false, for all the fixed stars are self-luminous, or shine by their own light. We may, in fact, state as a third Canon that—

3. *Two terms both disagreeing with one and the same third term may or may not agree with each other.*

Self-evident rules, of an exactly similar nature to these three Canons, are the basis of all mathematical reasoning, and are usually called axioms. Euclid's first axiom is that "Things which are equal to the same thing are equal to one another;" and whether we apply it to the length of lines, the magnitude of angles, areas, solids, numbers, degrees, or anything else which admits of being equal or unequal, it holds true. Thus if the lines *A* and *B* are each equal to *C* it is evident that each is equal to the other

Euclid does not give axioms corresponding to the second and third Canons, but they are really used in Geometry. Thus if *A* is equal to *B*, but *D* is not equal to *B*, it follows that *A* is not equal to *D*, or things of which one is equal, but the other unequal to the same third thing, are unequal to each other. Lastly, *A* and *E* are two lines both unequal to *D* and unequal to each other, whereas *A* and *B* are two lines both unequal to *D* but equal to each other; thus we plainly see that "two things both unequal to the same thing may or may not be equal to each other."

From what precedes it will be apparent that all rea soning requires that there should be one agreement at least; if there be two agreements we may reason to a third agreement; if there be one agreement and one difference we may reason to a second difference; but if there be two differences only we cannot reason to any conclusion whatever. These self-evident principles will in the next Lesson serve to explain some of the rules of the Syllogism.

Logicians however have not confined themselves to the use of these Canons, but have often put the same truth into a different form in axioms known as the *Dicta de omni et nullo* of Aristotle. This celebrated Latin phrase means "Statements concerning all and none," and the axiom, or rather pair of axioms, is usually given in the following words:

Whatever is predicated of a term distributed whether affirmatively or negatively, may be predicated in like manner of everything contained under it.

Or more briefly:

What pertains to the higher class pertains also to the lower.

This merely means, in untechnical language, that what may be said of all the things of any sort or kind may be said of any one or any part of those things; and, secondly, what may be denied of all the things in a class may be denied of any one or any part of them. Whatever may be said of "All planets" may be said of Venus, the Earth, Jupiter, or any other planet; and, as they may all be said to revolve in elliptic orbits, it follows that this may be asserted of Venus, the Earth, Jupiter, or any other planet. Similarly, according to the negative part of the Dicta, we may deny that the planets are self-luminous, and knowing that Jupiter is a planet may deny that Jupiter is self-luminous. A little reflection would show that the affirmative Dictum is really the first of the Canons in a less complete and general form, and that the negative Dictum is similarly the second Canon. These Dicta in fact only apply to such cases of agreement between terms as consist in one being the name of a smaller class, and another of the larger class containing it. Logicians have for the most part strangely overlooked the important cases in which one term agrees with another to the extent of being identical with it; but this is a subject which we cannot fitly discuss here at any length. It is treated in my little work called *The Substitution of Similars**.

Some logicians have held that in addition to the three laws which are called the Primary Laws of Thought,

* Macmillan and Co. 1869.

there is a fourth called "The Principle or Law of Suffi-cient Reason." It was stated by Leibnitz in the following words :

Nothing happens without a reason why it should be so rather than otherwise. For instance, if there be a pair of scales in every respect exactly alike on each side and with exactly equal weights in each scale, it must remain motionless and in equilibrium, because there is no reason why one side should go down more than the other. It is certainly a fundamental assumption in mechanical science that if a body is acted upon by two perfectly equal forces in different directions it will move equally between them, because there is no reason why it should move more to one side than the other. Mr Mansel, Sir W. Hamilton and others consider however that this law has no place in logic, even if it can be held self-evident at all ; and the question which appears open to doubt need not be dis-cussed here.

I have so freely used the word **axiom** in this lesson that it is desirable to clear up its meaning as far as pos-sible. Philosophers do not perfectly agree about its deri-vation or exact meaning, but it certainly comes from the verb ἀξιόω, which is rendered, *to think worthy.* It gene-rally denotes a self-evident truth of so simple a character that it must be assumed to be true, and, as it cannot be proved by any simpler proposition, must itself be taken as the basis of reasoning. In mathematics it is clearly used ·n this sense.

See Hamilton's *Lectures on Logic*, Lectures **5 and 6.**

LESSON XV.

THE RULES OF THE SYLLOGISM.

SYLLOGISM is the common name for Mediate Inference, or inference by a medium or middle term, and is to be distinguished from the process of Immediate Inference, or inference which is performed without the use of any third or middle term.

We are in the habit of employing a **middle term** or medium whenever we are prevented from comparing two things together directly, but can compare each of them with a certain third thing. We cannot compare the sizes of two halls by placing one in the other, but we can measure each by a foot rule or other suitable measure. which forms a common measure, and enables us to asce. tain with any necessary degree of accuracy their relative dimensions. If we have two quantities of cotton goods and want to compare them, it is not necessary to bring the whole of one portion to the other, but a sample is cut off, which represents exactly the quality of one portion, and, according as this sample does or does not agree with the other portion, so must the two portions of goods agree or differ.

The use of a middle term in syllogism is closely parallel to what it is in the above instances, but not exactly the same. Suppose, as an example, that we wish to ascertain whether or not "Whales are viviparous," and that we had not an opportunity of observing the fact directly; we could yet show it to be so if we knew that "whales are mammalian animals," and that "all mammalian animals are viviparous." It would follow that "whales are viviparous;" and so far as the inference is concerned it does not matter what is the meaning we attribute to the words viviparous and mammalian. In this case "mammalian animal" is the middle term.

The name **Syllogism** means the joining together in thought of two propositions, and is derived from the Greek words σύν, with, and λόγος, thought or reason. It is thus exactly the equivalent of the word *Computation,* which means thinking together (Latin *con,* together, *puto,* to think), or reckoning. In a syllogism we so unite in thought two **premises,** or propositions put forward, that we are enabled to draw from them or infer, by means of the middle term they contain, a third proposition called the **conclusion.** Syllogism may thus be defined as the act of thought by which from two given propositions we proceed to a third proposition, the truth of which necessarily follows from the truth of these given propositions. When the argument is fully expressed in language it is usual to call it concretely a syllogism.

The special rules of the syllogism are founded upon the Laws of Thought and the Canons considered in the previous Lesson. They serve to inform us exactly under what circumstances one proposition can be inferred from two other propositions, and are eight in number, as follows :—

1. *Every syllogism has three and only three terms.*

These terms are called the major term, the minor term, and the middle term.

2. *Every syllogism contains three, and only three propositions.*

These propositions are called the major premise, the minor premise, and the conclusion.

3. *The middle term must be distributed once at least, and must not be ambiguous.*

4. *No term must be distributed in the conclusio.*
which was not distributed in one of the premises.

5. *From negative premises nothing can be inferred.*

6. *If one premise be negative, the conclusion mus*
be negative; and vice versâ, *to prove a negative con*
clusion one of the premises must be negative.

From the above rules may be deduced two subor
dinate rules, which it will nevertheless be convenient t
state at once.

7. *From two particular premises no conclusion ca*
be drawn.

8. *If one premise be particular, the conclusion mu:*
be particular.

All these rules are of such extreme importance that
will be desirable for the student not only to acquire
perfect comprehension of their meaning and truth, but t
commit them to memory. During the remainder of th
lesson we shall consider their meaning and force.

As the syllogism consists in comparing two terms b
means of a middle term, there cannot of course be les
than three terms, nor can there be more ; for if ther
were four terms, say *A, B, C, D*, and we compared *
with *B* and *C* with *D*, we should either have no commo
medium at all between *A* and *D*, or we should require
second syllogism, so as first to compare *A* and *C* with *
and then *A* and *D* with *C.*

The **middle term** may always be known by the fac
;hat it does not occur in the conclusion. The **major ter.**
is always the predicate of the conclusion, and the **minc**
term the subject. These terms are thus called because i
the universal affirmative proposition (A) the predicate
necessarily a wider or greater or major term than th
subject ; thus in "all men are mortals," the predicate in
cludes all other animals as well as men, and is obvious
a major term or wider term than men.

Again, the syllogism necessarily consists of a premise called the major premise, in which the major and middle terms are compared together; of a minor premise which similarly compares the minor and middle terms; and of a conclusion, which contains the major and minor terms only. In a strictly correct syllogism the major premise always stands before the minor premise, but in ordinary writing and speaking this rule is seldom observed; and that premise which contains the major term still continues to be the major premise, whatever may be its position.

The third rule is a very important one, because many fallacies arise from its neglect. By the middle term being *distributed* once at least, we mean (see p. 74) that the whole of it must be referred to universally in one premise, if not both. The two propositions—

> All Frenchmen are Europeans,
> All Russians are Europeans,

do not distribute the middle term at all, because they are both affirmative propositions, which have (p. 75) undistributed predicates. It is apparent that Frenchmen are one part of Europeans, and Russians another part, as shown in Euler's method in Fig. 6, so that

Fig. 6.

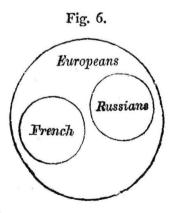

there is no real middle term. Those propositions would equally allow of Russians being or not being Frenchmen; for whether the two interior circles overlap or not they are equally within the larger circle of Europeans. Again, the two propositions

<blockquote>
All Frenchmen are Europeans,
All Parisians are Europeans,
</blockquote>

do not enable us to infer that all Parisians are Frenchmen. For though we know of course that all Parisians

Fig. 7.

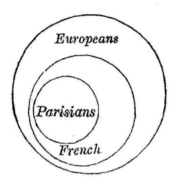

are included among Frenchmen, the premises would allow of their being placed anywhere within the circle of Europeans. We see in this instance that the premises and conclusion of an apparent argument may all be true and yet the argument may be fallacious.

The part of the third rule which refers to an ambi· guous middle term hardly requires explanation. It has been stated (Lesson IV.) that an ambiguous term is one which has two different meanings, implying different con· notations, and it is really equivalent to two different terms which happen to have the same form of spelling, so that they are readily mistaken for each other. Thus if we were to argue that because "all metals are elements and brass is metal, therefore it is an element," we should be committing a fallacy by using the middle term *metal* in two different senses, in one of which it means the pure simple substances known to chemists as metals, and in the other a mixture of metals commonly called metal in the arts, but known to chemists by the name alloy. In many examples which may be found in logical books the ·ambiguity of the middle term is exceedingly obvious, but the reader should always be prepared to meet with cases where exceedingly subtle and difficult cases of ambiguity occur. Thus it might be argued that "what is right should be enforced by law, and that charity is right and should therefore be enforced by the law." Here it is evident that *right* is applied in one case to what the conscience approves, and in another case to what public opinion holds to be necessary for the good of society.

The fourth rule forbids us to distribute a term in the conclusion unless it was distributed in the premises. As the sole object of the syllogism is to prove the conclusion by the premises, it is obvious that we must not make a statement concerning anything unless that thing was mentioned in the premises, in a way warranting the statement. Thus if we were to argue that "because many nations are capable of self-government and that nations capable of self-government should not receive laws from a despotic government, therefore no nation should receive laws from a despotic government," we should be clearly exceeding the contents of our premises. The minor term, *many nations*, was particular in the minor premise, and must not be made universal in the conclusion. The premises do not warrant a statement concerning anything but the *many nations* capable of self-government. The above argument would therefore be fallacious and would be technically called an **illicit process of the minor term,** meaning that we have improperly treated the minor term.

Such a breach of the fourth rule as is described above is exceedingly easy to detect, and is therefore very seldom committed.

But an **illicit process** or improper treatment of the major term is more common because it is not so transparently false. If we argued indeed that "because all Anglo-Saxons love liberty, and Frenchmen are not Anglo-Saxons, therefore they do not love liberty," the fallacy would be pretty apparent; but without a knowledge of logic it would not be easy to give a clear explanation of the fallacy. It is apparent that the major term *loving liberty*, is undistributed in the major premise, so that Anglo-Saxons must be assumed to be only a part of those who love liberty. Hence the exclusion of Frenchmen from the class Anglo-Saxons does not necessarily exclude them from the class who love liberty (see Fig. 8). The

Fig. 8.

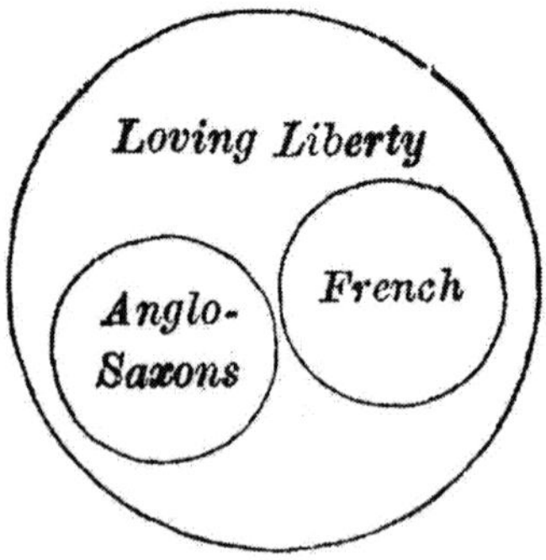

conclusion of the false argument being negative distributes its predicate, the major term, and as this is undistributed in the major premise we have an **illicit major** as we may briefly call this fallacy. The following is an obscurer example of the same fallacy;—" Few students are capable of excelling in many branches of knowledge, and such as can so excel are deserving of high commendation;" hence "few students are deserving of high commendation." The little word "few" has here the double meaning before explained (p. 67), and means that "a few are, &c., and the rest are not." The conclusion is thus really a negative proposition, and distributes the major term "deserving of high commendation." But this major term is clearly undistributed in the major premise, which merely asserts that those who can excel in many branches of knowledge are deserving, but says or implies nothing about other students.

The fifth rule is evidently founded on the principle noticed in the last lesson, that inference can only proceed where there is agreement, and that two differences or disagreements allow of no reasoning. Two terms, as the third Canon states, may both differ from a common term and yet may or may not differ from each other. Thus if

Fig. 9.

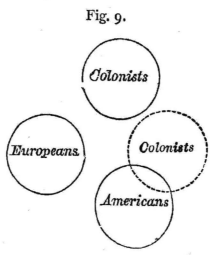

we were to argue that Americans are not Europeans, and Virginians are not Europeans, we see that both terms disagree with the middle term Europeans, and yet they

agree between themselves. In other cases the two negative premises may be plainly true while it will be quite
uncertain whether the major and minor terms agree or
not. Thus it is true, for **instance, that** "Colonists **are**
not Europeans, and Americans are not Europeans," but
this gives us no right to infer that Colonists are **or**
are not Americans. The two negative premises are represented in fig. 9, by excluding the circles of Colonists
and Americans from that of Europeans ; but this exclusion
may still be effected whether Colonists and Americans
coincide partially, or wholly, or not at all. A breach of
this rule of the syllogism may be conveniently called the
fallacy of **negative premises.** It must not however be
supposed that the mere occurrence of a negative particle
(*not* or *no*) in a proposition renders it negative in the
manner contemplated by this rule. Thus the argument

> " What is not compound is **an** element.
> Gold is not compound ;
> Therefore Gold is an element."

contains negatives in both premises, but is nevertheless
valid, because the negative in both cases affects the middle
term, which is really the negative term *not-compound.*

The truth of the sixth rule depends upon that of the
axiom, that if two terms agree with a common third term
they agree with each other, whence, remembering that a
negative proposition asserts disagreement, it is evident
that a negative conclusion could not be drawn from really
affirmative premises. The corresponding negative axiom
prevents our drawing an affirmative conclusion if either
premise should be really negative. Only practice however will enable the student to apply this and the
preceding rules of the syllogism with certainty, since
fallacy may be hidden and disguised by various forms of
expression. Numerous examples are given at the end of

the book by which the student may acquire facility in the analysis of arguments.

The remaining rules of the syllogism, the 7th and 8th, are by no means of a self-evident character and are in fact *corollaries* of the first six rules, that is *consequences* which follow from them. We shall therefore have to shew that they are true consequences in a future Lesson. We may call a breach of the 7th rule a *fallacy of particular premises*, and that of the 8th rule the fallacy of a *universal conclusion from a particular premise*, but these fallacies may really be resolved into those of Illicit Process, or Undistributed Middle.

> For many details concerning the Aristotelian and Scholastic Views of the Syllogism, and of Formal Logic generally, see the copious critical notes to Mansel's edition of Aldrich's *Artis Logicæ Rudimenta*. 2nd Ed. Oxford. 1852.

LESSON XVI.

THE MOODS AND FIGURES OF THE SYLLOGISM.

WE are now in full possession of those principles of reasoning, and the rules founded upon them, by which a true syllogism may be known from one which only seems to be a true one, and our task in the present Lesson is to ascertain the various shapes or fashions in which a process of mediate inference or syllogism may be met with. We know that every syllogistic argument must contain three propositions and three distinct terms each occurring twice in those propositions. Each proposition of the syllogism may, so far as we yet know, be either affirmative or negative, universal or particular, so that it is not difficult to calculate the utmost possible varieties of modes in which a syllogism might conceivably be constructed. Any one of the four propositions A, E, I, or O may in short be taken as a major premise, and joined with any one of the same form as a minor premise, and any one of the four again may be added as conclusion. We should thus obtain a series of the combinations or modes of joining the letters A, E, I, O, a few of which are here written out :

AAA	AEA	AIA	AOA	EAA	EEA
AAE	AEE	AIE	AOE	EAE	EEE
AAI	AEI	AII	AOI	EAI	EEI
AAO	AEO	AIO	AOO	EAO	&c.

It is obvious that there will be altogether 4 × 4 × 4 or 64 such combinations, of which 23 only are given above. The student can easily write out the remainder by carrying on the same systematic changes of the letters. Thus beginning with AAA we change the right-hand letter successively into E, I, and O, and then do the same beginning with AEA instead ; after the middle letter has been carried through all its changes we begin to change the left-hand letter. With each change of this we have to repeat all the sixteen changes of the other letters, so that there will obviously be altogether 64 different conceivable modes of arranging propositions into syllogisms.

We call each of these triplets of propositions a **mood** or form of the syllogism (Latin *modus*, shape), and we have to consider how many of such forms can really be used in valid arguments, as distinguished from those which break one or more of the rules of the syllogism. Thus the mood **AEA** would break the 6th rule, that if one premise be negative the conclusion must be so too; **AIE** breaks the converse part of the same rule, that a negative conclusion can only be proved by a negative premise; while **EEA**, **EEE** &c., break the 5th rule, which prohibits our reasoning at all from two negative premises. Examples of any of these moods can easily be invented, and their falsity would be very apparent ; thus for **AEA** we might take

> All Austrians are Europeans,
> No Australians are Europeans ;
> Therefore, all Australians are Austrians.

Many of the 64 conceivable moods are excluded by the 7th and 8th rules of the syllogism. Thus **AIA** and **EIE** break the rule, that if one premise be particular the conclusion must be so also, while **IIA**, **IOO**, **OIO** and many others, break the rule against two particular premises. Some combinations of propositions may break more than one rule; thus **OOO** has both negative premises and particular premises, and **OOA** also violates as well the 6th rule. It is an admirable exercise in the use of the syllogistic rules to write out all the 64 combinations and then strike out such as break any rule; the task if pursued systematically will not be so long or tedious as might seem likely. It will be found that there are only twelve moods which escape exclusion, and may so far be considered good forms of reasoning, and these are

AAA	**EAE**	**IAI**	**OAO**
AAI	**EAO**	**(IEO)**	
AEE	**EIO**		
AEO			
AII			
AOO			

Of these however **IEO** will have shortly to be rejected, because it will be found really to break the 4th rule, and involves Illicit process of the major term. There are, then, only *eleven* moods of the syllogism which are really valid; and we may thus account for the whole of the sixty-four moods.

Excluded by			Number of moods.
Negative premises, Rule	5	....	16
Particular premises	„ 7	....	12
One negative premise	„ 6	....	12
One premise particular	„ 8	....	8
Negative conclusion	„ 6	....	4
Illicit major	„ 4	....	1
Total excluded		....	53
Valid moods		....	11
Total		....	64

We have by no means exhausted as yet all the possible varieties of the syllogism, for we have only determined the character, affirmative or negative, general or particular of the propositions, but have not decided the ways in which the terms may be disposed in them. The major term must be the predicate of the conclusion, but it may either be subject or predicate of the major premise, and similarly the minor term or subject of the conclusion, may be either the subject or predicate of the minor premise. There thus arise four different ways, or as they are called **Figures**, in which the terms can be disposed. These four figures of the syllogism are shewn in the following scheme, taking

X to denote the major term
Y .... middle „
Z .... minor „

	1st Fig.	2nd Fig.	3rd Fig.	4th Fig.
Major Premise	$Y X$	$X Y$	$Y X$	$X Y$
Minor „	$Z Y$	$Z Y$	$Y Z$	$Y Z$
Conclusion	$Z X$	$Z X$	$Z X$	$Z X$

These figures must be carefully committed to memory, which will best be done by noting the position of the middle term. This term stands *first* as subject of the major premise in the 1st Figure, *second* as predicate in both premises of the 2nd Figure, *first* again as subject of both premises in the 3rd Figure, and in an intermediate position in the 4th Figure. In the conclusion, of course, the major and minor terms have one fixed position, and when the middle term is once correctly placed in any figure we easily complete the syllogism.

The reader will hardly be pleased to hear that each of the eleven valid moods will have to be examined in each of the four figures separately, so that there are 44 cases still possible, from which the valid syllogisms have to be selected. Thus the mood **AEE** in the first figure would be as follows :

$$\text{All } Y\text{'s are } X\text{'s,}$$
$$\text{No } Z\text{'s are } Y\text{'s ;}$$

Therefore $\text{No } Z\text{'s are } X\text{'s.}$

This would break the 4th rule and be an Illicit Major, because X is distributed in the conclusion, which is a negative proposition, and not in the major premise. In the second figure it would be valid:

$$\text{All } X\text{'s are } Y\text{'s,}$$
$$\text{No } Z\text{'s are } Y\text{'s ;}$$

Therefore $\text{No } Z\text{'s are } X\text{'s.}$

In the third figure it becomes

$$\text{All } Y\text{'s are } X\text{'s,}$$
$$\text{No } Y\text{'s are } Z\text{'s,}$$
$$\text{No } Z\text{'s are } X\text{'s,}$$

and again breaks the 4th rule, as regards the major term. Lastly in the 4th figure it is valid, as the reader may easily satisfy himself.

When all the valid moods are selected out of the 44 possible ones, there are found to be altogether 24, which are as follows:

Valid Moods of the Syllogism.

First Figure.	Second Figure.	Third Figure.	Fourth Figure.
AAA	EAE	AAI	AAI
EAE	AEE	IAI	AEE
AII	EIO	AII	IAI
EIO	AOO	EAO	EAO
		OAO	EIO
[AAI]	[EAO]	EIO	
[EAO]	[AEO]		[AEO]

Five of the above moods are set apart and enclosed in brackets, because though valid they are of little or no use. They are said to have a **weakened conclusion**, because the conclusion is particular when a general one might have been drawn. Thus **AAI**, in the first figure is represented by the example:

> All material substances gravitate,
> All metals are material substances;
> Therefore some metals gravitate.

It is apparent that the conclusion only states a part of the truth, and that in reality *all metals gravitate.* It is not actually an erroneous conclusion, because it must be carefully remembered (p. 77) that the affirming of a subaltern or particular proposition does not deny the corresponding general proposition. It is quite true that *some metals* gravitate, and it must be true because all of them do so. But when we can as readily prove that *all do gravitate* it is desirable to adopt this conclusion.

If we agree with most logicians to overlook the existence of the five syllogisms with weakened conclusions, there will remain *nineteen which are at once valid and useful.* In the next lesson certain ancient mnemonic lines will be furnished by which alone it would be possible for most persons to carry in the memory these 19 combinations; but the reader will in the mean time be able to gather from the statement of the moods in p. 140 the truth of the following remarks concerning the peculiar character of each figure of the syllogism.

The first figure is the only one which proves the proposition A, or has A for its conclusion. It is the only figure, too, which can prove any one of the four propositions A, E, I, O. As regards the premises, it is especially important to note that the major premise is always universal (A or E), and the minor premise affirmative (A or I): this peculiarity will be further considered in the next lesson.

The second figure only proves negative conclusions (E or O), and the reason is easily apparent. As the middle term in this figure is the predicate of both premises it would necessarily be undistributed in both premises if these were affirmatives, and we should commit the fallacy exemplified in p. 137. It follows that one premise must be negative and of course one only, so that of the major and minor terms one must be included or excluded wholly from the middle, and the other at the same time excluded or included at least partially. To illustrate this we may take *X, Y* and *Z* to represent, as before, the major, middle and minor terms of a syllogism, and the four moods of this figure are then

EAE	AEE
no *X*'s are *Y*'s,	all *X*'s are *Y*'s,
all *Z*'s are *Y*'s ;	no *Z*'s are *Y*'s;
∴ no *Z*'s are *X*'s.	∴ no *Z*'s are *X*'s.

EIO

no X's are Y's,
some Z's are Y's ;
∴ some Z's are not X's.

AOO

all X's are Y's,
some Z's are not Y's ;
∴ some Z's are not X's.

The nature of the moods of the second figure is clearly shewn in the following figures :

Fig. 10.
(Cesare.)

Fig. 11.
(Camestres.)

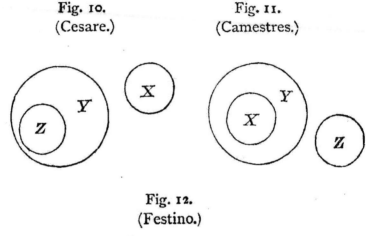

Fig. 12.
(Festino.)

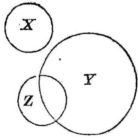

It will also be observed that in the second figure the minor premise may be any of the four **A, E, I, O**.

The third figure only proves particulars (**I** or **O**), and it always has an affirmative minor premise (**A** or **I**). It also contains the greatest number of moods, since in no case is the conclusion a weakened one.

The fourth figure is usually considered unnatural and comparatively useless, because the same arguments can be more clearly arranged in the form of the first figure, which in some respects it resembles. Thus it proves all the propositions except **A**, namely, **E, I, O**, and its first mood **AAI**, is in reality a weakened form of **AAA** in the first figure. Many logicians, including in recent times Sir W. Hamilton, have rejected the use of this figure altogether.

It is evident that the several figures of the syllogism possess different characters, and logicians have thought that each figure was best suited for certain special purposes. A German logician, Lambert, stated these purposes concisely as follows :—" The first figure is suited to the discovery or proof of the properties of a thing; the second to the discovery or proof of the distinctions between things; the third to the discovery or proof of instances and exceptions; the fourth to the discovery, or exclusion, of the different species of genus."

It may be added that the moods Cesare and Camestres are often used in disproving a statement, because they give a universal negative conclusion, founded upon the exclusion of one class from another. Thus if any one were still to assert that light consists of material particles it might be met by the following syllogism:

" Material particles communicate impetus to
whatever they strike,
Light does not communicate impetus to
whatever it strikes ;
Therefore light is not material particles."

The moods Baroko and Festino are less used, but allow of a particular conclusion being established.

When we wish however to establish objections or

exceptions to a general statement, which is indeed the natural way of meeting it, we employ the third figure. The statement that "all metals are solids" would at once be disproved by the exception *mercury*, as follows :

Mercury is not solid,
Mercury is a metal ;
Therefore some metal is not solid.

Were any one to assert that what is incomprehensible cannot exist, we meet it at once with the argument that Infinity is incomprehensible, but that infinity certainly exists, because we cannot otherwise explain the nature of a curve line, or of a quantity varying continuously; therefore something that is incomprehensible exists. In this case even one exception is sufficient entirely to negative the proposition, which really means that because a thing is incomprehensible it cannot exist. But if one incomprehensible thing does exist, others may also; and all authority is taken from the statement.

According to the Aristotelian system the third figure must also be employed whenever the middle term is a singular term, because in Aristotle's view of the subject a singular term could not stand as the predicate of a proposition.

LESSON XVII.

REDUCTION OF THE IMPERFECT FIGURES OF THE SYLLOGISM.

IN order to facilitate the recollection of the nineteen valid and useful moods of the syllogism, logicians invented, at least six centuries ago, a most curious system of artificial words, combined into mnemonic verses, which may be

readily committed to memory. This device, however in-
genious, is of a barbarous and wholly unscientific character; but a knowledge of its construction and use is still
expected from the student of logic, and the verses are
therefore given and explained below.

> *Barbara, Celarent, Darii, Ferio*que, prioris;
> *Cesare, Camestres, Festino, Baroko,* secundæ;
> Tertia, *Darapti, Disamis, Datisi, Felapton,*
> *Bokardo, Ferison,* habet; Quarta insuper addit
> *Bramantip, Camenes, Dimaris, Fesapo, Fresison.*

The words printed in ordinary type are real Latin
words, signifying that four moods whose artificial names
are Barbara, Celarent, Darii and Ferio, belong to the
first figure; that four others belong to the second; six
more to the third; while the fourth figure moreover
contains five moods. Each artificial name contains
three vowels, which indicate the propositions forming
a valid mood : thus, *CElArEnt* signifies the mood of the
first figure, which has E for a major premise, A for the
minor, and E for the conclusion. The artificial words
altogether contain exactly the series of combinations of
vowels shown in p. 140, excepting those in brackets.

These mnemonic lines also contain indications of the
mode in which each mood of the second, third and fourth
figures can be proved by **reduction** to a corresponding
mood of the first figure. Aristotle looked upon the first
figure as a peculiarly evident and cogent form of argument, the *Dictum de omni et nullo* being directly applicable to it, and he therefore called it the **Perfect Figure.**
The fourth figure was never recognised by him, and it is
often called the **Galenian** figure, because the celebrated
Galen is supposed to have discovered it. The second
and third figures were known to Aristotle as the **Imperfect
Figures,** which it was necessary to reduce to the first

figure by certain conversions and transpositions of the premises, for which directions are to be found in the artificial words. These directions are as follows :—

s indicates that the proposition denoted by the preceding vowel is to be converted *simply*.

p indicates that the proposition is to be converted *per accidens*, or by limitation.

m indicates that the premises of the syllogism are to be transposed, the major being made the minor of a new syllogism, and the old minor the new major. The *m* is derived from the Latin *mutare*, to change.

B, C, D, F, the initial consonants of the names, indicate the moods of the first figure, which are produced by reduction; thus Cesare, Camestres and Camenes are reducible to Celarent, Darapti, &c., to Darii, Fresison to Ferio and so on.

k denotes that the mood must be reduced or proved by a distinct process called **Indirect reduction,** or *reductio ad impossibile*, which will shortly be considered.

Let us now take some syllogism, say in *Camestres*, and follow the directions for reduction. Let the example be

All stars are self-luminous .... (1)
All planets are not self-luminous.............. (2)
Therefore no planets are stars................. (3)

The first *s* in Camestres shows that we are to convert simply the minor premise. The *m* instructs us to change the order of the premises, and the final *s* to convert the conclusion simply. When all these changes are made we obtain

No self-luminous bodies are planets.......Converse of (2)
All stars are self-luminous .... (1)
Therefore no stars are planets..............Converse of (3)

This, it will be found, is a syllogism in Celarent, as might be known from the initial *C* in Camestres.

As another example let us take Fesapo, for instance :
>No fixed stars are planets,
>All planets are round bodies ;
>Therefore some round bodies are not fixed stars.

According to the directions in the name, we are to convert simply the major premise, and by limitation the minor premise. We have then the following syllogism in *Ferio :*
>No planets are fixed stars,
>Some round bodies are planets ;
>Therefore some round bodies are not fixed stars.

The reader will easily apply the same process of conversion or transposition to the other moods, according to the directions contained in their names, and the only moods it will be necessary to examine especially are Bramantip, Baroko and Bokardo. As an example of Bramantip we may take :
>All metals are material substances,
>All material substances are gravitating bodies;
>Therefore some gravitating bodies are metals.

The name contains the letter m, which instructs us to transpose the premises, and the letter p, which denotes conversion by limitation ; effecting these changes we have :
>All material substances are gravitating bodies,
>All metals are material substances ;
>Therefore some metals are gravitating bodies.

This is not a syllogism in Barbara, as we might have expected, but is the weakened mood AAI of the first figure. It is evident that the premises yield the conclusion "all metals are gravitating bodies," and we must take the letter p to indicate in this mood that the conclusion is weaker than it might be. In truth the fourth figure is so

imperfect and unnatural in form, containing nothing but
ill-arranged syllogisms, which would have been better
stated in the first figure, that Aristotle, the founder of
logical science, never allowed the existence of the figure
at all.   It is to be regretted that so needless an addition
was made to the somewhat complicated forms of the
syllogism.

Indirect reduction.   The moods Baroko and Bokardo
give a good deal of trouble, because they cannot be reduced directly to the first figure.   To show the mode of
treating these moods we will take X, Y, Z to represent the
major, middle and minor terms of the syllogism, and
Baroko may then be stated as follows:

All X's are Y's,
Some Z's are not Y's ;
Therefore   Some Z's are not X's.

Now if we convert the major premise by **Contrapo-**
sition (p. 83) we have "all not-Y's are not-X's," and,
making this the major premise of the syllogism, we have

All not-Y's are not X's,
Some Z's are not-Y's ;
Therefore   Some Z's are not X's.

Although both the above premises appear to be negative, this is really a valid syllogism in Ferio, because
two of the negative particles merely affect the middle
term (see p. 134), and we have therefore effected the reduction of the syllogism.

Bokardo, when similarly stated, is as follows :

Some Y's are not X's,
All Y's are Z's ;
Therefore   Some Z's are not X's.

To reduce this, convert the major premise by negation, and then transpose the premises. We have:

> All Y's are Z's,
> Some not-X's are Y's;

Therefore   Some not-X's are Z's.

This conclusion is the converse by negation of the
former conclusion, the truth of which is thus proved by
reduction to a syllogism in Darii.

Both these moods, Baroko and Bokardo, may however
be proved by a peculiar process of **indirect reduction,**
closely analogous to the indirect proofs often employed by
Euclid in Geometry. This process consists in supposing
the conclusion of the syllogism to be false, and its contradictory therefore true, when a new syllogism can easily
be constructed which leads to a conclusion contradictory
of one of the original premises. Now it is absurd in logic
to call in question the truth of our own premises, for the
very purpose of argument or syllogism is to deduce a conclusion which will be true *when the premises are true.*
The syllogism enables us to restate in a new form the information which is contained in the premises, just as a
machine may deliver to us in a new form the material
which is put into it. The machine, or rather the maker
of the machine, is not responsible for the quality of the
materials furnished to it, and similarly the logician is not
responsible in the least for the truth of his premises, but
only for their correct treatment. He must treat them, if
he treat them at all, as true; and therefore a conclusion
which requires the falsity of one of our premises is altogether absurd.

To apply this method we may take Baroko, as before :

> All X's are Y's ....(1)
> Some Z's are not Y's ......(2)

Therefore   Some Z's are not X's ......(3)

If this conclusion be not true then its contradictory, 'all Z's are X's' must of necessity be regarded as true (pp. 76—79). Making this the minor premise of a new syllogism with the original major premise we have :

All X's are Y's .... (1)
All Z's are X's ....contradictory of (3)
Hence   All Z's are Y's.

Now this conclusion in **A**, is the contradictory of our old minor premise in **O**, and we must either admit one of our own premises to be false or allow that our original conclusion is true. The latter is of course the alternative we choose.

We treat Bokardo in a very similar manner ;

Some Y's are not X's..................(1)
All Y's are Z's............................(2)
Therefore   Some Z's are not X's ....(3)

If this conclusion be not true then 'all Z's are X's' must be true. Now we can make the syllogism :

All Z's are X's.........Contradictory of (3)
All Y's are Z's ....(2)
Hence   All Y's are X's.

This conclusion is the contradictory of (1), the original major premise, and as this cannot be allowed, we must either suppose (2) the original minor premise to be false, which is equally impossible, or allow that our original conclusion is true.

It will be observed that in both these cases of Indirect Reduction or Proof we use a syllogism in Barbara, which fact is indicated by the initial letters of Baroko and Bokardo. The same process of Indirect proof may be applied to any of the other moods, but it is not usual to do so, as the simpler process of direct or as it is often called ostensive reduction is sufficient.

It will be remembered that when in Lesson XV. (p. 135) we considered the rules of the syllogism, there were two supplementary rules, the 7th and 8th, concerning particular premises, which were by no means of a self-evident character, and which require to be proved by the six more fundamental rules. We have now sufficiently advanced to consider this proof with advantage. The 7th rule forbids us to draw any conclusion from two **particular premises**; now such premises must be either **II, IO, OI,** or **OO.** Of these **II** contain no distributed term at all, so that the 3rd rule, which requires the middle term to be distributed, must be broken. The premises **OO** evidently break the 5th rule, against negative premises. The conclusion of the pair **IO** must be negative by the 6th rule, because one premise is negative; the major term therefore will be distributed, but as the major premise is a particular affirmative it cannot be distributed without committing the fallacy of illicit process of the major, against rule 4. Lastly the premises **OI** contain only one distributed term, the predicate of the major premise. But as the conclusion must be negative by rule 6th, the major term must be distributed: we ought to have then in the premises two distributed terms, one for the middle term, the other for the major term; but as the premises contain only a single distributed term, we must commit the fallacy either of undistributed middle or of illicit process of the major term, if we attempt to draw any conclusion at all. We thus see that in no possible case can a pair of particular premises give a valid conclusion.

The 8th rule of the syllogism instructs us that if one premise of a syllogism be particular the conclusion must also be particular. It can only be shown to be true by going over all the possible cases and observing that the six principal rules of the syllogism always require the conclusion to be particular. Suppose for instance the premises are **A** and **I**; then they contain only one distributed term, the subject of **A**, and this is required for the middle term by rule 3. Hence the minor term cannot be distributed without breaking rule 4, so that the conclusion must be the proposition **I**. The premises **AO** would contain two distributed terms, the subject of **A** and the predicate of **O**; but if we were to draw from them the conclusion **E**, the major and minor terms would require to be distributed, so that the middle term would remain undistributed against rule 3. The reader can easily prove the other cases such as **EI** by calculating the number of distributed terms in a similar manner: it will always be found that there are insufficient terms distributed in the premises to allow of a universal conclusion.

LESSON XVIII.

IRREGULAR AND COMPOUND SYLLOGISMS.

IT may seem surprising that arguments which are met with in books or conversation are seldom or never thrown into the form of regular syllogisms. Even if a complete syllogism be sometimes met with, it is generally employed in mere affectation of logical precision. In former centuries it was, indeed, the practice for all students at the Universities to take part in public disputations, during which elaborate syllogistic arguments were put forward by one side and confuted by precise syllogisms on the other side. This practice has not been very long discontinued at the University of Oxford, and is said to be still maintained in some continental Universities; but except in such school disputations it must be allowed that perfectly formal syllogisms are seldom employed.

In truth, however, it is not syllogistic arguments which are wanting; wherever any one of the conjunctions, *therefore, because, for, since, hence, inasmuch as, consequently* occurs, it is certain that an inference is being drawn, and this will very probably be done by a true syllogism. It is merely the complete statement of the premises and conclusion, which is usually neglected because the reader is generally aware of one or other of the premises, or he can readily divine what is assumed; and it is tedious and even offensive to state at full length what the reader is already aware of. Thus, if I say "atmospheric air must have weight because it is a material substance," I certainly employ a syllogism; but I think it quite needless to state the premise, of which I clearly assume the truth, that "whatever is a material substance has weight." The conclusion of the syllogism is the first proposition, viz. "atmospheric air has weight." The middle term is "material substance," which does not occur in the conclusion; the minor is "atmospheric air," and the major, "having weight." The complete syllogism is evidently:

> All material substances have weight,
> Atmospheric air is a material substance;
> Therefore atmospheric air has weight.

This is in the very common and useful mood Barbara.

A syllogism when incompletely stated is usually called an **enthymeme,** and this name is often supposed to be derived from two Greek words (ἐν, in, and θυμός, mind), so as to signify that some knowledge is held by the mind and is supplied in the form of a *tacit,* that is a silent or understood premise. Most commonly this will be the major premise, and then the enthymeme may be said to be of the First Order. Less commonly the minor premise is unexpressed, and the enthymeme is of the Second

Order. Of this nature is the following argument: "Comets must be subject to the law of gravitation; for this is true of all bodies which move in elliptic orbits." It is so clearly implied that comets move in elliptic orbits, that it would be tedious to state this as the minor premise in a complete syllogism of the mood Barbara, thus :

All bodies moving in elliptic orbits are subject to the law of gravitation ;
Comets move in elliptic orbits ;
Therefore comets are subject to the law of gravitation.

It may happen occasionally that the conclusion of a syllogism is left unexpressed, and the enthymeme may then be said to belong to the Third Order. This occurs in the case of epigrams or other witty sayings, of which the very wit often consists in making an unexpressed truth apparent. Sir W. Hamilton gives as an instance of this kind of enthymeme the celebrated epigram written by Porson the English scholar upon a contemporary German scholar:

"The Germans in Greek
Are sadly to seek ;
Not five in five score,
But ninety-five more ;
All, save only Hermann,
And Hermann's a German."

It is evident that while pretending to make an exception of Hermann, the writer ingeniously insinuates that since he is a German he has not a correct knowledge of Greek. The wonderful speech of Antony over the body of Cæsar, in Shakspeare's greatest historical play, contains a series of syllogistic arguments of which the conclusions are suggested only.

Even a single proposition may have a syllogistic force if it clearly suggest to the mind a second premise which

XVIII.]   *SYLLOGISMS.*   155

thus enables a conclusion to be drawn. The expression of Horne Tooke, "Men who have no rights cannot justly complain of any wrongs," seems to be a case in point; for there are few people who have not felt wronged at some time or other, and they would therefore be likely to argue, whether upon true or false premises, as follows:

> Men who have no rights cannot justly complain of any wrongs;
> We can justly complain;
> Therefore we are not men who have no rights.

In other words, we have rights.

Syllogisms may be variously joined and combined together, and it is convenient to have special names for the several parts of a complex argument. Thus a syllogism which proves or furnishes a reason for one of the premises of another syllogism is called a **Prosyllogism**; and a syllogism which contains as a premise the conclusion of another syllogism is called an **Episyllogism**.

Take the example :

> All *B*'s are *A*'s,
> And all *C*'s are *B*'s;
> Therefore all *C*'s are *A*'s.
> But all *D*'s are *C*'s;
> Therefore   All *D*'s are *A*'s.

This evidently contains two syllogisms in the mood Barbara, the first of which is a Prosyllogism with respect to the second, while the second is an Episyllogism with respect to the first.

The peculiar name **Epicheirema** is given to a syllogism when either premise is proved or supported by a reason implying the existence of an imperfectly expressed prosyllogism; thus the form,

All *B*'s are *A*'s, for they are *P*'s,
And all *C*'s are *B*'s, for they are *Q*'s ;
Therefore all *C*'s are *A*'s,

is a double Epicheirema, containing reasons for both premises. The reader will readily decompose it into three complete syllogisms of the mood Barbara.

A more interesting form of reasoning is found in the chain of syllogisms commonly called the **Sorites**, from the Greek word σωρός, meaning *heap*. It is usually stated in this way :

All *A*'s are *B*'s,
All *B*'s are *C*'s,
All *C*'s are *D*'s,
All *D*'s are *E*'s ;
Therefore all *A*'s are *E*'s.

The chain can be carried on to any length provided it is perfectly consecutive, so that each term except the first and last occurs twice, once as subject and once as predicate. It hardly needs to be pointed out that the sorites really contains a series of syllogisms imperfectly expressed; thus

First Syllogism.	Second Syllogism.	Last Syllogism.
B's are *C*'s,	*C*'s are *D*'s,	*D*'s are *E*'s,
A's are *B*'s ;	*A*'s are *C*'s ;	*A*'s are *D*'s ;
∴ *A*'s are *C*'s.	∴ *A*'s are *D*'s.	∴ *A*'s are *E*'s.

Each syllogism furnishes a premise to the succeeding one, of which it is therefore the prosyllogism, and any syllogism may equally be considered the episyllogism of that which precedes.

In the above sorites all the premises were universal and affirmative, but a sorites may contain one particular premise provided it be the first, and one negative premise provided it be the last. The reader may easily assure himself by trial, that if any premise except the first were particular the fallacy of undistributed middle would be committed, because one of the middle terms would be the predicate of one affirmative premise and the subject of another particular premise. If any premise but the last were negative there would be a fallacy of illicit process of the major term.

It is not to be supposed that the forms of the syllogism hitherto described are all the kinds of reasoning actually employed in science or common life. In addition to the hypothetical and disjunctive syllogisms and some other forms to be described in succeeding lessons, there are really many modes of reasoning of which logicians have not taken much notice as yet. This was clearly pointed out more than two hundred years ago by the writers of the *Port Royal Logic,* a work first printed in the year 1662, but which has been since reprinted very often and translated into a great many languages. The book is named from a place near Paris where a small religious community lived, of which the authors of the book, namely Arnauld and Nicole, and a contributor to it the great philosopher and mathematician Pascal, were the most celebrated members. The *Port Royal Logic* was to a considerable extent the basis of the well-known Watts' *Logic,* but the reader can now be referred to an admirable translation of the original work made by Professor Spencer Baynes, of St Andrew's.

Many improvements of Logic may be found in this work, such as the doctrine of Extension and Intension explained in Lesson v. In the 9th Chapter of the 3rd Part moreover it is wisely pointed out that "little pains are taken in applying the rules of the syllogism to reasonings of which the propositions are complex, though this is often very difficult, and there are many arguments of this nature which appear bad, but which are nevertheless very good; and besides, the use of such reasonings is much more frequent than that of syllogisms which are quite simple." Some examples are given of the complex syllogisms here referred to; thus:

> The sun is a thing insensible,
> . The Persians worship the sun;
> Therefore the Persians worship a thing insensible.

This is an argument which cannot be proved by the rules of the syllogism, and yet it is not only evidently true, but is an exceedingly common kind of argument. Another example is as follows:

> The Divine Law commands us to honour kings;
> Louis XIV. is a king;
> Therefore the Divine Law commands us to honour Louis XIV.

The reader will also find that arguments which are really quite valid and syllogistic are expressed in language so that they appear to have four distinct terms and thus to break one of the rules of the syllogism. Thus if I say " Diamonds are combustible, for they are composed of carbon and carbon is combustible," there are four terms employed, namely, diamonds, combustible, composed of carbon, and carbon. But it is easy to alter the construction of the propositions so as to get a simple syllogism without really altering the sense, and we then have :

> What is composed of carbon is combustible;
> Diamonds are composed of carbon;
> Therefore diamonds are combustible.

Examples are given at the end of the book of concise arguments, taken from Bacon's *Essays* and other writings, which the student can reduce to the syllogistic form by easy alterations; but it should be clearly understood that these changes are of an extra-logical character, and belong more properly to the science of language.

I may here explain that the syllogism and the sorites can be expressed either in the order of extension or that of intension. In regard to the number of individual things the noble metals are part of the metals, and the metals are part of the elements; but in regard to intension, that is to say the qualities implied in the names, element is part of metal, and metal is part of noble metal. So again in extension the genus of plants Anemone is part of the order Ranunculaceæ, and this is part of the great class Exogens; but in intension the character of Exogen is part of the character of Ranunculaceæ, and this is part of the character of Anemone. Syllogistic reasoning is equally valid and evident in either case, and we might represent the two modes in ordinary language as follows:

Extensive Syllogism.

All Ranunculaceæ are Exogens;
The Anemone is one of the Ranunculaceæ;
Therefore the Anemone is an Exogen.

Intensive Syllogism.

All the qualities of Ranunculaceæ are qualities of Anemone;
All the qualities of Exogen are qualities of Ranunculaceæ;
Therefore all the qualities of Exogen are qualities of Anemone.

Any sorites can be similarly represented either in extension or intension.

Concerning the Aristotelian doctrine of the Enthymeme, see Mansel's Aldrich, App. Note F, and Hamilton's *Lectures on Logic*, Lecture XX. *Port Royal Logic*, translated by T. Spencer Baynes, 5th ed. Edinburgh, 1861.

LESSON XIX.

OF CONDITIONAL ARGUMENTS.

IT will be remembered that when treating of propositions we divided them into two distinct kinds, Categorical Propositions, and Conditional Propositions. The former kind alone has hitherto been considered, and we must now proceed to describe Conditional propositions and the arguments which may be composed of them.

Logicians have commonly described Conditional propositions as composed of *two or more Categorical propositions united by a conjunction.* This union may happen in two ways, giving rise to two very different species of conditionals, which we shall call **Hypothetical Propositions** and **Disjunctive Propositions.** The way in which the several kinds of propositions are related will be seen in the following diagram :

Propositions are { Categorical. / Conditional { Hypothetical. / Disjunctive.

A conditional proposition may be further described as one which makes a statement under a certain condition or qualification restricting its application. In the hypothetical form this condition is introduced by the conjunction *if,* or some other word equivalent to it. Thus—

"If iron is impure, it is brittle"

is a hypothetical proposition consisting of two distinct categorical propositions, the first of which, "Iron is impure," is called the **Antecedent**; the second, "It is brittle," the **Consequent.** In this case "impurity" is the condition or qualification which limits the application of the predicate brittle to iron. It was asserted by Horne Tooke in his celebrated work *The Diversions of Purley*, that all conjunctions are the remains or corrupted forms of verbs. This is certainly true in the case of the hypothetical conjunction; for the word *if* in old English is written *gif*, or *gyf*, and is undoubtedly derived from the verb *to give*. We may actually substitute at present any verb of similar meaning, as for instance—*grant, allow, suppose.* Thus we may say—

> "Grant that iron is impure, and it is brittle."
> "Supposing that iron is impure, it is brittle."

The hypothetical proposition might be employed in arguments of various form, but only two of these are of sufficient importance to receive special names. The **hypothetical syllogism** consists of two premises, called the major and minor, as in the case of the ordinary syllogism. The major premise is hypothetical in form; the minor premise is categorical, and according as it is affirmative or negative the argument is said to be a **Constructive** or a **Destructive hypothetical syllogism.** Thus the form,

> If *A* is *B*, *C* is *D*;
> But *A* is *B*;
> Therefore *C* is *D*,

is a constructive hypothetical syllogism.

It must be carefully observed that the minor premise affirms the antecedent of the major premise, whence the argument is said to be of the *modus ponens*, or mood which posits or affirms. It is probably one of the most familiar and common kinds of argument. The form,

> If *A* is *B*, *C* is *D*;
> But *C* is not *D*;
> Therefore *A* is not *B*,

represents the corresponding Destructive hypothetical syllogism, also called the *modus tollens*, or the mood which removes the consequent. It must be carefully ob- served again that it is the consequent, not the antecedent, which is denied.

The only rule which is requisite for testing the validity of such syllogisms embodies what we have observed above ; viz. that *either the antecedent must be affirmed, or the consequent denied.* If either part of this rule be broken, a serious fallacy will be committed. Thus the apparent argument,

> If A is B, C is D ;
> But C is D ;
> Therefore A is B,

is really a fallacy which we may call the *fallacy of affirm- ing the consequent*, and its fallacious nature is readily un- derstood by reflecting that "A being B" is not stated to be the only condition on which C is D. It may happen that when E is F, or G is H, or under a hundred other circumstances, C is D, so that the mere fact of C being D is no sufficient proof that A is B. Thus, if a man's cha- racter be avaricious he will refuse to give money for useful purposes ; but it does not follow that every person who refuses to give money for such purposes is avaricious. There may be many proper reasons or motives leading him to refuse ; he may have no money, or he may con- sider the purpose not a useful one, or he may have more useful purposes in view.

A corresponding fallacy arises from *denying the ante- cedent,* as in the form—

> If A is B, C is D ;
> But A is not B ;
> Therefore C is not D.

The error may be explained in the same way; for as "*A* being *B*" is not stated to be the only condition of *C* being *D*, we may deny this one condition to be true, but it is possible that the consequent may happen to be true for other reasons, of which we know nothing. Thus if a man is not avaricious we cannot conclude that he will be sure to give money whenever asked. Or take the following example :

"If the study of Logic furnished the mind with a multitude of useful facts like the study of other sciences, it would deserve cultivation; but it does not furnish the mind with a multitude of useful facts; therefore it does not deserve cultivation."

This is evidently a fallacious argument, because the acquiring of a multitude of useful facts is not the only ground on which the study of a science can be recommended. To correct and exercise the powers of judgment and reasoning is the object for which Logic deserves to be cultivated, and the existence of such other purpose is ignored in the above fallacious argument, which evidently involves *the denial of the antecedent.*

Although it is usual in logical works to describe the hypothetical proposition and syllogism as if they were different in nature from the categorical proposition and syllogism, yet it has long been known that the hypotheticals can be reduced to the categorical form, and brought under the ordinary rules of the syllogism. As a general rule the hypothetical proposition can be readily converted into a universal affirmative proposition (A) of exactly the same meaning. Thus our instance, "If iron is impure, it is brittle," becomes simply "Impure iron is brittle." In making this alteration in a hypothetical syllogism it will be found necessary to supply a new minor term; thus in the case,

> If iron is impure it is brittle ;
> But it is impure ;
> Therefore it is brittle,

we have to substitute for the indefinite pronoun *it,* the *iron in question,* and we obtain a correct categorical syllogism in the mood Barbara :

> Impure iron is brittle ;
> The iron in question is impure iron ;
> Therefore the iron in question is brittle.

Sometimes the reduction requires a more extensive change of language.   For instance,

> If the barometer is falling, bad weather is coming ;
> But the barometer is falling ;
> Therefore bad weather is coming,

may be represented in the following form:

The circumstances of the barometer falling are the circumstances of bad weather coming ;
But these are the circumstances of the **barometer** falling;
Therefore these are the circumstances of bad weather coming.

As an instance of the Destructive Hypothetical syllogism we may take :

> If Aristotle is right, slavery is a proper form of **society;**
> But slavery is not a proper form of society;
> Therefore Aristotle is not right.

This becomes as a categorical :

The case of Aristotle being right is the case of slavery being a proper form of society;
But this is not the case ;
Therefore this is not the case of Aristotle being right.

If not reducible by any other form of expression, hypotheticals can always be reduced by the use of the words *case of.*

It will now be easily made apparent that the fallacy of affirming the consequent is really a breach of the 3rd rule of the syllogism, leading to an undistributed middle term. Our example may be as before :

> If a man is avaricious he will refuse money ;
> But he does refuse money ;
> Therefore he is avaricious.

This becomes as a categorical syllogism,

> All avaricious men refuse money ;
> But **this** man refuses money ;
> Therefore this man is avaricious.

This is the mood AAA in the second figure ; and the niddle term, refusing money, is undistributed in both premises, so that the argument is entirely fallacious.

Again, the fallacy of *denying the antecedent* is equivalent to the *illicit process of the major.* Our former example (p. 163) may thus be represented:

"A science which furnishes the mind with a multitude of useful facts deserves cultivation; but Logic is not such a science; therefore Logic does not deserve cultivation."

This apparent syllogism is of the mood AEE in the first figure, which breaks the fourth rule of the syllogism, because the major term, *deserving cultivation*, is distributed in the negative conclusion, but not in the affirmative major premise.

We now pass to the consideration of the disjunctive proposition, which instead of a single predicate has several alternatives united by the disjunctive conjunction *or*, any one of which may be affirmed of the subject. "A member of the House of Commons is either a representative of a county, or of a borough, or of a University," is an instance of such a proposition, containing three alternatives ; but there may be any number of alternatives from two upwards.

The **disjunctive syllogism** consists of a disjunctive major premise with a categorical proposition, either affirmative or negative, forming the minor premise. Thu ι arise two moods, of which the affirmative mood is called by the Latin words *modus ponendo tollens* (the mood which by affirming denies), and may be thus stated:

A is either B or C,
But A is B;
Therefore A is not C.

This form of argument proceeds on the supposition that if one alternative of a disjunctive proposition be held true, the others cannot also be true. Thus "the time of year must be either spring, summer, autumn or winter," and if it be spring it cannot be summer, autumn or winter; and so on. But it has been objected by Whately, Mansel, Mill, as well as many earlier logicians, that this does not always hold true. Thus if we say that "a good book is valued either for the usefulness of its contents or the excellence of its style," it does not by any means follow because the contents of a book are useful that its style is not excellent. We generally choose alternatives which are inconsistent with each other; but this is not logically necessary.

The other form of disjunctive syllogism, called the *modus tollendo ponens* (the mood which by denying affirms), is always of necessity cogent, and is as follows:

A is either B or C,
But A is not B;
Therefore A is C.

Thus if we suppose a book to be valued only for the usefulness of its contents or the excellence of its style, it follows that if a book be valued but not for the former reason it must be for the latter; and *vice versa*. If the time of year be not spring, it must be summer, autumn or

winter; if it be not autumn nor winter, it must be eithe
spring or summer; and so on. In short if any alternatives
be denied, the rest remain to be affirmed as before. It
will be noticed that the disjunctive syllogism is governed
by totally different rules from the ordinary categorical
syllogism, since a negative premise gives an affirmative
conclusion in the former, and a negative conclusion in
the latter.

There yet remains a form of argument called the
Dilemma, because it consists in assuming two alternatives,
usually called the horns of the dilemma, and yet proves
something in either case (Greek δι- two ; λῆμμα, assumption). Mr Mansel defines this argument as " a syllogism,
having a conditional major premise with more than one
antecedent, and a disjunctive minor." There are at least
three forms in which it may be stated. The first form is
called the Simple Constructive Dilemma :

If A is B, C is D; and if E is F, C is D ;
But either A is B, or E is F;
Therefore C is D.

Thus "if a science furnishes useful facts, it is worthy o
being cultivated; and if the study of it exercises the
reasoning powers, it is worthy of being cultivated; but
either a science furnishes useful facts, or its study
exercises the reasoning powers ; therefore it is worthy of
being cultivated."

The second form of dilemma is the Complex Con·
structive Dilemma, which is as follows :

If A is B, C is D; and if E is F, G is H ;
But either A is B, or E is F;
Therefore either C is D, or G is H.

It is called complex because the conclusion is in the
disjunctive form As an instance we may take the argu-

ment, " If a statesman who sees his former opinions to
be wrong does not alter his course he is guilty of deceit;
and if he does alter his course he is open to a charge
of inconsistency; but either he does not alter his course
or he does; therefore he is either guilty of deceit, or he is
open to a charge of inconsistency." In this case as in
the greater number of dilemmas the terms A, B, C, D, &c.
are not all different.

The **Destructive Dilemma** is always complex, because
it could otherwise be resolved into two unconnected destructive hypothetical syllogisms.   It is in the following
form:

> If A is B, C is D; and if E is F, G is H;
> But either C is not D, or G is not H;
> Therefore either A is not B, or E is not F.

For instance, " If this man were wise, he would no
speak irreverently of Scripture in jest; and if he were
good, he would not do so in earnest; but he does it either
in jest or earnest; therefore he is either not wise, or not
good *."

Dilemmatic arguments are however more often fallacious than not, because it is seldom possible to find
instances where two alternatives exhaust all the possible
cases, unless indeed one of them be the simple negative
of the other in accordance with the law of excluded middle (p. 119).   Thus if we were to argue that " if a pupil is
fond of learning he needs no stimulus, and that if he dislikes learning no stimulus will be of any avail, but as he
is either fond of learning or dislikes it, a stimulus is either
needless or of no avail," we evidently assume improperly
the disjunctive minor premise.   Fondness and dislike are
not the only two possible alternatives, for there may be

* Whately.

some who are neither fond of learning nor dislike it, and
to these a stimulus in the shape of rewards may be desirable. Almost anything can be proved if we are allowed
thus to pick out two of the possible alternatives which are
in our favour, and argue from these alone.

A dilemma can often be retorted by producing as
cogent a dilemma to the contrary effect. Thus an Athe-
nian mother, according to Aristotle, addressed her son in
the following words : " Do not enter into public business ;
for if you say what is just, men will hate you ; and if you
say what is unjust, the Gods will hate you." To which
Aristotle suggests the following retort : " I ought to enter
into public affairs ; for if I say what is just, the Gods wi..
love me ; and if I say what is unjust, men will love me."

Mansel's Aldrich, App. Note I, on the Hypothetica.
Syllogism.

LESSON XX.

LOGICAL FALLACIES.

IN order to acquire a satisfactory knowledge of the rules
of correct thinking, it is essential that we should become
acquainted with the most common kinds of fallacy ; that
is to say, the modes in which, by neglecting the rules of
logic, we often fall into erroneous reasoning. In previous
lessons we have considered, as it were, how to find the
right road ; it is our task here to ascertain the turnings at
which we are most liable to take the wrong road.

In describing the fallacies I shall follow the order and
adopt the mode of classification which has been usual
for the last 2000 years and more, since in fact the great

teacher Aristotle first explained the fallacies. According to this mode of arrangement fallacies are divided into two principal groups, containing the logical and the material fallacies.

1. The **logical fallacies** are those which occur in the mere form of the statement ; or as it is said in the old Latin expressions, *in dictione,* or *in voce.* It is supposed accordingly that fallacies of this kind can be discovered without a knowledge of the subject-matter with which the argument is concerned.

2. The **material fallacies,** on the contrary, arise outside of the mere verbal statement, or as it is said, *extra dictionem;* they are concerned consequently with the subject of the argument, or *in re* (in the matter), and cannot be detected and set right but by those acquainted with the subject.

The first group of logical fallacies may be further divided into the *purely logical* and the *semi-logical,* and we may include in the former class the distinct breaches of the syllogistic rules which have already been described. Thus we may enumerate as **Purely Logical Fallacies :**

1. Fallacy of four terms (*Quaternio Terminorum*)— Breach of Rule 1 ;

2. Fallacy of undistributed middle—Breach of Rule 3 ;

3. Fallacy of illicit process, of the major or minor term—Breach of Rule 4 ;

4. Fallacy of negative premises—Breach of Rule 5 ; as well as breaches of the 6th rule, to which no distinct name has been given. Breaches of the 7th and 8th rules may be resolved into the preceding (p. 151), but they may also be described as in p. 135.

The other part of the class of logical fallacies contains **Semi-logical fallacies,** which are six in number, as follows :

1. Fallacy of Equivocation.
2. Fallacy of Amphibology.
3. Fallacy of Composition.
4. Fallacy of Division.
5. Fallacy of Accent.
6. Fallacy of Figure of Speech.

These I shall describe and illustrate in succession.

Equivocation consists in the same term being used in two distinct senses ; any of the three terms of the syllogism may be subject to this fallacy, but it is usually the middle term which is used in one sense in one premise and in another sense in the other. In this case it is often called *the fallacy of ambiguous middle,* and when we distinguish the two meanings by using other suitable modes of expression it becomes apparent that the supposed syllogism contains four terms. The fallacy of equivocation may accordingly be considered a disguised fallacy of four terms. Thus if a person were to argue that "all criminal actions ought to be punished by law; prosecutions for theft are criminal actions; therefore prosecutions for theft ought to be punished by law," it is quite apparent that the term "criminal action" means totally different things in the two premises, and that there is no true middle term at all. Often, however, the ambiguity is of a subtle and difficult character, so that different opinions may be held concerning it. Thus we might argue :

"He who harms another should be punished. He who communicates an infectious disease to another person harms him. Therefore he who communicates an infectious disease to another person should be punished."

This may or may not be held to be a correct argument according to the kinds of actions we should consider to come under the term *harm,* according as we regard negligence or malice requisite to constitute harm. Many

difficult legal questions are of this nature, as for instance :

> Nuisances are punishable by law ;
> To keep a noisy dog is a nuisance ;
> To keep a noisy dog is punishable by law.

The question here would turn upon the degree of
nuisance which the law would interfere to prevent. Or
again :

> Interference with another man's business is illegal;
> Underselling interferes with another man's business;
> Therefore underselling is illegal.

Here the question turns upon the *kind of interference*,
and it is obvious that underselling is not the kind of interference referred to in the major premise.

The Fallacy of **Amphibology** consists in an ambiguous
grammatical structure of a sentence, which produces mis-
conception. A celebrated instance occurs in the prophecy
of the spirit in Shakspeare's *Henry VI.:* "The Duke yet
lives that Henry shall depose," which leaves it wholly
doubtful whether the Duke shall depose Henry, or Henry
the Duke. This prophecy is doubtless an imitation of
those which the ancient oracle of Delphi is reported to
have uttered; and it seems that this fallacy was a great
resource to the oracles who were not confident in their
own powers of foresight. The Latin language gives great
scope to misconstructions, because it does not require
any fixed order for the words of a sentence, and when
there are two accusative cases with an infinitive verb, it
may be difficult to tell except from the context which
comes in regard to sense before the verb. The double
meaning which may be given to "twice two and three"
arises from amphibology; it may be 7 or 10, according
as we add the 3 after or before multiplying. In the
careless construction of sentences it is often impossible to

tell to what part any adverb or qualifying clause refers. Thus if a person says " I accomplished my business and returned the day after," it may be that the business was accomplished on the day after as well as the return ; but it may equally have been finished on the previous day. Any ambiguity of this kind may generally be avoided by a simple change in the order of the words; as for instance, " I accomplished my business, and, on the day after, returned." Amphibology may sometimes arise from confusing the subjects and predicates in a compound sentence, as if in "platinum and iron are very rare and useful metals" I were to apply the predicate useful to platinum and rare to iron, which is not intended. The word "respectively" is often used to shew that the reader is not at liberty to apply each predicate to each subject.

The Fallacy of **Composition** is a special case of equivocation, arising from the confusion of an universal and a collective term. In the premises of a syllogism we may affirm something of a class of things *distributively*, that is, of each and any separately, and then we may in the conclusion infer the same of the whole put together. Thus we may say that " all the angles of a triangle are less than two right angles," meaning that *any* of the angles is less than two right angles; but we must not infer that all the angles put together are less than two right angles. We must not argue that because every member of a jury is very likely to judge erroneously, the jury as a whole are also very likely to judge erroneously ; nor that because each of the witnesses in a law case is liable to give false or mistaken evidence, no confidence can be reposed in the concurrent testimony of a number of witnesses. It is by a fallacy of Composition that protective duties are still sometimes upheld. Because any one or any few trades which enjoy protective duties are benefited thereby, it is supposed that all trades at once might be benefited similarly; but this is impossible, because the protection of one trade by raising prices injures all others.

The Fallacy of **Division** is the converse of the preceding, and consists in using the middle term collectively in the major premise but distributively in the minor, so that the whole is divided into its parts. Thus it might be argued, "All the angles of a triangle are (together) equal to two right angles; ABC is an angle of a triangle; therefore ABC is equal to two right angles." Or again, "The inhabitants of the town consist of men, women and children of all ages; those who met in the Guildhall were inhabitants of the town; therefore they consisted of men, women and children of all ages;" or, "The judges of the court of appeal cannot misinterpret the law; Lord A. B. is a judge of the court of appeal; therefore he cannot misinterpret the law."

The Fallacy of **Accent** consists in any ambiguity arising from a misplaced accent or emphasis thrown upon some word of a sentence. A ludicrous instance is liable to occur in reading chapter xiii. of the First Book of Kings, verse 27, where it is said of the prophet "And he spake to his sons, saying, Saddle me the ass. And they saddled *him*." The italics indicate that the word *him* was supplied by the translators of the authorized version, but it may suggest a very different meaning. The Commandment "Thou shalt not bear false witness against thy neighbour" may be made by a slight emphasis of the voice on the last word to imply that we are at liberty to bear false witness against other persons. Mr De Morgan who remarks this also points out that the erroneous quoting of an author, by unfairly separating a word from its context or italicising words which were not intended to be italicised, gives rise to cases of this fallacy.

It is curious to observe how many and various may be the meanings attributable to the same sentence according as emphasis is thrown upon one word or another. Thus the sentence "The study of Logic is not supposed to communicate a knowledge of many useful facts," may be made to imply that the study of Logic *does* communicate such a knowledge although it is not supposed to; or that it communicates a knowledge of a *few* useful facts; or that it communicates a knowledge of many *useless* facts. This ambiguity may be explained by considering that if you deny a thing to have the group of qualities A, B, C, D, the truth of your statement will be satisfied by any one quality being absent, and an accented pronunciation will often be used to indicate that which the speaker believes to be absent. If you deny that a particular fruit is ripe and sweet and well-flavoured, it may be unripe and sweet and well-flavoured; or ripe and sour and well-flavoured; or ripe and sweet and ill-flavoured; or any two or even all three qualities may be absent. But if you deny it to be ripe and sweet and *well-flavoured,* the denial would be understood to refer to the last quality. Jeremy Bentham was so much afraid of being misled by this fallacy of accent that he employed a person to read to him, as I have heard, who had a peculiarly monotonous manner of reading.

The Fallacy of the **Figure of Speech** is the sixth and last of the semi-logical fallacies, and is of a very trifling character. It appears to consist in any grammatical mistake or confusion between one part of speech and another. Aristotle gravely gives the following instance: "Whatever a man walks he tramples on; a man walks the whole day; therefore he tramples on the day." Here an adverbial phrase is converted into a noun object.

LESSON XXI.

MATERIAL FALLACIES.

THE Material fallacies are next to be considered; and their importance is very great, although it is not easy to illustrate them by brief examples. There are altogether seven kinds of such fallacies enumerated by Aristotle and adopted by subsequent logicians, as follows :

1. The Fallacy of Accident.
2. The Converse Fallacy of Accident.
3. The Irrelevant Conclusion.
4. The Petitio Principii.
5. The Fallacy of the Consequent or Non sequitur.
6. The False Cause.
7. The Fallacy of Many Questions.

Of these the two first are conveniently described together. The fallacy of **accident** consists in arguing erroneously **from a general rule to a special case**, where a certain accidental circumstance renders the rule inapplicable. The converse fallacy consists in arguing **from a special case to a general one.** This latter fallacy is usually described by the Latin phrase *a dicto secundum quid ad dictum simpliciter*, meaning "from a statement under a condition to a statement *simply* or without that condition." Mr De Morgan has remarked in his very interesting Chapter on Fallacies* that we ought to add a third fallacy, which would consist in arguing *from one special case to another special case.*

* *Formal Logic*, Chapter XIII.

I will try by a few examples to illustrate these kinds of fallacy, but much difficulty is often encountered in saying to which of the three any particular example is best referred. A most ancient example repeated in almost every logical hand-book is as follows : "What you bought yesterday you eat to-day ; you bought raw meat yesterday; therefore you eat raw meat to-day." The assertion in the conclusion is made of meat with the accidental quality of rawness added, where the first premise evidently speaks of the substance of the meat without regard to its accidental condition. This then is a case of the direct fallacy. If it is argued again that because wine acts as a poison when used in excess it is always a poison, we fall into the converse fallacy.

It would be a case of the direct fallacy of accident to infer that a magistrate is justified in using his power to forward his own religious views, because every man has a right to inculcate his own opinions. Evidently a magistrate as a man has the rights of other men, but in his capacity of a magistrate he is distinguished from other men, and he must not infer of his special powers in this respect what is only true of his rights as a man. For another instance take the following : "He who thrusts a knife into another person should be punished ; a surgeon in operating does so ; therefore he should be punished." Though the fallacy of this is absurdly manifest, it is not so manifest how we are to classify the error. We may for instance say that as a general rule whoever stabs or cuts another is to be punished unless it can be shewn to have been done under exceptional circumstances, as by a duly qualified surgeon acting for the good of the person. In this case the example belongs to the direct fallacy of accident. In another view we might interpret the first premise to mean the special case of thrusting a knife *maliciously;* to argue from that to the

12

case of a surgeon would be to infer from one special case to another special case.

It is undoubtedly true that to give to beggars promotes mendicancy and causes evil; but if we interpret this to mean that assistance is never to be given to those who solicit it, we fall into the converse fallacy of accident, inferring of all who solicit alms what is only true of those who solicit alms as a profession. Similarly it is a very good rule to avoid lawsuits and quarrels, but only as a general rule, since there frequently arise circumstances in which resort to the law is a plain duty. Almost all the difficulties which we meet in matters of law and moral duty arise from the impossibility of always ascertaining exactly to what cases a legal or moral rule does or does not extend; hence the interminable differences of opinion, even among the judges of the land.

The Third Material Fallacy is that of the **Irrelevant Conclusion**, technically called the *Ignoratio Elenchi*, or literally Ignorance of the Refutation. It consists in arguing to the wrong point, or proving one thing in such a manner that it is supposed to be something else that is proved. Here again it would be difficult to adduce concise examples, because the fallacy usually occurs in the course of long harangues, where the multitude of words and figures leaves room for confusion of thought and forgetfulness. This fallacy is in fact the great resource of those who have to support a weak case. It is not unknown in the legal profession, and an attorney for the defendant in a lawsuit is said to have handed to the barrister his brief marked, " No case; abuse the plaintiff's attorney." Whoever thus uses what is known as *argumentum ad hominem*, that is an argument which rests, not upon the merit of the case, but the character or position of those engaged in it, commits this fallacy. If a man is accused of a crime it is no answer to say that the prosecutor is as bad. If a great change in the law is proposed in Parliament, it is an Irrelevant Conclusion to argue that the proposer is not the right man to bring it forward. Everyone who gives advice lays himself open to the retort that he who preaches ought to practise, or that those who live in glass houses ought not to throw stones. Nevertheless there is no necessary connection between the character of the person giving advice and the goodness of the advice.

The *argumentum ad populum* is another form of Irrelevant Conclusion, and consists in addressing arguments to a body of people calculated to excite their feelings and prevent them from forming a dispassionate judgment upon the matter in hand. It is the great weapon of rhetoricians and demagogues.

Petitio Principii is a familiar name, and the nature of the fallacy it denotes is precisely expressed in the phrase *begging the question*. Another apt name for the fallacy is *circulus in probando*, or "a circle in the proof." It consists in taking the conclusion itself as one of the premises of an argument. Of course the conclusion of a syllogism must always be contained or implied in the premises, but only when those premises are combined, and are distinctly different assertions from the conclusion. Thus in the syllogism,

$$B \text{ is } C,$$
$$A \text{ is } B,$$
$$\text{therefore } A \text{ is } C,$$

the conclusion is proved by being deduced from two propositions, neither of which is identical with it ; but if the truth of one of these premises itself depends upon the following syllogism,

$$C \text{ is } B,$$
$$A \text{ is } C,$$
$$\text{therefore } A \text{ is } B,$$

it is plain that we attempt to prove a proposition by itself, which is as reasonable as attempting to support a body upon itself. It is not easy to illustrate this kind of fallacy by examples, because it usually occurs in long arguments, and especially in wordy metaphysical writings We are very likely to fall into it however when we employ a mixture of Saxon and Latin or Greek words, so as to appear to prove one proposition by another which is really the same expressed in different terms, as in the following: "Consciousness must be immediate cognition of an object; for I cannot be said really to know a thing unless my mind has been affected by the thing itself."

In the use of the disjunctive syllogism this fallacy is likely to happen ; for by enumerating only those alternatives which favour one view and forgetting the others it is easy to prove anything. An instance of this occurs in the celebrated sophism by which some of the ancient Greek philosophers proved that motion was impossible. For, said they, a moving body must move either in the place where it is or the place where it is not ; now it is absurd that a body can be where it is not, and if it moves it cannot be in the place where it is; therefore it cannot move at all. The error arises in the assumption of a premise which begs the question; the fact of course is that *the body moves between the place where it is at one moment and the place where it is at the next moment.*

Jeremy Bentham however pointed out that the use even of a single name may imply a Petitio Principii. Thus in a Church assembly or synod, where a discussion is taking place as to whether a certain doctrine should be condemned, it would be a Petitio Principii to argue that the doctrine is *heresy,* and therefore it ought to be condemned. To assert that it is heresy is to beg the question, because every one understands by heresy a doctrine which is to be condemned. Similarly in Parliament a

bill is often opposed on the ground that it is unconstitu-
tional and therefore ought to be rejected; but as no
precise definition can be given of what is or is not constitutional, it means little more than that the measure is
distasteful to the opponent. Names which are used in
this fallacious manner were aptly called by Bentham
Question-begging Epithets. In like manner we beg the
question when we oppose any change by saying that it is
un-English.

The **Fallacy of the Consequent** is better understood
by the familiar phrase *non sequitur.* We may apply
this name to any argument which is of so loose and
inconsequent a character that no one can discover any
cogency in it. It thus amounts to little more than the
assertion of a conclusion which has no connection with
the premises. Prof. De Morgan gives as an example
the following: "Episcopacy is of Scripture origin; the
Church of England is the only episcopal Church in England; ergo, the Church established is the Church that
should be supported."

By the Fallacy of the **False Cause** I denote that which
has generally been referred to by the Latin phrase *non
causa pro causâ.* In this fallacy we assume that one
thing is the cause of another without any sufficient
grounds. A change in the weather is even yet attributed
to the new moon or full moon which had occurred shortly
before, although it has been demonstrated over and over
again that the moon can have no such effect. In former
centuries any plague or other public calamity which followed the appearance of a comet or an eclipse was
considered to be the result of it. The Latin phrase *post
hoc ergo propter hoc* (after this and therefore in consequence of this) exactly describes the character of these
fallacious conclusions. Though we no longer dread signs
and omens, yet we often enough commit the fallacy; as

when we assume that all the prosperity of England is the result of the national character, forgetting that the plentiful coal in the country and its maritime position have contributed to our material wealth. It is no doubt equally fallacious to attribute no importance to national character, and to argue that because England has in past centuries misgoverned Ireland all the present evils of Ireland are due to that misgovernment.

Lastly there is the somewhat trivial **Fallacy of Many Questions,** which is committed by those who so combine two or three questions into one that no true answer can be given to them. I cannot think of a better example than the vulgar pleasantry of asking, " Have you left off beating your mother?" Questions equally as unfair are constantly asked by barristers examining witnesses in a court of justice, and no one can properly be required to answer Yes or No to every question which may be addressed to him. As Aristotle says, " Several questions put as one should be at once decomposed into their several parts. Only a single question admits of a single answer: so that neither several predicates of one subject, nor one predicate of several subjects, but only one predicate of one subject, ought to be affirmed or denied in a single answer."

Read Prof. de Morgan's excellent and amusing Chapter on Fallacies, *Formal Logic,* Ch. XIII.
Whately's remarks on Fallacies, *Elements of Logic,* Book III., are often very original and acute.

LESSON XXII.

THE QUANTIFICATION OF THE PREDICATE.

THE syllogism has been explained in the preceding three lessons almost exactly in the form in which it has been taught for more than two thousand years. Just as Geometry has been taught in the way and order first adopted by the ancient Greek writer Euclid, so Logic has been taught nearly as Aristotle taught it about the year 335 B.C.

But within the last few years teachers have at last come to the conclusion in England that Euclid's ideas of Geometry are not as perfect as could be desired. During the last 30 or 40 years also it has been gradually made apparent that Aristotle's syllogism is not an absolutely perfect system of logical deduction. In fact, certain eminent writers, especially Sir William Hamilton, Professor De Morgan, Archbishop Thomson and Dr Boole, have shewn that we need to make improvements from the very basis of the science.

This reform in Logic is called by the somewhat mysterious name of the **quantification of the predicate**, but the reader who has found no insuperable difficulty in the preceding lessons need not fear one here. *To quantify the predicate is simply to state whether the whole or the part only of the predicate agrees with or differs from the subject.* In this proposition,

"All metals are elements,"

the subject is quantified, but the predicate is not; we know that all metals are elements, but the proposition does not distinctly assert whether metals make the whole of the elements or not. In the quantified proposition

" All metals are *some* elements,"

the little word *some* expresses clearly that in reality the metals form only a part of the elements. Aristotle avoided the use of any mark of quantity by assuming, as we have seen, that all affirmative propositions have a particular predicate, like the example just given; and that only negative propositions have a distributed or universal predicate. The fact however is that he was entirely in error, and thus excluded from his system an infinite number of affirmative propositions which are universal in both terms. It is true that—

"All equilateral triangles are *all* equiangular triangles,"

but this proposition could not have appeared in his system except in the mutilated form—

"All equilateral triangles are equiangular."

Such a proposition as

"London is the capital of England,"

or　　　　　" Iron is the cheapest metal,"

had no proper place whatever in his syllogism, since both terms are singular and identical with each other, and both are accordingly universal.

As soon as we allow the quantity of the predicate to be stated the forms of reasoning become much simplified. We may first consider the process of conversion. In our lesson on the subject it was necessary to distinguish between conversion by limitation and simple conversion. But now one single process of simple conversion is sufficient for all kinds of propositions. Thus the quantified proposition of the form A,

"All metals are some elements,"

is simply converted into
> "Some elements are all metals. '

The particular affirmative proposition
> " Some metals are some brittle substances "

becomes by mere transposition of terms
> " Some brittle substances are some metals."

The particular negative proposition
> " Some men are not (any) trustworthy persons "

is also converted simply into
> " Not any trustworthy persons are some men,"

though the result may appear less satisfactory in this form than in the affirmative form, as follows,
> " Some men are some not-trustworthy persons,"

converted simply into
> " Some not-trustworthy persons are some men."

The universal negative proposition **E** is converted simply as before, and finally we have a new affirmative proposition universal both in subject and predicate ; as in
> "All equilateral triangles are all equiangular triangles,"

which may obviously be converted simply into
> "All equiangular triangles are all equilateral triangles."

This doubly universal affirmative proposition is of most frequent occurrence; as in the case of all definitions and singular propositions ; I may give as instances "Honesty is the best policy," "The greatest truths are the simplest truths," "Virtue alone is happiness below," "Self-exaltation is the fool's paradise."

When affirmative propositions are expressed in the quantified form all immediate inferences can be readily drawn from them by this one rule, that *whatever we do with one term we should do with the other term.* Thus from the doubly universal proposition, "Honesty is the best policy," we infer that "what is not the best policy is not honesty," and also "what is not honesty is not the best policy." From this proposition in fact we can draw two contrapositives ; but the reader will carefully remember that from the ordinary unquantified proposition A we can only draw one contrapositive (see p. 84). Thus if "metals are elements" we must not say that "what are not metals are not elements." But if we quantify the predicate thus, "All metals are *some* elements," we may infer that "what are not metals are not *some* elements." Immediate inference by added determinant and complex conception can also be applied in either direction to quantified propositions without fear of the errors noticed in pp. 86-7.

It is clear that in admitting the mark of quantity before the predicate we shall double the number of propositions which must be admitted into the syllogism, because the predicate of each of the four propositions A, E, I, O may be either universal or particular. Thus we arrive at a list of eight conceivable kinds of propositions, which are stated in the following table.

U	All X is all Y.	
I	Some X is some Y.	*Affirmative*
A	All X is some Y.	*propositions.*
Y	Some X is all Y.	

E	No X is (any) Y.	
ω	Some X is not some Y.	*Negative*
η	No X is some Y.	*propositions.*
O	Some X is no Y.	

The letters X and Y are used to stand for any subject and predicate respectively, and the reader by substituting various terms can easily make propositions of each kind. The symbolic letters on the left-hand side were proposed by Archbishop Thomson as a convenient mode of refer-

ring to each of the eight propositions, and are very
suitably chosen. The doubly universal affirmative proposition is called **U**; the simple converse of **A** is called
Y; the Greek letter η (*Eta, ē*) is applied to the proposition obtained by changing the universal predicate of **E**
into a particular predicate; and the Greek ω (*Omega, ō*)
is applied to the proposition similarly determined from **O**.
All these eight propositions are employed by Sir W. Hamilton, but Archbishop Thomson considers that two of
them, η and ω, are never really used. It is remarkable
that a complete table of the above eight propositions was
given by Mr George Bentham in a work called *Outline
of a New System of Logic*, published in 1827, several
years previous to the earliest of the logical publications of
Sir W. Hamilton. But Mr Bentham considered that some
of the propositions are hardly to be distinguished from
others; as **Y** from **A**, of which it is the simple converse; or
η from **O**.

The employment even of the additional two propositions **U** and **Y** introduced by Thomson much extends
the list of possible syllogisms, making them altogether 62
in number, without counting the fourth figure, which is
not employed by Hamilton and Thomson. When the
whole eight propositions are admitted into use we are
obliged to extend the list of possible syllogisms so as to
contain 12 affirmative and 24 negative moods in each of
the three first figures. The whole of these moods are
conveniently stated in the table on the next page, given by
Archbishop Thomson at p. 188 of his *Laws of Thought*.

Sir W. Hamilton also devised a curious system of
notation for exhibiting all the moods of the syllogism in a
clear manner. He always employed the letter *M* to denote
the middle term of the syllogism, and the two letters *C*
and Γ (the Greek capital letter Gamma) for the two
terms appearing in the conclusion. The copula of the

Table of Moods of the Syllogism.

	FIRST FIGURE.		SECOND FIG.		THIRD FIGURE.	
	Affirm.	Neg.	Affirm.	Neg.	Affirm.	Neg.
i	U U U	E U E U E E	U U U	E U E U E E	U U U	E U E U E E
ii	A Y I	η Y ω A O ω	Y Y I	O Y ω Y O ω	A A I	η A ω A η,ω
iii	A A A	η A η A η η	Y A A	O A η Y η η	A Y A	η Y η A O η
iv	Y Y Y	O Y O Y O O	A Y Y	η Y O A O O	Y A Y	O A O Y η O
v	A I I	η I ω A ω ω	Y I I	O I ω Y ω ω	A I I	η I ω A ω ω
vi	I Y I	ω Y ω I O ω	I Y I	ω Y ω I O ω	I A I	ω A ω I η ω
vii	U Y Y	E Y O U O O	U Y Y	E Y O U O O	U A Y	E A O U η O
viii	A U A	η U η A E η	Y U A	O U η Y E η	A U A	η U η A E η
ix	U A A	E A E U η η	U A A	E A E U η η	U Y A	E Y E U O η
x	Y U Y	O U O Y E E	A U Y	η U O A E E	Y U Y	O U O Y E E
xi	U I I	E I O U ω ω	U I I	E I O U ω ω	U I I	E I O U ω ω
xii	I U I	ω U ω I E η	I U I	ω U ω I E η	I U I	ω U ω I E η

proposition was indicated by a line thickened towards the subject; thus *C* ▬▬▬▬ *M* means that "*C* is *M*." To indicate the quantity of the terms Hamilton inserted a

colon (:) between the term and the copula when the
quantity is universal, and a comma (,) when the quantity
is particular.   Thus we readily express the following
affirmative propositions.

C : ━━━━━━━━ , M All C's are some M's   (A)

C : ━━━━━━━━ : M All C's are all M's   (U)

C , ━━━━━━━━ , M Some C's are some M's   (I)

and so on.   Any affirmative proposition can be converted
into the corresponding negative proposition by drawing a
stroke through the line denoting the copula, as in the
following—

C : ━━━┿━━━ : M No C is any M (E)

C , ━━━┿━━━ : M Some C is not any M (O)

C , ━━━┿━━━ , M Some C is not some M (ω)

Any syllogism can be represented by placing M the
middle term in the centre and connecting it on each side
with the other terms.   The copula representing the conclusion can then be placed below ; Barbara is expressed
as follows—

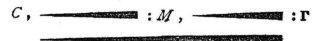

The negative mood Celarent is similarly—

Cesare in the second figure is thus represented—

Sir W. Hamilton also proposed a new law or supreme
canon of the syllogism by which the validity of all forms

of the syllogism might be tested. This was stated in the following words : "What worse relation of subject and predicate subsists between either of two terms and a common third term, with which both are related, and one at least positively so—that relation subsists between these two terms themselves."

By a *worse relation*, Sir William means that a negative relation is worse than an affirmative and a particular than a universal. This canon thus expresses the rules that if there be a negative premise the conclusion must be negative, and if there be a particular premise the conclusion must be particular. Special canons were also developed for each of the three figures, but in thus rendering the system complex the advantages of the quantified form of proposition seem to be lost.

Prof. De Morgan also discovered the advantages of the quantified predicate, and invented a system differing greatly from that of Sir W. Hamilton. It is fully explained in his *Formal Logic, The Syllabus of a new System of Logic,* and various important memoirs on the Syllogism in the *Transactions of the Cambridge Philosophical Society.* In these works is also given a complete explanation of the "Numerically Definite Syllogism." Mr De Morgan pointed out that two particular premises may often give a valid conclusion provided that the actual quantities of the two terms are stated, and when added together exceed the quantity of the middle term. Thus if the majority of a public meeting vote for the first resolution, and a majority also vote for the second, it follows necessarily that some who voted for the first voted also for the second. The two majorities added together exceed the whole number of the meeting, so that they could not consist of entirely different people. They may indeed consist of exactly the same people; but all that we can deduce from the premises is that the excess of the two majorities added together over the number of the meeting must have voted in favour of each resolution. This kind of inference has by Sir W. Hamilton been said to depend on *ultra-total* distribution ; and the name of **Plurative Propositions** has been proposed for all those which give a distinct idea of the fraction or number of the subject involved in the assertion.

> T. Spencer Baynes, *Essay on the new Analytic of Logical Forms;* Edinburgh, 1850.
>
> Prof. Bowen's *Treatise on Logic or the Laws of Pure Thought*, Cambridge, U. S. 1866 (Trübner and Co.) gives a full and excellent account of Hamilton's Log c.

LESSON XXIII.

BOOLE'S SYSTEM OF LOGIC.

IT would not in the least be possible to give in an elementary work a notion of the system of indirect inference first discovered by the late Dr Boole, the Professor of Mathematics at the Queen's College, Cork. This system was founded as mentioned in the last lesson upon the Quantification of the Predicate, but Dr Boole regarded Logic as a branch of Mathematics, and believed that he could arrive at every possible inference by the principles of algebra. The process as actually employed by him is very obscure and difficult ; and hardly any attempt to introduce it into elementary text-books of Logic has yet been made.

I have been able to arrive at exactly the same results

as Dr Boole without the use of any mathematics; and though the very simple process which I am going to describe can hardly be said to be strictly Dr Boole's logic, it is yet very similar to it and can prove everything that Dr Boole proved.   This **Method of Indirect Inference** is founded upon the three primary Laws of Thought stated in Lesson XIV., and the reader who may have thought them mere useless truisms will perhaps be surprised to find how extensive and elegant a system of deduction may be derived from them.

The law of excluded middle enables us to assert that anything must either have a given quality or must have it not.   Thus if *iron* be the thing, and *combustibility* the quality, anyone must see that

"Iron is either combustible or incombustible."

This division of alternatives may be repeated as often as we like.   Thus let Book be the class of things to be divided, and English and Scientific two qualities.   Then any book must be either English or not English; again an English book must be either Scientific or not Scientific, and the same may be said of books which are not English. Thus we can at once divide books into four classes—

Books, English and Scientific.
Books, English and not-Scientific.
Books, not-English and Scientific.
Books, not-English and not-Scientific.

This is what we may call an **exhaustive division** of the class Books; for there is no possible book which does not fall into one division or other of these four, on account of the simple reason, that if it does not fall into any of the three first it must fall into the last.   The process can be repeated without end, as long as any new circumstance can be suggested as the ground of division. Thus we might divide each class again according as the

books are octavo or not octavo, bound or unbound, published in London or elsewhere, and so on. We shall call
this process of twofold division, which is really the process of Dichotomy mentioned in p. 107, the development
of a term, because it enables us always to develope the
utmost number of alternatives which need be considered.

As a general rule it is not likely that all the alternatives thus unfolded or developed can exist, and the next
point is to ascertain how many do or may exist. The Law
of Contradiction asserts that nothing can combine contradictory attributes or qualities, and if we meet with any
term which is thus self-contradictory we are authorized at
once to strike it out of the list. Now consider our old
example of a syllogism :

> Iron is a metal ;
> All metals are elements ;
> Therefore iron is an element.

We can readily prove this conclusion by the indirect
method. For if we develope the term iron, we have four
alternatives; thus—

> Iron, metal, element.
> Iron, metal, not-element.
> Iron, not-metal, element.
> Iron, not-metal, not-element.

But if we compare each of these alternatives with the
premises of the syllogism, it will be apparent that several
of them are incapable of existing. Iron, we are informed,
is a metal. Hence no class of things "iron, not-metal"
can exist. Thus we are enabled by the first premise to
strike out both of the last two alternatives which combine
iron and not-metal. The second alternative, again, combines metal and not-element ; but as the second premise
informs us that "all metals are elements," it must be
struck out. There remains, then, only one alternative

which is capable of existing if the premises be true, and as there cannot conceivably be more alternatives than those considered, it follows demonstratively that iron occurs only in combination with the qualities of metal and element, or, in brief, that it is an element.

We can, however, prove not only the ordinary syllogistic conclusion, but any other conclusion which can be drawn from the same premises; the syllogistic conclusion is in fact only one out of many which can usually be obtained from given premises. Suppose, for instance, that we wish to know what is the nature of the term or class *not-element*, so far as we can learn it from the premises just considered. We can develope the alternatives of this term, just as we did those of iron, and get the following—

Not-element, iron, metal.
Not-element, iron, not-metal.
Not-element, not-iron, metal.
Not-element, not-iron, not-metal.

Compare these combinations as before with the premises. The first it is easily seen cannot exist, because all metals are elements; for the same reason the third cannot exist; the second is likewise excluded, because iron is a metal and cannot exist in combination with the qualities of not-metal. Hence there remains only one combination to represent the class desired—namely,

Not-element, not-iron, not-metal.

Thus we learn from the premises that every not-element is not a metal and is not iron.

As another example of this kind of deductive process I will take a case of the Disjunctive Syllogism, in the negative mood, as follows:—

A fungus is either plant or animal,
A fungus is not an animal;
Therefore it is a plant.

Now if we develope all the possible ways in which fungus, plant and animal can be combined together, we obtain for the term fungus—

(1)   Fungus, plant, animal.
(2)   Fungus, plant, not-animal.
(3)   Fungus, not-plant, animal.
(4)   Fungus, not-plant, not-animal.

Of these however the 4th cannot exist because by the premise a fungus must be a plant, or if not a plant an animal. The 1st and 3rd again cannot exist because the minor premise informs us that a fungus is not an animal. There remains then only the second combination,

Fungus, plant, not-animal,

from which we learn the syllogistic conclusion that " a fungus is a plant."

The chief excellence of this mode of deduction consists in the fact that it is not restricted to any definite series of forms like the syllogism, but is applicable, without any additional rules, to all kinds of propositions or problems which can be conceived and stated. There may be any number of premises, and they may contain any number of terms ; all we have to do to obtain any possible inference is to develope the term required into all its alternatives and then to examine how many of these agree with the premises. What remain after this examination necessarily form the description of the term. The only inconvenience of the method is that, as the number of terms increases, the number of alternatives to be examined increases very rapidly, and it soon becomes tĕdious to write them all out. This work may be abbreviated if we substitute single letters to stand for the terms, somewhat as in algebra ; thus we may take A, B, C, D, &c., to stand for the affirmative terms, and a, b, c, d, &c., for the corresponding negative ones.   Let us take as a first example the premises—

Organic substance is either vegetable or animal.

Vegetable substance consists mainly of carbon, hydrogen, and nitrogen.

Animal substance consists mainly of carbon, hydrogen, and nitrogen.

It would take a long time to write out all the combinations of the four terms occurring in the above; but if we substitute letters as follows—

A = organic substance,
B = vegetable substance,
C = animal substance,
D = consisting mainly of carbon, hydrogen, and nitrogen,

we can readily represent all the combinations which can belong to the term A.

(1)	$ABCD$	$AbCD$	(5)
(2)	$ABCd$	$AbCd$	(6)
(3)	$ABcD$	$AbcD$	(7)
(4)	$ABcd$	$Abcd$	(8)

Now the premises amount to the statements, that

A must be either B or C,
B must be D,
C must be D.

The combinations (7) and (8) are inconsistent with the first premise; the combinations (2) and (4) with the second premise; and (6) is inconsistent with the third premise. There remain only,

$ABCD$
$ABcD$
$AbCD$.

Whence we learn at once that "organic substance (A) always consists mainly of carbon, hydrogen and nitrogen," because it always occurs in connexion with *D*. The reader may perhaps notice that the term *ABCD* implies that organic substance may be both vegetable (*B*) and animal (*C*), If the first premise be interpreted as meaning that this is not possible, of course this combination should also be struck out. It is an unsettled point whether the alternatives of a disjunctive proposition can coexist or not (see p. 166), but I much prefer the opinion that they can; and as a matter of fact it is quite likely that there exist very simple kinds of living beings, which cannot be distinctly asserted to be vegetable only or animal only, but partake of the nature of each.

As a more complicated problem to shew the powers of this system, let us consider the premises which were treated by Dr Boole in his *Laws of Thought*, p. 125, as follows :

" Similar figures consist of all whose corresponding angles are equal, and whose corresponding sides are proportional.

Triangles whose corresponding angles are equal have their corresponding sides proportional; and *vice versâ*.

Triangles whose corresponding sides are proportional have their corresponding angles equal."

Now if we take our symbol letters as follows :

A = similar figure,
B = triangle,
C = having corresponding angles equal,
D = having corresponding sides proportional,

the premises will be seen to amount to the statements that

A is identical with CD,

and that

BC is identical with BD;

in other words, all A's ought to be CD's, CD's ought to be A's, all BC's ought to be BD's and all BD's ought to be BC's.

The possible combinations in which the letters may be united are 16 in number and are shewn in the following table:

$ABCD$	$aBCD$
$ABCd$	$aBCd$
$ABcD$	$aBcD$
$ABcd$	$aBcd$
$AbCD$	$abCD$
$AbCd$	$abCd$
$AbcD$	$abcD$
$Abcd$	$abcd$

Comparing each of these combinations with the premises we see that $ABCd$, $ABcD$, $ABcd$, and others, are to be struck out because every A is also to be CD. The combinations $aBCD$ and $abCD$ are struck out because every CD should also be A. Again, $aBCd$ is inconsistent with the condition that every BC is also to be BD; and if the reader carefully follows out the same process of examination, there will remain only six combinations, which agree with all the premises, thus—

$ABCD$	$aBcd$
$AbCD$	$abCd$
	$abcD$
	$abcd$

From these combinations we can draw any description we like of the classes of things agreeing with the premises. The class A or similar figures is represented by only two combinations or alternatives; the negative class a or dissimilar figures, by four combinations, whence we may draw the following conclusion: "Dissimilar figures consist of all triangles which have not their corresponding angles equal, and sides proportional ($aBcd$), and of all figures, not being triangles, which have either their angles equal and sides not proportional (*abCd*), or their corresponding sides proportional and angles not equal (*abcD*), or neither their corresponding angles equal nor corresponding sides proportional (*abcd*)."

In performing this method of inference it is soon seen to proceed in a very simple mechanical manner, and the only inconvenience is the large number of alternatives or combinations to be examined. I have, therefore, devised several modes by which the labour can be decreased; the simplest of these consists in engraving the series of 16 combinations on the opposite page, which occur over and over again in problems, with larger and smaller sets, upon a common writing slate, so that the excluded ones may be readily struck out with a common slate pencil, and yet the series may be employed again for any future logical question. A second device, which I have called the "Logical abacus," is constructed by printing the letters upon slips of wood furnished with pins, contrived so that any part or class of the combinations can be picked out mechanically with very little trouble; and a logical problem is thus solved by the hand, rather than by the head. More recently however I have reduced the system to a completely mechanical form, and have thus embodied the whole of the indirect process of inference in what may be called a Logical Machine. In the front of the machine are seen certain moveable wooden rods carrying the set of 16 combinations of letters which are seen on the preceding page. At the foot are 21 keys like those of a piano; eight keys towards the left hand are marked with the letters *A, a, B, b, C, c, D, d,* and are intended to represent these terms when occurring in the subject of a proposition. Eight other keys towards the right hand represent the same letters or terms when occurring in the predicate. The copula of a proposition is represented by a key in the middle of the series; the full stop by one to the extreme right, while there are two other keys which serve for the disjunctive conjunction *or*, according as it occurs in subject or predicate. Now if the letters be taken to stand for the terms of a syllogism or any other logical argument, and the keys of the instrument be pressed exactly in the order corresponding to the words of the premises, the 16 combinations will be so selected and arranged thereby that at the end only the possible combinations will remain in view. Any question can then be asked of the machine, and an infallible answer will be obtained from the combinations remaining. The internal construction of the machine is such, therefore, as actually to perform the work of inference which, in Dr Boole's system, was performed by a very complicated mathematical calculation. It should be added, that there is one remaining key to the extreme left which has the effect of obliterating all previous operations and restoring all the combinations to their original place, so that the machine is then ready for the performance of any new problem.

An account of this logical machine may be found in the *Proceedings of the Royal Society* for Jan. 20th, 1870, the machine having on that day been exhibited in action to the Fellows of the Society. The principles of the method of inference here described are more completely stated in *The Substitution of Similars**, and the *Pure Logic*†, which I published in the years 1869 and 1864. I may add, that the first-named of these works contains certain views as to the real nature of the process of inference which I do

---

* *The Substitution of Similars, the true Principle of Reasoning, derived from a modification of Aristotle's Dictum.* Macmillan and Co. 1869.

† *Pure Logic, or the Logic of Quality apart from Quantity, &c.* Edward Stanford, Charing Cross.

n>t think it desirable to introduce into an elementary work like the present, on account of their speculative character. The process of inference, on the other hand, which I have derived from Boole's system is of so self-evident a character, and is so clearly proved to be true by its reduction to a mechanical form, that I do not hesitate to bring it to the reader's notice.

> George Boole, *Mathematical Analysis of Logic,* 1847. *An Investigation of the Laws of Thought.* Londor Walton and Maberly, 1854.

LESSON XXIV.

ON METHOD, ANALYSIS AND SYNTHESIS.

IT has been held by many writers on Logic that, in addition to the three parts of logical doctrine which treat successively of Terms, Propositions and Syllogisms, there was a fourth part, which treats of method. Just as the doctrine of Judgment considers the arranging of terms and their combination into Propositions, and the doctrine of Syllogism considers the arranging of propositions that they may form arguments, so there should in like manner be a fourth part, called Method, which should govern the arrangement of syllogisms and their combination into a complete discourse. Method is accordingly defined as consisting in *such a disposition of the parts of a discourse that the whole may be most easily intelligible.*

The celebrated Peter Ramus, who perished in the massacre of St Bartholomew, first proposed to make method in this manner a part of the science of Logic; but it may well be doubted whether any definite set of rules or principles can be given to guide us in the arrangement of arguments. Every different discourse must consist of arguments arranged in accordance with the peculiar nature of the subject; and no general rules can be given for treating things which are infinitely various in the mode of treatment required. Accordingly the supposed general rules of method are no better than truisms, that is, they tell us nothing more than we must be supposed to know beforehand. Thus, we are instructed in composing any discourse to be careful that—

1.   Nothing should be wanting or redundant.

2.   The separate parts should agree with each other.

3.   Nothing should be treated unless it is suitable to the subject or purpose.

4.   The separate parts should be connected by suit. able transitions.

But it is evident that the whole difficulty consists in deciding what is wanting or redundant, suitable or consistent. Rules of this kind simply tell us to do what we ought to do, without defining what that is.

There exist nevertheless certain general modes of treating any subject which can be clearly distinguished. and should be well understood by the logical student. Logic cannot teach him exactly how and when to use each kind of method, but it can teach him the natures and powers of the methods, so that he will be more likely to use them rightly. We must distinguish,

1.   The method of discovery,

2.   The method of instruction.

The **method of discovery** is employed in the acquisition of knowledge, and really consists in those processes of inference and induction, by which general truths are ascertained from the collection and examination of particular facts. This method will be the subject of most of our remaining Lessons. The second method only applies when knowledge has already been acquired and expressed in the form of general laws, rules, principles or truths, so that we have only to make ourselves acquainted with these and observe the due mode of applying them to particular cases, in order to possess a complete acquaintance with the subject.

A student, for example, in learning Latin, Greek, French, German, or any well-known language, receives a complete Grammar and Syntax setting forth the whole of the principles, rules and nature of the language. He receives these instructions, and takes them to be true on the authority of the teacher, or the writer of the book; and after rendering them familiar to his mind he has nothing to do but to combine and apply the rules in reading or composing the language. He follows, in short, the method of Instruction. But this is an entirely different and opposite process to that which the scholar must pursue who has received some writings in an unknown language, and is endeavouring to make out the alphabet, words, grammar, and syntax of the language. He possesses not the laws of grammar, but words and sentences obeying those laws, and he has to detect the laws if possible by observing their effects on the written language. He pursues, in short, the method of discovery consisting in a tedious comparison of letters, words, and phrases, such as shall disclose the more frequent combinations and forms in which they occur. The process would be a strictly inductive one, such as I shall partially exemplify in the Lessons on Induction ; but it is far more difficult than the method of Instruction, and depends to a great extent on the happy use of conjecture and hypothesis which demands a certain skill and inventive ability.

Exactly the same may be said of the investigation of

natural things and events. The principles of mechanics, of the lever, inclined plane, and other Mechanical Powers, or the Laws of Motion, seem comparatively simple and obvious as explained to us in books of instruction. But the early philosophers did not possess such books; they had only the Book of Nature, in which is set forth not the laws but the results of the laws, and it was only after the most patient and skilful investigation, and after hundreds of mistakes, that those laws were ascertained. It is very easy now to understand the Copernican system of Astronomy, which represents the planets as revolving round the sun in orbits of various magnitude. Once knowing the theory we can readily see why the planets have such various movements and positions, and why they sometimes stand still; it is easy to see, too, why in addition to their own proper motions they all go round the earth apparently every day in consequence of the earth's diurnal rotation. But all these changes were exceedingly puzzling to the ancients, who regarded the earth as standing still.

The method of discovery thus begins with facts apparent to the senses, and has the difficult task of detecting those universal laws or general principles which can only be comprehended by intellect. It has been aptly said that the method of discovery thus proceeds *from things better known to us*, or our senses (*nobis notiora*), to those which are more simple or *better known in nature* (*notiora naturæ*). The method of Instruction proceeds in the opposite direction, beginning with the things *notiora naturæ*, and proceeding to show or explain the things *nobis notiora*. The difference is almost like that between *hiding* and *seeking*. He who has hidden a thing knows where to find it; but this is not the position of a discoverer, who has no clue except such as he may meet in his own diligent and sagacious search.

Closely corresponding to the distinction between the methods of Discovery and Instruction is that between the methods of Analysis and Synthesis. It is very important indeed that the reader should clearly apprehend the meanings of these terms in their several applications. Analysis is the process of separating a whole into its parts, and synthesis the combination of parts into a whole. The analytical chemist, who receives a piece of mineral for examination, may be able to separate completely the several chemical elements of which it is composed and ascertain their nature and comparative quantities; this is chemical analysis. In other cases the chemist mixes together carefully weighed quantities of certain simple substances and combines them into a new compound substance; this is chemical synthesis. Logical analysis and synthesis must not be confused with the physical actions, but they are nevertheless actions of mind of an analogous character.

In logical synthesis we begin with the simplest possible notions or ideas, and combine them together. We have the best possible example in the elements of Geometry. In Euclid we begin with certain simple notions of points, straight lines, angles, right angles, circles, &c. Putting together three straight lines we make a triangle; joining to this the notion of a right-angle, we form the notion of a right-angled triangle. Joining four other equal lines at right angles to each other we gain the idea of a square, and if we then conceive such a square to be formed upon each of the sides of a right-angled triangle, and reason from the necessary qualities of these figures, we discover that the two squares upon the sides containing the right angle must together be exactly equal to the square upon the third side, as shewn in the 47th Proposition of Euclid's first book. This is a perfect instance of combining simple ideas into more complex ones.

We have often, however, in Geometry to pursue the opposite course of Analysis. A complicated geometrical figure may be given to us, and we may have, in order to prove the properties which it possesses, to resolve it into its separate parts, and to consider the properties of those parts each distinct from the others.

A similar distinction between the analytical and synthetic methods can be traced throughout the natural sciences. By keeping exact registers of the appearance and changes of the weather we may readily acquire an immense collection of facts, each such recorded fact implying a multitude of different circumstances occurring together. Thus in any storm or shower of rain we have to consider the direction and force of the wind; the temperature and moistness of the air; the height and forms of the clouds; the quantity of rain which falls, or the lightning and thunder which occur with it. If we proceed by analysis only to explain the changes of the weather we should have to try resolving each storm or change of weather into its separate circumstances, and comparing each with every other to discover what circumstances usually go together. We might thus ascertain no doubt with considerable certainty what kinds of clouds, and what changes of the wind, temperature, moisture, &c., usually precede any kind of storm, and we might even in time give some imperfect explanation of what takes place in the atmosphere.

But we might also apply with advantage the synthetical method. By previous chemical investigations we know that the atmosphere consists mainly of the two fixed gases, oxygen and nitrogen, with the vapour of water, the latter being very variable in quantity. We can try experimentally what takes place when portions of such air of various degrees of moistness are compressed or allowed to expand, or are mixed together, as often happens in the atmosphere. It is thus discovered that whenever moist air is allowed to expand cloud is produced, and it may be drops of rain. Dr Hutton, too, found that whenever cold moist air is mixed with warm moist air cloud is again produced. We can safely argue from such small experiments to what takes place in the atmosphere. Putting together synthetically, from the sciences of chemistry, mechanics, and electricity, all that we know of air, wind, cloud and lightning, we are able to explain what takes place in a thunder-storm far more completely than we could do by merely observing directly what happens in the storm. We are here however anticipating the methods of inductive investigation, which we must consider in the following lessons. It will appear that **Induction** is equivalent to analysis, and that the deductive kinds of reasoning which we have treated in prior lessons are of a synthetic character.

It has been said that the synthetic method usually corresponds to the method of instruction and the analytic method to that of discovery. But it may be possible to discover new truths by synthesis and to teach old ones by analysis. Sir John Herschel in his well-known *Outlines of Astronomy* partially adopts the analytic method: he supposes a spectator in the first place to survey the appearances of the heavenly bodies and the surface of the earth, and to seek an explanation; he then leads him through a course of arguments to show that these appearances really indicate the rotundity of the earth, its revolution about its own axis and round the sun, and its subordinate position as one of the smaller planets of the solar system. Mr Norman Lockyer's *Elementary Lessons in Astronomy* is a clear example of the synthetic method of instruction; for he commences by describing the sun, the centre of the system, and successively adds the planets and other members of the system, until at last we have the complete picture ; and the reader who has temporarily received everything on the writer's authority, sees that the description corresponds with the truth. Each method, it must be allowed, has its own advantages.

It must be carefully observed that the meaning of analysis, and therefore that of synthesis, varies according as we look to the intension or extension of terms. To divide or analyse a class of things in extension I must add a quality or difference. Thus I divide the class *organism* when I add the quality *vegetable*, and separate vegetable organism from what is not vegetable. Analysis in extension is therefore the same process as synthesis in intension; and *vice versâ*, whenever I separate or analyse a group of qualities each part belongs to a larger class of things in extension. When I analyse the notion vegetable organism, and regard the notion organism apart from vegetable, it is apparent that I really add the whole class of animal organisms to the class I am considering—so that analysis in intension is synthesis in extension. The reader who has well considered the contents of Lessons V. and XII. will probably see that this connection of the two processes is only a re-statement of the law, (p. 40), that "as the intension of a term is increased the extension is decreased."

To express the difference between knowledge derived deductively and that obtained inductively the Latin phrases *à priori* and *à posteriori* are often used. By A priori reasoning we mean argument based on truths previously known ; A posteriori reasoning, on the contrary, proceeds to infer from the consequences of a general truth what that general truth is. Many philosophers consider that the mind is naturally in possession of certain laws or truths which it must recognise in every act of thought; all such, if they exist, would be *à priori* truths. It cannot be doubted, for instance, that we must always recognise in thought the three Primary Laws of Thought considered in Lesson XIV. We have there an *à priori* knowledge that "matter cannot both have weight and be without weight," or that "every thing must be either self-luminous or not self-luminous." But there is no law of thought which can oblige us to think that matter has weight, and luminous ether has not weight; that Jupiter and Venus are not self-luminous, but that comets are to some extent self-luminous. These are facts which are no doubt necessary consequences of the laws of nature and the general constitution of the world; but as we are not naturally acquainted with all the secrets of creation, we have to learn them by observation, or by the *à posteriori* method.

It is not however usual at the present time to restrict the name *à priori* to truths obtained altogether without recourse to observation. Knowledge may originally be of an *à posteriori* origin, and yet having been long in possession, and having acquired the greatest certainty, it may be the ground of deductions, and may then be said to give *à priori* knowledge. Thus it is now believed by all scientific men that force cannot be created or destroyed by any of the processes of nature. If this be true the force which disappears when a bullet strikes a target must be converted into something else, and on *à priori* grounds we may assert that heat will be the result. It is true that we might easily learn the same truth *à posteriori*, by picking up portions of a bullet which has just struck a target and observing that they are warm. But there is a great advantage in *à priori* knowledge; we can often apply it in cases where experiment or observation would be difficult. If I lift a stone and then drop it, the most delicate instruments could hardly show that the stone was heated by striking the earth; yet on *à priori* grounds I know that it must have been so, and can easily calculate the amount of heat produced. Similarly we know, without the trouble of observation, that the Falls of Niagara and all other waterfalls produce heat. This is fairly an instance of *à priori* knowledge because no one that I have heard of has tried the fact or proved it *à posteriori;* nevertheless the knowledge is originally founded on the experiments of Mr Joule, who observed in certain well-chosen cases how much force is equivalent to a certain amount of heat. The reader, however, should take care not to confuse the meaning of *à priori* thus explained with that given to the words by the philosophers who hold the mind to be in the possession of knowledge independently of all observation.

It is not difficult to see that the *à priori* method is equivalent to the synthetic method (see p. 205) considered in intension, the *à posteriori* method of course being equivalent to the analytic method. But the same difference is really expressed in the words deductive and inductive; and we shall frequently need to consider it in the following lessons.

For general remarks upon Method see the *Port Royal Logic*, Part IV.

LESSON XXV.

PERFECT INDUCTION AND THE INDUCTIVE SYLLOGISM.

WE have in previous lessons considered deductive reasoning, which consists in combining two or more general propositions synthetically, and thus arriving at a conclusion which is a proposition or truth of less generality than the premises, that is to say, it applies to fewer individual instances than the separate premises from which it was inferred. When I combine the general truth that "metals are good conductors of heat," with the truth that 'aluminium is a metal," I am enabled by a syllogism in the mood Barbara to infer that "aluminium is a good conductor of heat." As this is a proposition concerning one metal only, it is evidently less general than the premise, which referred to all metals whatsoever. In induction, on the contrary, we proceed from less general, or even from individual facts, to more general propositions, truths, or, as we shall often call them, Laws of Nature. When it is known that Mercury moves in an elliptic orbit round the Sun, as also Venus, the Earth, Mars, Jupiter, &c., we are able to arrive at the simple and general truth that "all the planets move in elliptic orbits round the sun." This is an example of an inductive process of reasoning.

It is true that we may reason without rendering our conclusion either more or less general than the premises, as in the following:—

Snowdon is the highest mountain in England or Wales.
Snowdon is not so high as Ben Nevis.
Therefore the highest mountain in England or Wales is
  not so high as Ben Nevis.

Again:
Lithium is the lightest metal known.
Lithium is the metal indicated by one bright red line in
  the spectrum *.
Therefore the lightest metal known is the metal indicated
  by a spectum of one bright red line.

In these examples all the propositions are singular propositions, and merely assert the identity of singular

---

* Roscoe's *Lessons in Elementary Chemistry*, p. 199.

14—2

terms, so that there is no alteration of generality. Each conclusion applies to just such an object as each of the premises applies to. To this kind of reasoning the apt name of **Traduction** has been given.

Induction is a much more difficult and more important kind of reasoning process than Traduction or even Deduction; for it is engaged in detecting the general laws or uniformities, the relations of cause and effect, or in short all the general truths that may be asserted concerning the numberless and very diverse events that take place in the natural world around us. The greater part, if not, as some philosophers think, the whole of our knowledge, is ultimately due to inductive reasoning. The mind, it is plausibly said, is not furnished with knowledge in the form of general propositions ready made and stamped upon it, but is endowed with powers of observation, comparison, and reasoning, which are adequate, when well educated and exercised, to procure knowledge of the world without us and the world within the human mind. Even when we argue synthetically and deductively from simple ideas and truths which seem to be ready in the mind, as in the case of the science of geometry, it may be that we have gathered those simple ideas and truths from previous observation or induction of an almost unconscious kind. This is a debated point upon which I will not here speak positively; but if the truth be as stated, **Induction** will be the mode by which all the materials of knowledge are brought to the mind and analysed. **Deduction** will then be the almost equally important process by which the knowledge thus acquired is utilised, and by which new Inductions of a more complicated character, as we shall see, are rendered possible.

An Induction, that is an act of Inductive reasoning, is called **Perfect** when all the possible cases or instances to which the conclusion can refer, have been examined and enumerated in the premises. If, as usually happens, it is impossible to examine all cases, since they may occur at future times or in distant parts of the earth or other regions of the universe, the Induction is called **Imperfect** The assertion that all the months of the year are of less length than thirty-two days is derived from Perfect Induction, and is a certain conclusion because the calendar is a human institution, so that we know beyond doubt how many months there are, and can readily ascertain that each of them is less than thirty-two days in length. But the assertion that all the planets move in one direction round the sun, from West to East, is derived from Imperfect Induction; for it is possible that there exist planets more distant than the most distant-known planet Neptune, and to such a planet of course the assertion would apply.

Hence it is obvious that there is a great difference between Perfect and Imperfect Induction. The latter includes some process by which we are enabled to make assertions concerning things that we have never seen or examined or even known to exist. But it must be carefully remembered also that no Imperfect Induction can give a certain conclusion. It may be highly probable or nearly certain that the cases unexamined will resemble those which have been examined, but it can never be certain. It is quite possible, for instance, that a new planet might go round the sun in an opposite direction to the other planets. In the case of the satellites belonging to the planets more than one exception of this kind has been discovered, and mistakes have constantly occurred in science from expecting that all new cases would exactly resemble old ones. Imperfect Induction thus gives only a certain degree of probability or likelihood that all instances will agree with those examined. **Perfect** Induction, on the other hand, gives a necessary and certain conclusion, but it asserts nothing beyond what was asserted in the premises.

Mr Mill, indeed, differs from almost all other logicians in holding that Perfect Induction is improperly called Induction, because it does not lead to any new knowledge. He defines **Induction** as *inference from the known to the unknown,* and considers the unexamined cases which are apparently brought into our knowledge as the only gain from the process of reasoning. Hence Perfect Induction seems to him to be of no scientific value whatever, because the conclusion is a mere reassertion in a briefer form, a mere summing up of the premises. I may point out, however, that if Perfect Induction were no more than a process of abbreviation it is yet of great importance, and requires to be continually used in science and common life. Without it we could never make a comprehensive statement, but should be obliged to enumerate every particular. After examining the books in a library and finding them to be all English books we should be unable to sum up our results in the one proposition, "all the books in this library are English books;" but should be required to go over the list of books every time we desired to make any one acquainted with the contents of the library. The fact is, that the power of expressing a great number of particular facts in a very brief space is essential to the progress of science. Just as the whole science of arithmetic consists in nothing but a series of processes for abbreviating addition and subtraction, and enabling us to deal with a great number of units in a very short time, so Perfect Induction is absolutely necessary to enable us to deal with a great number of particular facts in a very brief space.

It is usual to represent Perfect Induction in the form of an **Inductive Syllogism,** as in the following instance :—

Mercury, Venus, the Earth, &c., all move round the sun from West to East.

Mercury, Venus, the Earth, &c., are all the known Planets. Therefore all the known planets move round the sun from West to East.

This argument is a true Perfect Induction because the conclusion only makes an assertion of all *known* planets, which excludes all reference to possible future discoveries; and we may suppose that all the known planets have been enumerated in the premises. The form of the argument appears to be that of a syllogism in the third figure, namely *Darapti*, the middle term consisting in the group of the known planets. In reality, however, it is not an ordinary syllogism. The minor premise states not that Mercury, Venus, the Earth, Neptune, &c., are *contained among* the known planets, but that they *are* those planets, or are identical with them. This premise is then a doubly universal proposition of a kind (p. 184—7) not recognised in the Aristotelian Syllogism. Accordingly we may observe that the conclusion is a universal proposition, which is not allowable in the third figure of the syllogism.

As another example of a Perfect Induction we may take—

January, February,............December, each contain less than 32 days.
January.........December are all the months of the year.
Therefore all the months of the year contain less than 32 days.

Although Sir W. Hamilton has entirely rejected the notion, it seems worthy of inquiry whether the Inductive Syllogism be not really of the Disjunctive form of Syllogism. Thus I should be inclined to represent the last example in the form:

A month of the year is either January, or February, or March............or December; but January has less than 32 days; and February has less than 32 days; and so on until we come to December, which has less than 32 days.

It follows clearly that a month must in any case have less than 32 days; for there are only 12 possible cases, and in each case this is affirmed. The fact is that the major premise of the syllogism on the last page is a compound sentence with twelve subjects, and is therefore equivalent to twelve distinct logical propositions. The minor premise is either a disjunctive proposition, as I have represented it, or something quite different from anything we have elsewhere had.

From Perfect Induction we shall have to pass to **Imperfect Induction**; but the opinions of Logicians are not in agreement as to the grounds upon which we are warranted in taking a part of the instances only, and concluding that what is true of those is true of all. Thus if we adopt the example found in many books and say—

This, that, and the other magnet attract iron;
This, that, and the other magnet are all magnets;
Therefore all magnets attract iron,

we evidently employ a false minor premise, because this, that, and the other magnet which we have examined, cannot possibly be all existing magnets. In whatever form we put it there must be an assumption that the magnets which we have examined are a fair specimen of all magnets, so that what we find in some we may expect in all. Archbishop Whately considers that this assumption should be expressed in one of the premises, and he represents Induction as a Syllogism in *Barbara* as follows:—

That which belongs to this, that, and the other magnet,
    belongs to all;
Attracting iron belongs to this, that, and the other;
Therefore it belongs to all.

xxv.] *THE INDUCTIVE SYLLOGISM* 217

But though this is doubtless a correct expression of the assumptiŏn made in an Imperfect Induction, it does not in the least explain the grounds on which we are allowed to make the assumption, and under what circumstances such an assumption would be likely to prove true. Some writers have asserted that there is a Principle called the **Uniformity of Nature**, which enables us to affirm that what has often been found to be true of anything will continue to be found true of the same sort of thing. It must be observed, however, that if there be such a principle it is liable to exceptions; for many facts which have held true up to a certain point have afterwards been found not to be always true. Thus there was a wide and unbroken induction tending to show that all the Satellites in the planetary system went in one uniform direction round their planets. Nevertheless the Satellites of Uranus when discovered were found to move in a *retrograde* direction, or in an opposite direction to all Satellites previously known, and the same peculiarity attaches to the Satellite of Neptune more lately discovered.

We may defer to the next lesson the question of the varying degree of certainty which belongs to induction in the several branches of knowledge.

The advanced student may consult the following with advantage :—Mansel's Aldrich, Appendix, Notes G and H. Hamilton's *Lectures on Logic*, Lecture XVII., and Appendix VII., *On Induction and Example*, Vol. II., p. 358. J. S. Mill's *System of Logic*, Book III. Chap. 2, *Of Inductions improperly so-called.*

LESSON XXVI.

GEOMETRICAL AND MATHEMATICAL INDUC-
TION, ANALOGY AND EXAMPLE.

IT is now indispensable that we should consider with
great care upon what grounds Imperfect Induction is
founded. No difficulty is encountered in Perfect Induction because all possible cases which can come under the
general conclusion are enumerated in the premises, so
that in fact there is no information in the conclusion which
was not given in the premises. In this respect the Inductive Syllogism perfectly agrees with the general principles of deductive reasoning, which require that the information contained in the conclusion should be shown
only from the data, and that we should merely unfold,
or transform into an explicit statement what is contained
in the premises implicitly.

In **Imperfect Induction** the process seems to be of a
wholly different character, since the instances concerning
which we acquire knowledge may be infinitely more
numerous than those from which we acquire the knowledge. Let us consider in the first place the process of
Geometrical Reasoning which has a close resemblance to
inductive reasoning. When in the fifth proposition of the
first book of Euclid we prove that the angles at the base
of an isosceles triangle are equal to each other, it is done
by taking one particular triangle as an example. A
figure is given which the reader is requested to regard as
having two equal sides, and it is conclusively proved that
if the sides be really equal then the angles opposite to
those sides must be equal also. But Euclid says nothing
about other isosceles triangles; he treats one single
triangle as a sufficient specimen of all isosceles triangles,

and we are asked to believe that what is true of that is **true** of any other, whether its sides be so small as to be only visible in a microscope, or so large as to reach to the furthest fixed star. There may evidently be an infinite number of isosceles triangles as regards the length of the equal sides, and each of these may be infinitely varied by increasing or diminishing the contained angle, so that the number of possible isosceles triangles is infinitely infinite; and yet we are asked to believe of this incomprehensible number of objects what we have proved only of one single specimen. This might seem to be the most extremely Imperfect Induction possible, and yet every one allows that it gives us really certain knowledge. We do know with as much certainty as knowledge can possess, that if lines be conceived as drawn from the earth to two stars equally distant, they will make equal angles with the line joining those stars; and yet we can never have tried the experiment.

The generality of this geometrical reasoning evidently depends upon the certainty with which we know that all isosceles triangles exactly resemble each other. The proposition proved does not in fact apply to a triangle unless it agrees with our specimen in all the qualities essential to the proof. The absolute length of any of the sides or the absolute magnitude of the angle contained between any of them were not points upon which the proof depended—they were purely accidental circumstances; hence we are at perfect liberty to apply to all new cases of an isosceles triangle what we learn of one case. Upon a similar ground rests all the vast body of certain knowledge contained in the mathematical sciences—not only all the geometrical truths, but all general algebraical truth. It was shown, for instance, in p. 58, that if a and b be two quantities, and we multiply together their sum and difference, we get the difference of the squares of a and b. However often we try this it will be found true; thus if $a = 10$ and $b = 7$, the product of the sum and difference is $17 \times 3 = 51$; the squares of the quantities are 10×10 or 100 and 7×7 or 49, the difference of which is also 51. But however often we tried the rule no certainty would be added to it; because when proved algebraically there was no condition which restricted the result to any particular numbers, and a and b might consequently be any numbers whatever This generality of algebraical reasoning by which a property is proved of infinite varieties of numbers at once, is one of the chief advantages of algebra over arithmetic. There is also in algebra a process called **Mathematical Induction** or **Demonstrative Induction**, which shows the powers of reasoning in a very conspicuous way. A good example is found in the following problem :—If we take the first *two* consecutive odd numbers, 1 and 3, and add them together the sum is 4, or exactly *twice two;* if we take *three* such numbers $1 + 3 + 5$, the sum is 9 or exactly *three times three;* if we take *four,* namely $1 + 3 + 5 + 7$ the sum is 16, or exactly *four times four;* or generally, if we take any given number of the series, $1 + 3 + 5 + 7 + \dots$ the sum is equal to the number of the terms multiplied by itself. Anyone who knows a very little algebra can prove that this remarkable law is universally true, as follows— Let n be the number of terms, and assume for a moment that this law is true up to n terms, thus—

$$1 + 3 + 5 + 7 + \dots + (2n - 1) = n^2.$$

Now add $2n + 1$ to each side of the equation. It follows that—

$$1 + 3 + 5 + 7 + \dots + (2n - 1) + (2n + 1) = n^2 + 2n + 1.$$

But the last quantity $n^2 + 2n + 1$ is just equal to $(n + 1)^2$; so that if the law is true for n terms it is true also for $n + 1$ terms. We are enabled to argue from each single case of the law to the next case; but we have already shown that it is true of the first few cases, therefore it must be true ot all. By no conceivable labour could a person ascertain by trial what is the sum of the first billion odd numbers, and yet symbolically or by general reasoning we know with certainty that they would amount to a billion billion, and neither more nor less even by a unit. This process of Mathematical Induction is not exactly the same as Geometrical Induction, because each case depends upon the last, but the proof rests upon an equally narrow basis of experience, and creates knowledge of equal certainty and generality.

Such mathematical truths depend upon observation of a few cases, but they acquire certainty from the perception we have of the exact similarity of one case to another, so that we undoubtingly believe what is true of one case to be true of another. It is very instructive to contrast with these cases certain other ones where there is a like ground of observation, but not the same tie of similarity. It was at one time believed that if any integral number were multipled by itself, added to itself and then added to 41, the result would be a prime number, that is a number which could not be divided by any other integral number except unity; in symbols,

$$x^2 + x + 41 = \text{prime number.}$$

This was believed solely on the ground of trial and experience, and it certainly holds for a great many values of x. Thus when x is successively made equal to the numbers in the first line below, the expression $x^2 + x + 41$ gives the values in the second line, and they are all prime numbers :

0	1	2	3	4	5	6	7	8	9	10
41	43	47	53	61	71	83	97	113	131	151

No reason however could be given why it should

always be true, and accordingly it is found that the rule does not always hold true, but fails when $x=40$. Then we have $40 \times 40 + 40 + 41 = 1681$, but this is clearly equal to $41 \times 40 + 41$ or 41×41, and is not a prime number.

In that branch of mathematics which treats of the peculiar properties and kinds of numbers, other propositions depending solely upon observation have been asserted to be always true. Thus Fermat believed that $2^{2^x} + 1$ always represents a prime number, but could not give any reason for the assertion. It holds true in fact until the product reaches the large number 4294967297, which was found to be divisible by 641, so that the generality of the statement was disproved.

We find then that in some cases a single instance proves a general and certain rule, while in others a very great number of instances are insufficient to give any certainty at all; all depends upon the perception we have of similarity or identity between one case and another. We can perceive no similarity between all prime numbers which assures us that because one is represented by a certain formula, also another is; but we do find such similarity between the sums of odd numbers, or between isosceles triangles.

Exactly similar considerations apply to inductions in physical science. When a chemist analyses a few grains of water and finds that they contain exactly 8 parts of oxygen and 1 of hydrogen for 9 parts of water, he feels warranted in asserting that the same is true of all pure water whatever be its origin, and whatever be the part of the world from which it comes. But if he analyse a piece of granite, or a sample of sea-water from one part of the world, he does not feel any confidence that it will resemble exactly a piece of granite, or a sample of sea-water from another part of the earth; hence he does not venture to assert of all granite or sea-water, what he finds true of

a single sample. Extended experience shows that granite is very variable in composition, but that sea-water is
rendered pretty uniform by constant mixture of currents.
Nothing but experience in these cases could inform us
how far we may assert safely of one sample what we have
ascertained of another. But we have reason to believe
that chemical compounds are naturally fixed and invariable in composition, according to Dalton's laws of combining proportions. No *à priori* reasoning from the
principles of thought could have told us this, and we only
learn it by extended experiment. But having once shown
it to be true with certain substances we do not need to
repeat the trial with all other substances, because we have
every reason to believe that it is a natural law in which
all chemical substances resemble each other. It is only
necessary then for a single accurate analysis of a given
fixed compound to be made in order to inform us of the
composition of all other portions of the same substance.

It must be carefully observed however that **all inductions in physical science are only probable**, or that if certain, it is only hypothetical certainty they possess. Can
I be absolutely certain that all water contains one part
of hydrogen in nine? I am certain only on two conditions :—

1. That this was certainly the composition of the
   sample tried.
2. That any other substance I call water exactly
   resembles that sample.

But even if the first condition be undoubtedly true, I
cannot be certain of the second. For how do I know
what is water except by the fact of its being a transparent
liquid, freezing into a solid and evaporating into steam,
possessing a high specific heat, and a number of other
distinct properties? But can I be absolutely certain that
every liquid possessing all these properties is water?

Practically I can be certain, but theoretically I cannot. Two substances may have been created so like each other that we should never yet have discovered the difference; we might then be constantly misled by assuming of the one what is only true of the other. That this should ever happen with substances possessing the very distinct qualities of water is excessively improbable, but so far is it from being impossible or improbable in other cases, that it has often happened. Most of the new elements discovered in late years have, without doubt, been mistaken previously for other elements. Cæsium and Rubidium had been long mistaken for each other, and for Potassium, before they were distinguished by Bunsen and Kirchhoff by means of the spectroscope. As they are now known to be widely distributed, although in small quantities, it is certain that what was supposed to be Potassium in many thousands of analyses was partly composed of different substances. Selenium had probably been confused with Sulphur, and there are certain metals—for instance, Rhodium, Ruthenium, Iridium, Osmium, and Beryllium—Yttrium, Erbium, Cerium, Lanthanum, and Didymium—Cadmium and Indium—which have only recently been distinguished. The progress of science will doubtless show that we are mistaken in many of our identifications, and various difficulties thus arising will ultimately be explained.

Take again a very different case of induction. Are we certain that the sun will rise again to-morrow morning as it has risen for many thousand years, and probably for some hundred million years? We are certain only on this condition or hypothesis, that the planetary system proceeds to-morrow as it has proceeded for so long. Many causes may exist which might at any moment defeat all our calculations; our sun is believed to be a variable star, and for what we know it might at any moment suddenly

explode or flare up, as certain other stars have been observed to do, and we should then be all turned into thin
luminous vapour in a moment of time. It is not at all
impossible that a collision did once occur in the planetary system, and that the minute planets or asteroids are
the result. Even if there is no large meteor, comet or
cther body capable of breaking up the earth by collision,
yet it is probable that the sun moves through space at the
rate of nearly 300 miles per minute, and if some other
star should meet us at a similar rate the consequences
would be inconceivably terrible. It is highly improbable
however that such an event should come to pass even in
the course of a million years.

The reader will now see that no mere Imperfect Induction can give certain knowledge; all inference proceeds
upon the assumption that new instances will exactly resemble old ones in all material circumstances; but in
natural phenomena this is purely hypothetical, and we
may constantly find ourselves in error. In Mathematical
Induction certainty arose from the cases being hypothetical in their own nature, or being made so as exactly to
correspond with the conditions. We cannot assert that
any triangle existing in nature has two equal sides or two
equal angles, and it is even impossible in practice that
any two lines or angles can be absolutely equal. But it
is nevertheless true that if the sides are equal the angles
are equal. All certainty of inference is thus relative and
hypothetical. Even in the syllogism the certainty of the
conclusion only rests on the hypothesis of certainty in the
premises. It is probable, in fact, that all reasoning reduces
itself to a single type—that what is true of one thing will
be true of another thing, on condition of there being an
exact resemblance between them in all material circumstances.

The reader will now understand with ease the nature

of reasoning by analogy.   In strictness an analogy is not an identity of one thing with another, but an identity of relations.   In the case of numbers 7 is not identical with 10 nor 14 with 20, but the ratio of 7 to 10 is identical with the ratio of 14 to 20, so that there is an analogy between these numbers.   To multiply two by two is not the same thing as to construct a square upon a line two units long; but there is this analogy—that there will be just as many units of area in the square as there are units in the product of two by two.   This analogy is so evident that we fearlessly assert a square mile to consist of 1760 x 1760 square yards without any trial of the truth.   In ordinary language, however, analogy has come to mean any resemblance between things which enables us to believe of one what we know of the other.

Thus the planet Mars possesses an atmosphere, with clouds and mist closely resembling our own; it has seas distinguished from the land by a greenish colour, and polar regions covered with snow.   The red colour of the planet seems to be due to the atmosphere, like the red colour of our sunrises and sunsets.   So much is similar in the surface of Mars and the surface of the Earth that we readily argue there must be inhabitants there as here.   All that we can certainly say however is, that if the circumstances be really similar, and similar germs of life have been created there as here, there must be inhabitants.   The fact that many circumstances are similar increases the probability.   But between the Earth and the Sun the analogy is of a much fainter character; we speak indeed of the sun's atmosphere being subject to storms and filled with clouds, but these clouds are heated probably beyond the temperature of our hottest furnaces; if they produce rain it must resemble a shower of melted iron; and the sun-spots are perturbations of so tremendous a size and character, that the earth together with half-a-dozen of the other planets could readily be swallowed up in one of them*. It is plain then that there is little or no analogy between the Sun and the Earth, and we can therefore with difficulty form a conception of anything going on in a sun or star.

Argument from analogy may be defined as direct inductive inference from one instance to any similar instance. It may, as Mr Mill says, be reduced to the following formula :—

"Two things resemble each other in one or more respects ; a certain proposition is true of the one ; therefore it is true of the other." This is no doubt the type of all reasoning, and the certainty of the process depends entirely upon the degree of resemblance or identity between the cases. In geometry the cases are absolutely identical in all material points by hypothesis, and no doubt attaches to the inference ; in physical science the identity is a question of probability, and the conclusion is in a like degree probable. It should be added that Mr Mill considers Geometrical and Mathematical Induction not to be properly called Induction, for reasons of which the force altogether escapes my apprehension ; but the reader will find his opinions in the 2nd chapter of the 3rd book of his *System of Logic.*

One form of analogical or inductive argument consists in the constant use of **examples** and **instances**. The best way to describe the nature of a class of things is to present one of the things itself, and point out the properties which belong to the class as distinguished from those peculiar to the thing. Throughout these Lessons, as throughout every work on Logic, instances of propositions, of compound or complex sentences, of syllogisms, &c., are continually used, and the reader is asked to apply to all

* Lockyer's *Elementary Lessons in Astronomy*, § 108.

similar cases what he observes in the examples given.
It is assumed that the writer selects such examples as
truly exhibit the properties in question.

While all inductive and analogical inferences rest
upon the same principles there are wide differences between the sources of probability. In **analogy** we have two
cases which resemble each other in a great many properties, and we infer that some additional property in one is
probably to be found in the other. The very narrow
basis of experience is compensated by the high degree of
similarity. In the processes more commonly treated
under the name **Induction**, the things usually resemble
each other only in two or three properties, and we require
to have more instances to assure us that what is true of
of these is probably true of all similar instances. The
less, in short, the intension of the resemblance the greater
must be the extension of our inquiries.

We proceed to the ordinary processes of Induction in
the following Lessons.

> Mr Mill's *System of Logic*, Book III. Chap. XX. *Of
> Analogy*. Mansel's *Aldrich*, App. Note H. *On
> Example and Analogy*.

LESSON XXVII.

OBSERVATION AND EXPERIMENT.

ALL knowledge, it may be safely said, must be ultimately
founded upon **experience**, which is but a general name for
the various feelings impressed upon the mind at any period
of its existence. The mind never creates entirely new
knowledge independent of experience, and all that the
reasoning powers can do is to arrive at the full meaning

of the facts which are in our possession. In previous centuries men of the highest ability have held that the mind of its own power alone could, by sufficient cogitation, discover what things outside us should be, and would be found to be on examination. They thought that we were able *to anticipate Nature* by evolving from the human mind an idea of what things would be made by the Creator. The celebrated philosopher Descartes thus held that whatever the mind can clearly conceive may be considered true; but we can conceive the existence of mountains of gold or oceans of fresh water, which do not as a fact exist. Anything that we can clearly conceive must be conformable to the laws of thought, and its existence is then not impossible, so far as our intellect is concerned; but the forms and sizes and manners in which it has pleased the Creator to make things in this or any other part of the universe, cannot possibly be anticipated by the exceedingly limited wisdom of the human mind, and can only be learnt by actual examination of existing things.

In the latter part of the 13th century the great Roger Bacon clearly taught in England the supreme importance of experience as the basis of knowledge; but the same doctrine was also, by a curious coincidence, again upheld in the 17th century by the great Chancellor Francis Bacon, after whom it has been called the **Baconian Philosophy**. I believe that Roger Bacon was even a greater man than Francis, whose fame is best known; but the words in which **Francis Bacon** proclaimed the importance of experience and experiment must be ever memorable. In the beginning of his great work, the **Novum Organum**, or *New Instrument*, he thus points out our proper position as learners in the world of nature.

"Man, the Servant and Interpreter of Nature, can do and understand as much as he has observed concerning the order of nature in outward things or in the mind; more, he can neither know nor do."

The above is the first of the aphorisms or paragraphs with which the *Novum Organum* commences. In the second aphorism he asserts that the unaided mind can effect little and is liable to err; assistance in the form of a definite logical method is requisite, and this it was the purpose of his New Instrument to furnish. The 3rd and 4th aphorisms must be given entire; they are:—

"Human science and human power coincide, because ignorance of a cause deprives us of the effect. For nature is not conquered except by obedience; and what we discover as a cause by contemplation becomes a rule in operation."

"Man can himself do nothing else than move natural bodies to or from each other; nature working within accomplishes the rest."

It would be impossible more clearly and completely to express the way in which we discover science by interpreting the changes we observe in nature, and then turn our knowledge to a useful purpose in the promotion of the arts and manufactures. We cannot create and we cannot destroy a particle of matter; it is now known that we cannot even create or destroy force; nor can we really alter the inner nature of any substance that we have to deal with. All that we can do is to observe carefully how one substance by its natural powers acts upon another substance, and then by moving them together at the right time we can effect our object; as Bacon says, "Nature working within does the rest." Had it not been the nature of heat when applied to water to develope steam possessing elastic power, it is needless to say that the steam-engine could never have been made, so that the invention of the steam-engine arose from observing the utility of the force of steam, and employing it accordingly.

It is in this sense that Virgil has proclaimed him happy who knows the causes of things—

Felix qui potuit rerum cognoscere causas,

and that Bacon has said, *Knowledge is Power.* So far as we have observed how things happen in nature, and on what occasion particular effects are brought to pass, we are enabled to avoid or utilise those effects as we may desire, not by altering the natures of things, but by allowing them in suitable times and circumstances to manifest their own proper powers. It is thus, as Tennyson has excellently said, that we

" Rule by obeying Nature's Powers."

Inductive logic treats of the methods of reasoning by which we may successfully interpret nature and learn the natural laws which various substances obey in different circumstances. In this lesson we consider the first requisite of induction, namely, the **experience** or examination of nature which is requisite to furnish us with facts. Such experience is obtained either by **observation** or **experiment**. *To observe* is merely to notice events and changes which are produced in the ordinary course of nature, without being able, or at least attempting, to control or vary those changes. Thus the early astronomers observed the motions of the sun, moon and planets among the fixed stars, and gradually detected many of the laws or periodical returns of those bodies. Thus it is that the meteorologist observes the ever-changing weather, and notes the height of the barometer, the temperature and moistness of the air, the direction and force of the wind, the height and character of the clouds, without being in the least able to govern any of these facts. The geologist again is genenerally a simple observer when he investigates the nature and position of rocks. The zoologist, the botanist, and the mineralogist usually employ mere observation when they examine animals, plants, and minerals, as they are met with in their natural condition.

In experiment, on the contrary, we vary at our will the combinations of things and circumstances, and then observe the result. It is thus that the chemist discovers the composition of water by using an electric current to separate its two constituents, oxygen and hydrogen. The mineralogist may employ experiment when he melts two or three substances together to ascertain how a particular mineral may have been produced. Even the botanist and zoologist are not confined to passive observation; for by removing animals or plants to different climates and different soils, and by what is called domestication, they may try how far the natural forms and species are capable of alteration.

It is obvious that experiment is the most potent and direct mode of obtaining facts where it can be applied. We might have to wait years or centuries to meet accidentally with facts which we can readily produce at any moment in a laboratory; and it is probable that most of the chemical substances now known, and many excessively useful products, would never have been discovered at all by waiting till nature presented them spontaneously to our observation. Many forces and changes too may go on in nature constantly, but in so slight a degree as to escape our senses, and render some experimental means necessary for their detection. Electricity doubtless operates in every particle of matter, perhaps at every moment of time; and even the ancients could not but notice its action in the loadstone, in lightning, in the Aurora Borealis, or in a piece of rubbed amber (*electrum*). But in lightning electricity was too intense and dangerous; in the other cases it was too feeble to be properly understood. The science of electricity and magnetism could only advance by getting regular supplies of electricity from the common electric machine or the galvanic battery, and by making powerful electro-magnets. Most if not all the effects which electricity produces must go on in nature, but altogether too obscurely for observation.

Experiment, again, is rendered indispensable by the fact that on the surface of the earth we usually meet substances under certain uniform conditions, so that we could never learn by observation what would be the nature of such substances under other conditions. Thus carbonic acid is only met in the form of a gas, proceeding from the combustion of carbon; but when exposed to extreme pressure and cold, it is condensed into a liquid, and may even be converted into a snow-like solid substance. Many other gases have in like manner been liquefied or solidified; and there is reason to believe that every substance is capable of taking all the three forms of solid, liquid and gas, if only the conditions of temperature and pressure can be sufficiently varied. Mere observation of nature would have led us, on the contrary, to suppose that nearly all substances were fixed in one condition only, and could not be converted from solid into liquid and from liquid into gas.

It must not be supposed however that we can draw any precise line between observation and experiment, and say where the one ends and the other begins. The difference is rather one of degree than of kind; and all we can say is that the more we vary the conditions artificially the more we employ experiment. I have said that meteorology is a science of *nearly* pure observation, but if we purposely ascend mountains to observe the rarefaction and cooling of the atmosphere by elevation, or if we make balloon ascents for the same purpose, like Gay Lussac and Glaisher, we so vary the mode of observation as almost to render it experimental. Astronomers again

may almost be said to experiment instead of merely observing when they simultaneously employ instruments as
far to the north, and as far to the south, upon the earth's
surface as possible, in order to observe the apparent difference of place of Venus when crossing the sun in a
transit, so as thus to compare the distances of Venus and
the sun with the dimensions of the earth.

Sir John Herschel has excellently described the difference in question in his *Discourse on the Study of Natural Philosophy**. " Essentially they are much alike,
and differ rather in degree than in kind; so that perhaps
the terms *passive* and *active observation* might better
express their distinction; but it is, nevertheless, highly
important to mark the different states of mind in inquiries carried on by their respective aids, as well as their
different effects in promoting the progress of science.
In the former, we sit still and listen to a tale, told us, perhaps obscurely, piecemeal, and at long intervals of time,
with our attention more or less awake. It is only by after
rumination that we gather its full import; and often, when
the opportunity is gone by, we have to regret that our
attention was not more particularly directed to some point
which, at the time, appeared of little moment, but of
which we at length appreciate the importance. In the
latter, on the other hand, we cross-examine our witness,
and by comparing one part of his evidence with the other,
while he is yet before us, and reasoning upon it in his
presence, are enabled to put pointed and searching questions, the answer to which may at once enable us to make
up our minds. Accordingly it has been found invariably,
that in those departments of physics where the phenomena are beyond our control, or into which experimental
enquiry, from other causes, has not been carried, the pro

* p. 77.

gress of knowledge has been slow, uncertain and irregular; while in such as admit of experiment, and in which mankind have agreed to its adoption, it has been rapid, sure, and steady."

Not uncommonly, however, nature has, so to speak, made experiments upon a scale and for a duration with which we cannot possibly compete. Thus we do not need to try the soil and situation which suits any given plant best; we have but to look about and notice the habitat or situation in which it is naturally found in the most flourishing condition, and that, we may be sure, indicates the result of ages of natural experiment. The distances of the fixed stars would probably have been for ever unknown to us did not the earth by describing an orbit with a diameter of 182,000,000 miles make a sort of experimental base for observation, so that we can see the stars in very slightly altered positions, and thus judge their distances compared with the earth's orbit*. Eclipses, transits, occultations and remarkable conjunctures of the planets, are also kinds of natural experiments which have often been recorded in early times, and thus afford data of the utmost value.

Logic can give little or no aid in making an acute or accurate observer. There are no definite rules which can be laid down upon the subject. To observe well is an art which can only be acquired by practice and training; and it is one of the greatest advantages of the pursuit of the Natural Sciences that the faculty of clear and steady observation is thereby cultivated. Logic can however give us this caution, which has been well pointed out by Mr Mill—*to discriminate accurately between what we really do observe and what we only infer from the facts observed.* So long as we only record and describe what our senses

---

* See Lockyer's *Elementary Lessons in Astronomy*, Nos. XLVI, XLVII.

have actually witnessed, we cannot commit an error; but the moment we presume or infer anything we are liable to mistake. For instance, we examine the sun's surface with a telescope and observe that it is intensely bright except where there are small breaks or circular openings in the surface with a dark interior. We are irresistibly led to the conclusion that the inside of the sun is colder and darker than the outside, and record as a fact that we saw the dark interior of the sun through certain openings in its luminous atmosphere. Such a record, however, would involve mistaken inference, for we saw nothing but dark spots, and we should not have done more in observation than record the shape, size, appearance and change of such spots. Whether they are dark clouds above the luminous surface, glimpses of the dark interior, or, as is now almost certainly inferred, something entirely different from either, can only be proved by a comparison of many unprejudiced observations.

The reader cannot too often bear in mind the caution against **confusing facts observed with inferences from those facts.** It is not too much to say that nine-tenths of what we seem to see and hear is inferred, not really felt. Every sense possesses what are called **acquired perceptions,** that is, the power of judging unconsciously, by long experience, of many things which cannot be the objects of direct perception. The eye cannot see distance, yet we constantly imagine and say that we see things at such and such distances, unconscious that it is the result of judgment. As Mr Mill remarks, it is too much to say " I saw my brother." All I positively know is that J saw some one who closely resembled my brother as far as could be observed. It is by judgment only I can assert he was my brother, and that judgment may possibly be wrong.

Nothing is more important in observation and experi-

ment than to be uninfluenced by any prejudice or theory
in correctly recording the facts observed and allowing to
them their proper weight. He who does not do so will
almost always be able to obtain facts in support of an
opinion however erroneous. Thus the belief still exists
with great force in the majority of uneducated persons,
that the moon has great influence over the weather. The
changes of the moon, full, new and half moon, occur four
times in every month, and it is supposed that any change
may influence the weather at least on the day preceding
or following that of its occurrence. There will thus be
twelve days out of every 28 on which any change of weather would be attributed to the moon, so that during the
year many changes will probably be thus recorded as
favourable to the opinion. The uneducated observer is
struck with these instances and remembers them carefully, but he fails to observe, or at least to remember, that
changes of weather often occur also when there is no
change of the moon at all. The question could only
be decided by a long course of careful and unbiassed
observation in which all facts favourable or unfavour-
able should be equally recorded. All observations which
have been published negative the idea that there can be
any such influence as the vulgar mind attributes to the
moon.

But it would at the same time be an error to suppose
that the best observer or experimentalist is he who holds
no previous opinions or theories on the subject he investigates. On the contrary, the great experimentalist is he
who ever has a theory or even a crowd of theories or ideas
upon his mind, but is always putting them to the test of
experience and dismissing those which are false. The
number of things which can be observed and experimented
on are infinite, and if we merely set to work to record
facts without any distinct purpose, our records will have

no value. We must have some opinion or some theory to direct our choice of experiments, and it is more probable that we hit upon the truth in this way than merely by haphazard. But the great requisite of the true philosopher is that he be perfectly unbiassed and abandon every opinion as soon as facts inconsistent with it are observed.

It has been well said by the celebrated Turgot, that "the first thing is to invent a system; the second thing is to be disgusted with it;" that is to say, we ought to have some idea of the truth we seek, but should immediately put it to a severe trial as if we were inclined to distrust and dislike it rather than be biassed in its favour. Few men probably have entertained more false theories than Kepler and Faraday; few men have discovered or established truths of greater certainty and importance. Faraday has himself said that—

"The world little knows how many of the thoughts and theories which have passed through the mind of a scientific investigator, have been crushed in silence and secrecy by his own severe criticism and adverse examination; that in the most successful instances not a tenth of the suggestions, the hopes, the wishes, the preliminary conclusions have been realized *."

The student is strongly recommended to read Sir J. Herschel's *Preliminary Discourse on the Study of Natural Philosophy* (Lardner's *Cabinet Cyclopædia*), especially Part II. Chaps. 4 to 7, concerning Observation, Experiment, and the Inductive Processes generally.

* *Modern Culture*, edited by Youmans, p. 222. [Macmillan and Co.]

LESSON XXVIII.

METHODS OF INDUCTION.

WE have now to consider such methods as can be laid down for the purpose of guiding us in the search for general truths or laws of nature among the facts obtained by observation and experiment. Induction consists in inferring from particulars to generals, or detecting a general truth among its particular occurrences. But in physical science the truths to be discovered generally relate to the connection of cause and effect, and we usually call them **laws of causation** or **natural laws**. By the Cause of an event we mean the circumstances which must have preceded in order that the event should happen. Nor is it generally possible to say that an event has one single cause and no more. There are usually many different things, conditions or circumstances necessary to the production of an effect, and all of them must be considered causes or necessary parts of the cause. Thus the cause of the loud explosion in a gun is not simply the pulling of the trigger, which is only the last apparent cause or occasion of the explosion; the qualities of the powder; the proper form of the barrel; the existence of some resisting charge; the proper arrangement of the percussion cap and powder; the existence of a surrounding atmosphere, are among the circumstances necessary to the loud report of a gun: any of them being absent it would not have occurred.

The cause of the boiling of water again is not merely the application of heat up to a certain degree of temperature, but the possibility also of the escape of the vapour when it acquires a certain pressure. The freezing of water similarly does not depend merely upon the withdrawal of heat below the temperature of 0° Centigrade. It is the work of Induction then to detect those circumstances which uniformly will produce any given effect; and as soon as these circumstances become known, we have a law or uniformity of nature of greater or less generality.

In this and the following Lessons I shall often have to use, in addition to cause and effect, the words antecedent and consequent, and the reader ought to notice their meanings. By an **antecedent** we mean any thing, condition, or circumstance which exists before or, it may be, at the same time with an event or phenomenon. By a **consequent** we mean any thing, or circumstance, event, or phenomenon, which is different from any of the antecedents and follows after their conjunction or putting together. It does not follow that an antecedent is a cause, because the effect might have happened without it. Thus the sun's light may be an antecedent to the burning of a house, but not the cause, because the house would burn equally well in the night. A *necessary or indispensable antecedent is* however *identical with a cause*, being that without which the effect would not take place.

The word **phenomenon** will also be often used. It means simply *anything which appears*, and is therefore observed by the senses; the derivation of the word from the Greek word φαινόμενον, *that which appears*, exactly corresponds to its logical use.

The first method of Induction is that which Mr Mill has aptly called the **Method of agreement**. It depends upon the rule that "If two or more instances of the phenomenon under investigation have only one circumstance in common, the circumstance in which alone all the instances agree, is the cause (or effect) of the given phenomenon." The meaning of this **First Canon** of inductive inquiry might, I think, be more briefly expressed by saying that *the sole invariable antecedent of a phenomenon is probably its cause.*

To apply this method we must collect as many instances of the phenomenon as possible, and compare together their antecedents. Among these the causes will lie, but if we notice that certain antecedents are present or absent without appearing to affect the result, we conclude that they cannot be necessary antecedents. Hence it is the one antecedent or group of antecedents always present, when the effect follows, that we consider the cause. For example, bright prismatic colours are seen on bubbles, on films of tar floating upon water, on thin plates of.mica, as also on cracks in glass, or between two pieces of glass pressed together. On examining all such cases they seem to agree in nothing but the presence of a very thin layer or plate, and it appears to make no appreciable difference of what kind of matter, solid, liquid, or gaseous, the plate is made. Hence we conclude that such colours are caused merely by the thinness of the plates, and this conclusion is proved true by the theory of the interference of light. Sir David Brewster beautifully proved in a similar way that the colours seen upon Mother-of-pearl are not caused by the nature of the substance, but by the form of the surface. He took impressions of the Mother-of-pearl in wax, and found that although the substance was entirely different the colours were exactly the same. And it was afterwards found that if a plate of metal had a surface marked by very fine close grooves, it would have iridescent colours like those of Mother-of-pearl. Hence it is evident that the form of the surface, which is the only invariable antecedent or condition requisite for the production of the colours, must be their cause.

16

The method of agreement is subject to a serious difficulty, called by Mr Mill the Plurality of Causes, consisting in the fact that the same effect may in different instances be owing to different causes. Thus if we inquire accurately into the cause of heat we find that it is produced by friction, by burning or combustion, by electricity, by pressure, &c.; so that it does not follow that if there happened to be one and the same thing present in all the cases we examined this would be the cause. The second method of induction which we will now consider is free from this difficulty, and is known as the Method of Difference. It is stated in Mr Mill's Second Canon as follows:—

"If an instance in which the phenomenon under investigation occurs, and an instance in which it does not occur, have every circumstance in common save one, that one occurring only in the former; the circumstance in which alone the two instances differ, is the effect, or the cause, or an indispensable part of the cause, of the phenomenon."

In other words, we may say that the antecedent which is invariably present when the phenomenon follows, and invariably absent when it is absent, other circumstances remaining the same, is the cause of the phenomenon in those circumstances.

Thus we can clearly prove that friction is *one* cause of heat, because when two sticks are rubbed together they become heated; when not rubbed they do not become heated. Sir Humphry Davy showed that even two pieces of ice when rubbed together in a vacuum produce heat, as shown by their melting, and thus completely demonstrated that the friction is the source and cause of the heat. We prove that air is the cause of sound being communicated to our ears by striking a bell in the receiver of an air-pump, as Hawksbee first did in 1705, and then observing that when the receiver is full of air we hear the bell ; when it contains little or no air we do not hear the bell. We learn that sodium or any of its compounds produces a spectrum having a bright yellow double line by noticing that there is no such line in the spectrum of light when sodium is not present, but that if the smallest quantity of sodium be thrown into the flame or other source of light, the bright yellow line instantly appears. Oxygen is the cause of respiration and life, because if an animal be put into a jar full of atmospheric air, from which the oxygen has been withdrawn, it soon becomes suffocated.

This is essentially the great **method of experiment**, and its utility mainly depends upon the precaution of only *varying one circumstance at a time, all other circumstances being maintained just as they were.* This is expressed in one of the rules for conducting experiments given by Thomson and Tait in their great treatise on *Natural Philosophy*, Vol. I. p. 307, as follows:—

"In all cases when a particular agent or cause is to be studied, experiments should be arranged in such a way as to lead if possible to results depending on it alone ; or, if this cannot be done, they should be arranged so as to increase the effects due to the cause to be studied till these so far exceed the unavoidable concomitants, that the latter may be considered as only disturbing, not essentially modifying the effects of the principal agent."

It would be an imperfect and unsatisfactory experiment to take air of which the oxygen has been converted into carbonic acid by the burning of carbon, and argue that, because an animal dies in such air, oxygen is the cause of respiration. Instead of merely withdrawing the oxygen we have a new substance, carbonic acid, present, which is quite capable of killing the animal by its own poisonous properties. The animal in fact would be suffocated even when a considerable proportion of oxygen remained, so that the presence of the carbonic acid is a disturbing circumstance which confuses and vitiates the experiment.

It is possible to prove the existence, and even to measure the amount of the force of gravity, by delicately suspending a small ball about the size of a marble and then suddenly bringing a very heavy leaden ball weighing a ton or more close to it. The small ball will be attracted and set in motion; but the experiment would not be of the least value unless performed with the utmost precaution. It is obvious that the sudden motion of the large leaden ball would disturb the air, shake the room, cause currents in the air by its coldness or warmth, and even occasion electric attractions or repulsions; and these would probably disturb the small ball far more than the force of gravitation.

Beautiful instances of experiment according to this method are to be found, as Sir John Herschel has pointed out, in the researches by which Dr Wells discovered the cause of dew. If on a clear calm night a sheet or other covering be stretched a foot or two above the earth, so as to screen the ground below from the open sky, dew will be found on the grass around the screen but not beneath it. As the temperature and moistness of the air, and other circumstances, are exactly the same, the open sky must be an indispensable antecedent to dew. The same experiment is indeed tried for us by nature, for if we make observations of dew during two nights which differ in nothing but the absence of clouds in one and their presence in the other, we shall find that the clear open sky is requisite to the formation of dew.

It may often happen that we cannot apply the method of difference perfectly by varying only one circumstance at a time. Thus we cannot, generally speaking, try the

qualities of the same substance in the solid and liquid
condition without any other change of circumstances, because it is necessary to alter the temperature of the substance in order to liquefy or solidify it. The temperature
might thus be the cause of what we attribute to the liquid
or solid condition. Under such circumstances we have
to resort to what Mr Mill calls the **joint method of agreement and difference**, which consists in a double application of the method of agreement, first to a number of
instances where an effect is produced, and secondly, to a
number of quite different instances where the effect is not
produced. It is clearly to be understood, however, that
the negative instances differ in several circumstances
from the positive ones; for if they differed only in one
circumstance we might apply the simple method of difference. Iceland spar, for instance, has a curious power of
rendering things seen through it apparently double. This
phenomenon, called double refraction, also belongs to
many other crystals; and we might at once prove it to be
due to crystalline structure could we obtain any transparent substance crystallized and uncrystallized, but subject
to no other alteration. We have, however, a pretty satisfactory proof by observing that uniform transparent uncrystallized substances agree in not possessing double
refraction, and that crystalline substances, on the other
hand, with certain exceptions which are easily explained,
agree in possessing the power in question. The principle
of the **joint method** may be stated in the following rule,
which is Mr Mill's **Third Canon** :—

  " If two or more instances in which the phenomenon
occurs have only one circumstance in common, while two
or more instances in which it does not occur have nothing
in common save the absence of that circumstance; the
circumstance in which alone the two sets of instances
(always or invariably) differ, is the effect, or the cause,

or an indispensable part of the cause, of the phenomenon."

I have inserted the words in parentheses, as without
them the canon seems to me to express exactly the opposite of what Mr Mill intends.

It may facilitate the exact comprehension of these inductive methods if I give the following symbolic representation of them in the manner adopted by Mr Mill.
Let A, B, C, D, E, &c., be antecedents which may be
variously combined, and let a, b, c, d, e, &c., be effects
following from them. If then we can collect the following
sets of antecedents and effects—

Antecedents.	Consequents.
ABC	abc
ADE	ade
AFG	afg
AHK	ahk
......	......
......	......

we may apply the **method of agreement**, and little doubt
will remain that A, the sole invariable antecedent, is the
cause of a.

The method of difference is sufficiently represented by—

Antecedents.	Consequents.
ABC	abc
BC	bc

Here while B and C remain perfectly unaltered we find
that the presence or absence of A occasions the presence
or absence of a, of which it is therefore the cause, in the
presence of B and C. But the reader may be cautioned
against thinking that this proves A to be the cause of a
under all circumstances whatever.

The joint method of agreement and difference is similarly
represented by—

Antecedents.	Consequents.
ABC	*abc*
ADE	*ade*
AFG	*afg*
AHK	*ahk*
......	...
PQ	*pq*
RS	*rs*
TV	*tv*
XY	*xy*
...	...

Here the presence of *A* is followed as in the simple method of agreement by *a*; and the absence of *A*, in circumstances differing from the previous ones, is followed by the absence of *a*. Hence there is a very high probability that *A* is the cause of *a*. But it will easily be seen that *A* is not the only circumstance in which the two sets of instances differ, otherwise to any pair we might apply the simple method of difference. But the presence of *A* is a circumstance in which one set invariably, or uniformly, or always, differs, from the other set. This joint method is thus a substitute for the simpler method of difference in cases where that cannot be properly brought into action.

Herschel's *Discourse*, part II. chap. 6, p. 144.
Mill's *System of Logic*, book III. chaps. 8 and 9.

LESSON XXIX.

METHODS OF QUANTITATIVE INDUCTION.

THE methods of Induction described in the last Lesson related merely to the happening or not happening of the event, the cause of which was sought. Thus we learnt that friction was one cause of heat by observing that two solid bodies, even two pieces of ice, rubbed together, produced heat, but that when they were not rubbed there was no such production of heat. This, however, is a very elementary sort of experiment ; and in the progress of an investigation we always require to measure the exact quantity of an effect, if it be capable of being more or less, and connecting it with the quantity of the cause. There is in fact a natural course of progress through which we proceed in every such inquiry, as may be stated in the following series of questions.

1. Does the antecedent invariably produce an effect?
2. In what direction is that effect?
3. How much is that effect in proportion to the cause?
4. Is it uniformly in that proportion?
5. If not, according to what law does it vary?

Take for instance the effect of heat in altering the dimensions of bodies. The first question is, whether the heating of a solid body, say a bar of iron, alters its length ; the simple method of difference enables us to answer that it does. The next inquiry shows that almost all substances are lengthened or increased in dimensions by heat, but that a very few, such as india rubber, and water below $4\cdot08^\circ$ Cent., are decreased. We next ascertain the proportion of the change to each degree of temperature, which is called the coefficient of expansion. Thus iron expands $0\cdot0000122$ of its own length for every 1° Centigrade between 0° and 100°.

Still more minute inquiry shows, however, that the expansion is not uniformly proportional to temperature; most metals expand more and more rapidly the hotter they are, but the details of the subject need not be considered here.

The fixed stars, again, have often been mentioned in these Lessons, but the reader is probably aware that they are not really fixed. Taking any particular star, the astronomer has really to answer the several five questions stated below.

Firstly. Does the star move?

2ndly. In what direction does it move?

3rdly. How much does it move in a year or a century?

4thly. Does it move uniformly?

5thly. If not, according to what law does the motion vary in direction and rapidity?

Every science and every question in science is first a matter of fact only, then a matter of quantity, and by degrees becomes more and more precisely quantitative. Thirty years ago most of the phenomena of electricity and electro-magnetism were known merely as facts; now they can be for the most part exactly measured and calculated.

As soon as phenomena can thus be measured we can apply a further Method of Induction of a very important character. It is the **Method of Difference** indeed applied under far more favourable circumstances, where every degree and quantity of a phenomenon gives us a new experiment and proof of connection between cause and effect. It may be called the **Method of Concomitant Variations**, and is thus stated by Mr Mill, in what he entitles the **Fifth Canon** of Induction:

"Whatever phenomenon varies in any manner whenever another phenomenon varies in some particular manner, is either a cause or an effect of that phenomenon, or is connected with it through some fact of causation."

Sir John Herschel's statement of the same method is as follows:—"Increase or diminution of the effect, with the increased or diminished intensity of the cause, in cases which admit of increase and diminution," to which he adds, "Reversal of the effect with that of the cause."

The illustrations of this method are infinitely numerous. Thus Mr Joule, of Manchester, conclusively proved that friction is a cause of heat by expending exact quantities of force in rubbing one substance against another, and showed that the heat produced was exactly greater or less in proportion as the force was greater or less. We can apply the method to many cases which had previously been treated by the simple method of difference; thus instead of striking a bell in a complete vacuum we can strike it with a very little air in the receiver of the air-pump, and we then hear a very faint sound, which increases or decreases every time we increase or decrease the density of the air. This experiment conclusively satisfies any person that air is the cause of the transmission of sound.

It is this method which often enables us to detect the material connection which exists between two bodies. For a long time it had been doubtful whether the red flames seen in total eclipses of the sun belonged to the sun or the moon ; but during the last eclipse of the sun it was noticed that the flames *moved with the sun*, and were gradually covered and uncovered by the moon at successive instants of the eclipse. No one could doubt thenceforth that they belonged to the sun.

Whenever, again, phenomena go through **Periodic Changes**, alternately increasing and decreasing, we should seek for other phenomena which go through changes in exactly the same periods, and there will probably be a connection of cause and effect. It is thus that the tides are proved to be due to the attraction of the moon and sun, because the periods of high and low, spring and neap tides, succeed each other in intervals corresponding to the *apparent* revolutions of those bodies round the earth. The fact that the moon revolves upon its own axis in *exactly* the same period that it revolves round the earth, so that for unknown ages past the same side of the moon has always been turned towards the earth, is a most perfect case of concomitant variations, conclusively prov·

ing that the earth's attraction governs the motions of the moon on its own axis.

The most extraordinary case of variations howevei consists in the connection which has of late years been shown to exist between the Aurora Borealis, magnetic storms, and the spots on the sun. It has only in the last 30 or 40 years become known that the magnetic compass needle is subject at intervals to very slight but curious movements ; and that at the same time there are usually natural currents of electricity produced in tele-graph-wires so as to interfere with the transmission of messages. These disturbances are known as magnetic storms, and are often observed to occur when a fine display of the Northern or Southern Lights is taking place in some part of the earth. Observations during many years have shown that these storms come to their worst at the end of every eleven years, the maximum taking place about the present year 1870, and then diminish in intensity until the next period of eleven years has passed. Close observations of the sun during 30 or 40 years have shown that the size and number of the dark spots, which are gigantic storms going on upon the sun's surface, increase and decrease exactly at the same periods of time as the magnetic storms upon the earth's surface. No one can doubt, then, that these strange phenomena are connected together, though the mode of the connection is quite unknown. It is now believed that the planets Jupiter, Saturn, Venus and Mars, are the real causes of the disturbances; for Balfour Stewart and Warren de la Rue have shown that an exact correspondence exists between the motions of these planets and the periods of the sunspots. This is a most remarkable and extensive case of concomitant variations.

We have now to consider a method of Induction which must be employed when several causes act at once and their effects are all blended together, producing a joint effect of the same kind as the separate effects. If in one experiment friction, combustion, compression and electric action are all going on at once, each of these causes will produce quantities of heat which will be added together, and it will be difficult or impossible to say how much is due to each cause separately. We may call this a case of the **homogeneous intermixture of effects**, the name indicating that the joint effect is of the same kind as the separate effects. It is distinguished by Mr Mill from cases of the **heterogeneous**, or, as he says, the *heteropathic* intermixture of effects, where the joint effect is totally different in kind from the separate effects. Thus if we bend a bow too much it breaks instead of bending further; if we warm ice it soon ceases to rise in temperature and melts; if we warm water it rises in temperature **homogeneously** for a time but then suddenly ceases, and an effect of a totally different kind, the production of vapour, or possibly an explosion, follows.

Now when the joint effect is of a heterogeneous kind the method of difference is sufficient to ascertain the cause of its occurrence. Whether a bow or a spring will break with a given weight may easily be tried, and whether water will boil at a given temperature in any given state of the barometer may also be easily ascertained. But in the homogeneous intermixture of effects we have a more complicated task. There are several causes each producing a part of the effect, and we want to know how much is due to each. In this case we must employ a further Inductive Method, called by Mr Mill the **Method of Residues**, and thus stated in his **Fourth Canon :—**

"Subduct from any phenomenon such part as is known by previous inductions to be the effect of certain antecedents, and the residue of the phenomenon is the effect of the remaining antecedents."

If we know that the joint effect *a*, *b*, *c* is due to the causes *A*, *B*, and *C*, and can prove that *a* is due to *A* and *b* to *B*, it follows that *c* must be due to *C*. There cannot be a simpler case of this than ascertaining the exact weight of any commodity in a cart by weighing the cart and load, and then subtracting the tare or weight of the cart alone, which had been previously ascertained. We can thus too ascertain how much of the spring tides is due to the attraction of the sun, provided we have previously determined the height of the tide due to the moon, which will be about the average height of the tides during the whole lunar month. Then subtracting the moon's tide the remainder is the sun's tide.

Newton employed this method in a beautiful experiment to determine the elasticity of substances by allowing balls made of the substances to swing against each other, and then observing how far they rebounded compared with their original fall. But the loss of motion is due partly to imperfect elasticity and partly to the resistance of the air. He determined the amount of the latter effect in the simplest manner by allowing the balls to swing without striking each other, and observing how much each vibration was less than the last. In this way he was enabled easily to calculate the quantity that must be subtracted for the resistance of the air.

It is this method that we employ in making allowance for the errors or necessary corrections in observations. Few thermometers are quite correct; but if we put a thermometer into melting snow, which has exactly the temperature of 0^0 Centigrade, or 32^0 Fahr., we can observe exactly how much below or above the true po'nt the mercury stands, and this will indicate how much we ought to add or subtract from readings of the thermometer to make them correct. The height of the barometer is affected by several causes besides the variation of the pressure of the air. It is decreased by the capillary repulsion between the glass tube and the mercury; it is increased by the expansion of the mercury by heat, if the temperature be above 32° Fahr.; and it may be increased or decreased by any error in the length of the measure employed to determine the height. In an accurate observation all these effects are calculated and allowed for in the final result.

In chemical analysis this method is constantly employed to determine the proportional weight of substances which combine together. Thus the composition of water is ascertained by taking a known weight of oxide of copper, passing hydrogen over it in a heated tube, and condensing the water produced in a tube containing sulphuric acid. If we subtract the original weight of the condensing tube from its final weight we learn how much water is produced; the quantity of oxygen in it is found by subtracting the final weight of the oxide of copper from its original weight. If we then subtract the weight of the oxygen from that of the water we learn the weight of the hydrogen, which we have combined with the oxygen. When the experiment is very carefully performed, as described in Dr Roscoe's *Lessons in Elementary Chemistry*, (p. 38), we find that 88·89 parts by weight of oxygen unite with 11·11 parts of hydrogen to form 100 parts of water.

In all sciences which allow of measurement of quantities this method is employed, but more especially in astronomy, the most exact of all the sciences. Almost all the causes and effects in astronomy have been found out as residual phenomena, that is, by calculating the effects of all known attractions upon a planet or satellite, and then observing how far it is from the place thus predicted. When this was very carefully done in the case of Uranus, it was still found that the planet was sometimes before and sometimes behind its true place. This residual effect pointed to the existence of some cause of attraction not then known, but which was in consequence soon discovered in the shape of the planet Neptune. The motions of several comets have in this way been calculated, but it is observed that they return each time a little later than they ought. This retardation points to the existence of some obstructive power in the space passed through, the nature of which is not yet understood.

> Mill's *System of Logic*, Book iii. Chap. 10, *Of the Plurality of Causes; and of the Intermixture of Effects.*

LESSON XXX.

EMPIRICAL AND DEDUCTIVE METHODS.

WE have hitherto treated of Deduction and Induction as if they were entirely separate and independent methods. In reality they are frequently blended or employed alternately in the pursuit of truth; and it may be said that all the more important and extensive investigations of science rely upon one as much as upon the other. It is probably the greatest merit in Mr Mill's logical writings that he points out the entire insufficiency of what is called the Baconian Method to detect the more obscure and difficult laws of nature. Bacon advised that we should always begin by collecting facts, classifying them according to their agreement and difference, and gradually gathering from them laws of greater and greater generality. He protested altogether against "anticipating nature," that is, forming our own hypotheses and theories as to what the laws of nature probably are, and he seemed to think that systematic arrangement of facts would take the place of all other methods. The reader will soon see that the progress of Science has not confirmed his opinions.

When a law of nature is ascertained purely by induction from certain observations or experiments, and has no other guarantee for its truth, it is said to be an **empirical law.** As Mr Mill says, "Scientific inquirers give the name of Empirical Laws to uniformities which observation or experiment has shown to exist, but on which they hesitate to rely in cases varying much from those which have been actually observed, for want of seeing any reason *why* such a law should exist." The name is derived from the Greek word ἐμπειρία, meaning experience or trial. Instances of such laws are abundant. We learn empirically that a certain strong yellow colour at sunset, or an unusual clearness in the air, portends rain ; that a quick pulse indicates fever ; that horned animals are always ruminants ; that quinine affects beneficially the nervous system and the health of the body generally ; that strychnine has a terrible effect of the opposite nature : all these are known to be true by repeated observation, but we can give no other reason for their being true, that is, we cannot bring them into harmony with any other scientific facts ; nor could we at all have deduced them or anticipated them on the ground of previous knowledge. The connection between the sun's spots, magnetic storms, auroras, and the motions of the planets mentioned in the last Lesson, is perhaps the most remarkable known instance of an empirical induction ; for no hint has yet been given of the way in which these magnetic influences are exerted throughout the vast dimensions of the planetary system. The qualities of the several alloys of metals are also good instances of empirical knowledge. No one can tell before mixing two or three metals for the first time in any given proportions what the qualities of the mixture will be—that brass should be both harder and more ductile than either of its constituents, copper and zinc; that copper alloyed with the very soft metal tin should make hard and sonorous bell-metal; that a certain mixture of lead, bismuth, tin and cadmium, should melt with a temperature (65° cent.) far below that of boiling water*.

However useful may be empirical knowledge, it is yet of slight importance compared with the well-connected and perfectly explained body of knowledge which constitutes an advanced and deductive science. It is in fact in proportion as a science becomes deductive, and enables us to grasp more and more apparently unconnected facts under the same law, that it becomes perfect. He who knows exactly why a thing happens, will also know exactly in what cases it will happen, and what difference in the circumstances will prevent the event from happening. Take for instance the simple effect of hot water in cracking glass. This is usually learnt empirically. Most people have a confused idea that hot water has a natural and inevitable tendency to break glass, and that thin glass, being more fragile than other glass, will be more easily broken by hot water. Physical science, however, gives a very clear reason for the effect, by showing that it is only one case of the general tendency of heat to expand substances. The crack is caused by the successful effort of the heated glass to expand in spite of the colder glass with which it is connected. But then we shall see at once that the same will not be true of thin glass vessels; the heat will pass so quickly through that the glass will be nearly equally heated; and accordingly chemists habitually use thin uniform glass vessels to hold or boil hot liquids without fear of the fractures which would be sure to take place in thick glass vessels or bottles.

The history of science would show conclusively that

* Roscoe's *Lessons in Elementary Chemistry*, p. 175.

deduction was the clue to all the greatest discoveries. Newton, after Galileo the chief founder of experimental philosophy, possessed beyond all question the greatest power of deductive thought which has ever been enjoyed by man. It is striking indeed to compare his results in optics with those in chemistry or alchemy. It is not generally known that Newton was really an alchemist, and spent days and nights in constant experiments in his laboratory, trying to discover the secret by which metals could be transmuted into gold. But in these researches all was purely empirical, and he had no clue to guide him to successful experiments. A few happy guesses given in his celebrated Queries are all the result of this labour. But in the science of Optics it was quite otherwise; here he grasped general laws, and every experiment only led him to devise and anticipate the results of several others, each more beautiful than the last. Thus he was enabled to establish beyond all doubt the foundations of the science of the Spectrum, now bearing such wonderful results. Some persons may suppose that Newton, living shortly after Bacon, adopted the Baconian method, but I believe that there is no reference to Bacon in Newton's works; and it is certain that he did not employ the method of Bacon. The *Principia*, though containing constant appeals to experiment and observation, is nevertheless the result of a constant and sustained effort of deductive mathematical reasoning.

What Mr Mill has called the **Deductive Method**, but which I think might be more appropriately called the **Combined** or **Complete Method**, consists in the alternate use of induction and deduction. It may be said to have three steps, as follows:—

1. Direct Induction.
2. Deduction, or, as Mr Mill calls it, Ratiocination.
3. Verification.

The first process consists in such a rough and simple appeal to experience as may give us a glimpse of the laws which operate, without being sufficient to establish their truth. Assuming them as provisionally true, we then proceed to argue to their effects in other cases, and a further appeal to experience either verifies or negatives the truth of the laws assumed. There are, in short, two appeals to experience connected by the intermediate use of reasoning. Newton, for instance, having passed a ray of sun-light through a glass prism found that it was spread out into a series of colours resembling those of the rainbow. He adopted the theory that white light was actually composed of a mixture of different coloured lights, which became separated in passing through the prism. He saw that if this were true, and he were to pass an isolated ray of the spectrum, for instance, the yellow ray, through a second prism, it ought not to be again broken up into different colours, but should remain yellow whatever was afterwards done with it. On trial he found this to be the case, and afterwards devised a succession of similar confirmatory experiments which verified his theory beyond all possible doubt.

It was no mere accident that led Pascal to have a barometer carried up to the top of the mountain Puy de Dôme in France. Galileo, indeed, became acquainted by accident with the fact that water will not rise in an ordinary pump more than 33 feet, and was thus led to assert that the limited weight of the atmosphere caused it to rise. Torricelli, reasoning from this theory, saw that mercury, which is fourteen times as heavy as water, should not rise more than one-fourteenth part of the distance, or about 29 or 30 inches. The experiment being tried verified the theory. It was the genius of Pascal, however, which saw that the experiment required to be varied in another way by carrying the mercurial barome-

ter to the top of a mountain.   If the weight of the atmosphere were really the cause of the suspension of the mercury, it ought to stand lowei on the mountain than below,
because only the higher parts of the atmosphere pressed
upon the mountain.   The success of the experiment completely verified the original hypothesis.   The progress of
the experimental sciences mainly depends upon the mode
in which one experiment thus leads to others, and dis-
closes new facts, which would in all probability have never
come under our notice had we confined ourselves to the
purely Baconian method of collecting the facts first and
performing induction afterwards.

The greatest result of the deductive method is no less
than the **theory of gravitation,** which makes a perfect
instance of its procedure.   In this case the preliminary
induction consisted, we may suppose, in the celebrated
fall of the apple, which occurred while Newton was sitting
in an orchard during his retirement from London, on
account of the Great Plague.   The fall of the apple, we
are told, led Newton to reflect that there must be a power
tending to draw bodies towards the earth, and he asked
himself the question why the moon did not on that account
fall upon the earth.   The Lancashire astronomer Horrocks
suggested to his mind another fact, namely, that when a
stone is whirled round attached to a string, it exerts a
force upon the string, often called centrifugal force.   Horrocks remarked that the planets in revolving round the
sun must tend in a similar way to fly off from the centre.
Newton was acquainted with Horrocks' views, and was
thus possibly led to suppose that the earth's attractive
force might exactly neutralise the moon's centrifugal
tendency, so as to maintain that satellite in constant
rotation.

But it happened that the world was in possession of
certain empirical laws concerning the motions of the pla-

nets, without which Newton could scarcely have proceeded further. Kepler had passed a lifetime in observing the heavenly bodies, and forming hypotheses to explain their motions. In general his ideas were wild and unfounded, but the labours of a lifetime were rewarded in the establishment of the three laws which bear his name, and describe the nature of the orbits traversed by the planets, and the relation between the size of such orbit and the time required by the planet to traverse it. Newton was able to show by geometrical reasoning that if one body revolved round another attracted towards it by a force decreasing as the square of the distance increases, it would necessarily describe an orbit of which Kepler's laws would be true, and which would therefore exactly resemble the orbits of the planets. Here was a partial verification of his theory by appeal to the results of experience. But several other philosophers had gone so far in the investigation of the subject. It is Newton's chief claim to honour, that he carried on his deductions and verifications until he attained complete demonstration. To do this it was necessary first of all to show that the moon actually does fall towards the earth just as rapidly as a stone would if it were in the same circumstances. Using the best information then attainable as to the distance of the moon, Newton calculated that the moon falls through the space of 13 feet in one minute, but that a stone, if elevated so high, would fall through 15 feet. Most men would have considered this approach to coincidence as a proof of his theory, but Newton's love of certain truth rendered him different even from most philosophers, and the discrepancy caused him to lay " aside at that time any further thoughts of this matter."

It was not till many years afterwards (probably 15 or 16) that Newton, hearing of some more exact data from which he could calculate the distance of the moon,

was able to explain the discrepancy. His theory of gravitation was then verified so far as the moon was concerned; but this was to him only the beginning of a long
course of deductive calculations, each ending in a verification. If the earth and moon attract each other, and also
the sun and the earth, similarly there is no reason why
the sun and moon should not attract each other. Newton
followed out the consequences of this inference, and showed
that the moon would not move as if attracted by the
earth only, but sometimes faster and sometimes slower.
Comparisons with Flamsteed's observations of the moon
showed that such was the case. Newton argued again,
that as the waters of the ocean are not rigidly attached to
the earth, they might attract the moon, and be attracted
in return, independently of the rest of the earth. Certain
daily motions would then be caused thereby exactly
resembling the tides, and there were the tides to verify
the fact. It was the almost superhuman power with
which he traced out geometrically the consequences of his
theory, and submitted them to repeated comparison with
experience, which constitutes his preeminence over all
philosophers.

What he began has been going on ever since. The
places of the moon and planets are calculated for each
day on the assumption of the absolute truth of Newton's
law of gravitation. Every night their places are observed
as far as possible at Greenwich or some other observatory;
comparison of the observed with the predicted place is
always in some degree erroneous, and if coincident would
be so only by accident. The theory is never proved completely true, and never can be; but the more accurately the
results of the theory are calculated, and the more perfect
the instruments of the astronomer are rendered, the more
close is the correspondence. Thus the rude observations
of Kepler and the few slight facts which worked on New-

ton's mind, were the foundation of a theory which yielded indefinite means of anticipating new facts, and by constant verification, as far as human accuracy can go, has been placed beyond all reasonable doubt.

Were space available it might be shown that all other great theories have followed nearly the same course. The undulatory theory of sound was in fact almost verified by Newton himself, though when he calculated from it the velocity of sound there was again a discrepancy, which only subsequent investigation could explain. This theory no doubt suggested the corresponding theory of light, which when followed out by Young, Fresnel, and others, always gave results which were ultimately in harmony with observation. It even enabled mathematicians to anticipate results which the most ardent imagination could hardly have guessed, and which mere haphazard experiment might never have revealed. Dalton's laws of equivalent proportions in chemistry, if not his atomic theory, were founded on experiments made with the simplest and rudest apparatus, but results deduced from them are daily verified in the nicest processes of modern chemical analysis. The still more modern theory of the Conservation of Energy, which had been vaguely anticipated by Bacon, Rumford, Montgolfier, Seguin, Mayer and possibly others, was by Mr Joule brought to the test of experimental verification in some of the most beautiful and decisive experiments which are on record. It will be long before scientific men shall have traced out all the consequences of this grand principle, but its correspondence with fact already places it far beyond doubt.

It will now be apparent, I think, that though observation and induction must ever be the ground of all certain knowledge of nature, their unaided employment could never have led to the results of modern science. He who merely collects and digests facts will seldom acquire a comprehension of their laws. He who frames a theory and is content with his own deductions from it, like Descartes, will only surprise the world with his misused genius ; but the best student of science is he who with a copious store of theories and fancies has the highest power of foreseeing their consequences, the greatest diligence in comparing them with undoubted facts, and the greatest candour in confessing the ninety-nine mistakes he has made in reaching the one true law of nature.

LESSON XXXI.

EXPLANATION, TENDENCY, HYPOTHESIS, THEORY, AND FACT.

IN the preceding Lessons I have used several expressions of which the meaning has not been defined. It will now be convenient to exemplify the use of these terms, and to arrive as far as possible at a clear understanding of their proper meanings.

Explanation is literally the making plain or clear, so that there shall be nothing uneven or obscure to interrupt our view. **Scientific explanation** consists in harmonizing fact with fact, or fact with law, or law with law, so that we may see them both to be cases of one uniform law of causation. If we hear of a great earthquake in some part of the world and subsequently hear that a neighbouring volcano has broken out, we say that the earthquake is thus partially explained. The eruption shows that there were great forces operating beneath the earth's surface, and the earthquake is obviously an effect of such causes. The scratches which may be plainly seen upon the surface of rocks in certain parts of Wales and Cumberland, are explained by the former existence of glaciers in those mountains; the scratches exactly harmonize with the effects of glaciers now existing in Switzerland, Greenland, and elsewhere. These may be considered **ex-planations of fact by fact.**

A fact may also be explained by a general law of nature, that is the cause and mode of its production may be pointed out and shown to be the same as operates in many apparently different cases. Thus the cracking of glass by heat was explained (p. 257) as one result of the universal law that heat increases the dimensions of solid bodies. The trade-winds are explained as one case of the general tendency of warm air to rise and be displaced by cold and dense air. The very same simple laws of heat and mechanics which cause a draught to flow up a chimney when there is a fire below, cause winds to blow from each hemisphere towards the equator. At the same time the easterly direction from which the winds come is explained by the simplest laws of motion; for as the earth rotates from west to east, and moves much more rapidly at the equator than nearer the poles, the air tends to preserve its slower rate of motion, and the earth near the equator moving under it occasions an apparent motion of the wind from east to west.

There are, according to Mr Mill, three distinct ways in which one law may be explained by other laws, or brought into harmony with them.

The first is the case where there are really two or more separate causes in action, the results of which are combined or added together, homogeneously. As was before explained, **homogeneous intermixture of effects** (p. 252) means that the joint effect is simply the sum of the separate effects, and is of the same kind with them. Our last example of the trade-winds really comes under this case, for we find that there is one law or tendency which causes winds to blow from the arctic regions towards the equator, and a second tendency which causes then to blow from east to west. These tendencies are combined together, and cause the trade-winds to blow from the North-East in the northern hemisphere, and from the South-East in the southern hemisphere. The law according to which the temperature of the air is governed in any part of the earth is a very complicated one, depending partly on the law by which the sun's heating power is governed, partly on the power of the earth to radiate the heat away into space, but even more perhaps on the effect of currents of air or water in bringing warmth or carrying it away. The path of a cannon-ball or other projectile is determined by the joint action of several laws; firstly, the simple law of motion, by which any moving body tends to move onward at an uniform rate in a straight line; secondly, the law of gravity, which continually deflects the body towards the earth's surface; thirdly, the resistance of the air, which tends to diminish its velocity.

The reader will perhaps have noticed the frequent use of the word **tendency**, and I have repeatedly spoken of a cause as tending to produce its effect. If the joint and homogeneous action of causes has been clearly explained, it will now be clear that a tendency means a cause which will produce an effect unless there be opposite causes, which, in combination with it, counteract and disguise that effect. Thus when we throw a stone into the air the attractive power of the earth tends to make it fall, but the upward motion we have impressed upon it disguises the result for a certain time. The interminable revolving motion of the moon round the earth is the result of two balanced tendencies, that towards the earth, and that to proceed onward in a straight line. The laws of motion and gravity are such that this balance must always be preserved; if the moon by any cause were brought nearer to the earth its tendency to fly off would be increased, and would exceed the effect of gravity until it had regained its proper distance. *A tendency then is a cause which may or may not be counteracted.*

In the second case of explanation an effect is shown to be due, not to the supposed cause directly, but to an **intermediate effect of that cause.** Instead of *A* being the cause of *C*, it is found that *A* is the cause of *B*, and *B* the cause of *C*, so that *B* constitutes an **intermediate link.** This explanation may seem to increase the complexity of the matter, but it really simplifies it; for the connection of *A* with *B* may be a case of a familiar and simple law, and so may that of *B* with *C*; whereas the law that *A* produces *C* may be purely empirical and apparently out of harmony with everything else. Thus in lightning it seems as if electricity had the power of creating a loud explosion; but in reality electricity only produces heat, and it is the heat which occasions sound by suddenly expanding the air. Thus thunder comes into harmony with the sound of artillery, which is also occasioned by the sudden expansion of the heated gases emitted by the powder. When chlorine was discovered it was soon found to have a strong power of bleaching, and at the present day almost all bleaching is done by chlorine instead of the sun, as formerly. Inquiry showed however that it was not really the chlorine which destroyed colour, but that oxygen is the intermediate and active agent. Chlorine decomposes water, and taking the hydrogen leaves the oxygen in a state of great activity and ready to destroy the organic colouring matter. Thus a number of facts are harmonized; we learn why dry chlorine does not bleach, and why there are several other substances which resemble chlorine in its bleaching power, for instance, ozone, peroxide of hydrogen, sulphurous acid, and a peculiar oxide of vanadium, lately discovered by Dr Roscoe. It would be impossible to understand the effect at all unless we knew that it is probably due to active oxygen or ozone in all the cases, even in the old method of bleaching by exposure to the sun *.

The third and much more important case of explanation is where one law is shown to be **a case of a more general law.** As was explained in Lesson XXIV. we naturally discover the less general first, and gradually penetrate to the more simple but profound secrets of nature. It has often been found that scientific men were in possession of several well-known laws without perceiving the bond which connected them together. Men, for instance, had long known that all heavy bodies tended to fall towards the earth, and before the time of Newton it was known to Hooke, Huyghens, and others, that some force probably connected the earth with the sun and moon. It was Newton, however, who clearly brought these and many other facts under one general law, so that each fact or less general law throws light upon every other.

The science of Electricity now harmonizes a vast series of partial laws and facts between which it was a truly difficult task to discover any resemblance. The chief properties of the magnet had been fairly known since the time of Gilbert, the physician of Queen Elizabeth ; common frictional electricity was carefully studied by Otto von Guericke, Epinus, Coulomb, and others ; Galvanism was elaborately investigated almost as soon as Galvani and Volta discovered the fact that the chemical action of one substance on another may produce electricity. In the early part of this century there were three distinct sciences, Magnetism, Electricity and Galvanism ; now there is but one science. Oersted of Copenhagen gave in 1819 the first link between them, by pointing out that an electric current may cause movements in a compass-needle. Ampère and Faraday worked

* Watts' *Dictionary of Chemistry,* Vol. I. p. 601.

out the complicated relations of the three sciences, comprehending them finally in a wider science, which may be called Electro-magnetism, or we may perhaps conveniently generalize the name Electricity so as to comprehend all the phenomena connected with it.

A number of minor laws and detached facts are comprehended and explained in the theory now generally accepted, that heat, electricity, light, and in fact all the phenomena of nature, are but manifestations in different forms of one same kind of energy. The total amount of energy existing in the universe is held to be fixed and unalterable, like the quantity of matter ; sometimes it is disguised by affecting only the insensible molecules ; at other times it is seen to produce palpable mechanical effects, as in the fall of a stone, or the expansion of steam. Now it had been previously known, ever since the time of the Greeks, that a simple lever, although greatly altering the character of force by making its action slower or faster, does not alter its amount, because the more intense the force the slower and more limited is its action. In modern times a similar truth was proved of every kind of machine ; and it was recognised that, apart from friction, no kind of mechanism either creates or destroys energy. It had been independently recognised that electricity produced in the galvanic battery was exactly proportional to the amount of chemical action, and that almost any one of the forces named could be converted into any one of the others. All such facts are now comprehended under one general theory, the details of which are being gradually rendered more certain and accurate, but the main principle of which is that a certain amount of mechanical energy is equal to a certain amount of heat, a certain amount of electricity, of chemical action, or even of muscular exertion.

The word hypothesis is much used in connection with

the subject we are discussing, and its meaning must be considered. It is derived from the Greek words ὑπό, *under*, and θέσις, *placing*, and is therefore exactly synonymous with the Latin word *suppositio*, a placing under, whence our common word *supposition*. It appears to mean in science the imagining of some thing, force or cause, which underlies the phenomena we are examining, and is the agent in their production without being capable of direct observation. In making a hypothesis we assert the existence of a cause on the ground of the effects observed, and the probability of its existence depends upon the number of diverse facts or partial laws that we are thus enabled to explain or reduce to harmony. To be of any value at all a hypothesis must harmonize at least two different facts. If we account for the effects of opium by saying with Molière that it possesses a *dormitive power*, or say that the magnet attracts because it has a *magnetic power*, every one can see that we gain nothing. We know neither more nor less about the dormitive or magnetic power than we do about opium or the magnet. But if we suppose the magnet to attract because it is occupied by circulating currents of electricity the hypothesis may seem a very improbable one, but is valid, because we thus draw a certain analogy between a magnet and a coil of wire conveying electricity. Such a coil of wire attracts other coils exactly in the way that one magnet attracts another ; so that this hypothesis enables us to harmonize several different facts. The existence of intense heat in the interior of the earth is hypothetical in so far as regards the impossibility of actually seeing and measuring the heat directly, but it harmonizes so many facts derived from different sources that we can hardly doubt its existence. Thus the occurrence of hot springs and volcanoes are some facts in its favour, though they might be explained on other grounds ; the empirical law that the heat increases as we sink mines in any part of the earth's surface is stronger evidence. The intensely heated condition of the sun and other stars is strongly confirmatory as showing that other bodies do exist in the supposed condition of the earth's interior. The cool state of the earth's surface is perfectly consistent with its comparatively small size and the known facts and laws concerning the conduction and radiation of heat. And the more we learn concerning the way in which the sun's heat is supplied by the fall of meteoric matter, the more it is probable that the earth may have been intensely heated like the sun at some former time, although for an immense period it has been growing slowly colder. A supposition coinciding with so many facts, laws, and other probable hypotheses, almost ceases to be hypothetical, and its high probability causes it to be regarded as a known fact.

Provided it is consistent with the laws of thought there is nothing that we may not have to accept as a probable hypothesis, however difficult it may be to conceive and understand. The force of gravity is hypothetical in so far that we know it only by its effects upon the motions of bodies. Its decrease at a distance harmonizes exactly indeed with the way in which light, sound, electric or magnetic attractions, and in fact all influences which emanate from a point and spread through space, decrease ; hence it is probable that the law of the inverse square is absolutely true. But in other respects gravity is strongly opposed to all our ideas. If sound could travel to the sun as rapidly as in the earth's atmosphere it would require nearly fourteen years to reach its destination ; were the sun and earth united by a solid continuous bar of iron, a strong pull at one end would not be felt at the other until nearly three years had passed. Light indeed comes from the sun in rather more than eight minutes ; but what are we to think of the force of gravity, which appears to reach the sun in an instant—so short that no calculations have yet been able to detect any interval at all? In fact there seems some reason to suppose that gravity is felt instantaneously throughout the immeasurable regions of space.

The undulatory hypothesis of light presents features equally extraordinary and inconceivable. That light does consist of minute but excessively rapid vibrations of something occupying space, is almost certain, because of the great harmony which this hypothesis introduces into the exceedingly various and complicated phenomena of light, and the explanation which it affords of the analogy of light to sound. It is difficult indeed to imagine that anything can oscillate so rapidly as to strike the retina of the eye 831,479,000,000,000 in one second, as must be the case with violet light according to this hypothesis. But this is nothing to the difficulty of imagining space to be filled with solid ether of extreme rigidity and elasticity, but which nevertheless offers no appreciable resistance to the passage through it of ordinary matter, and does not itself possess any gravity *. It has been asserted indeed that the retardation in the return of comets is due to friction against this ether, and Mr Balfour Stewart believes he has produced heat by friction of a metallic disc against the ether in a vacuum. Should these assertions prove to be true we have new facts in harmony with the theory of light, which would thereby become less hypothetical than before.

There is no difficulty now in perceiving the part which hypothesis plays in the **deductive method** of scientific investigation considered in the last lesson. The preliminary induction is replaced more or less completely by

* See Sir John Herschel's *Familiar Lectures,* p. 315, &c.

imagining the existence of agents which we think adequate to produce the known effects in question. If it is our object to explain the causes of ebbing and flowing wells, which occur in many parts of the world, we cannot possibly proceed by first exploring the interior of the earth, until we can discover the source of a spring, and observe its circumstances. We are obliged to imagine cavities and channels of various forms, until we conceive such an apparatus as will, in accordance with known laws of hydrostatics, occasion the irregular flowing of water in the way observed. If we can show that cavities of a particular form will produce that effect, and can think of no other mode in which it could be produced, the hypo-thesis becomes established as almost a certain fact.

It is the same with any great hypothesis like that of the theory of light. We have no means of directly observing and measuring the qualities of the ether which is the medium of light. All we know about this ether at present is derived from the observed phenomena of light. Hence we are driven to invent something and endow it with qualities from which we may calculate, according to some of the principles of mechanics, the effect to be expected ; and finding that these effects may be made to harmonize with those actually observed, we depend upon this coinci-dence to prove the existence of the ether. The truth of a hypothesis thus altogether depends upon subsequent verification and accordance with observed facts. To invent hypotheses which cannot thus be verified, or to invent them and then neglect the verification, leads to no result at all, or to fallacy. But when the verification is careful and complete no reproach can be brought against the employment of hypothesis. It becomes, perhaps, as certain as any other mode of investigation, and is at any rate indispensable. There was, in fact, little truth or reason in Newton's celebrated protest against the use of hypothesis—"Hypotheses non fingo." The fact is that as his theory of gravitation rested upon the greatest and most successful of hypotheses, so his views of the material nature of light and the causes of its peculiar phenomena involved a false hypothesis, which has long since been completely disproved.

The word **theory** has constantly been used in the last few lessons, and deserves some examination. It comes from the Greek θεωρία, meaning contemplation, reflection or speculation; but this gives us little clue to its modern use. In reality the word is highly ambiguous, being sometimes used as equivalent to hypothesis, at other times as equivalent to general law or truth. When people form theories concerning comets, the sun, the cause of earthquakes, &c., they imagine a great many things which may or may not exist; such theories are really complicated hypotheses, and should be so called. In this sense there are two theories of electricity, one of which supposes the existence of a single fluid which accumulates in some places and has then a tendency to discharge itself towards places where there is a deficiency, just as water always tends to find its level; the other supposes the existence of two fluids which are commonly united, but when separated tend to rush back into union again. These so-called theories are really hypotheses, because we have no independent evidence of the existence of any fluid, and it is now almost certain that there is no such thing. The atomic theory, again, is really a hypothesis suggested by Dalton to explain the remarkable laws which he detected in the proportions of chemical elements which combine together. It is a valid hypothesis in so far as it does really explain the fixedness of the quantities which combine; but it is purely hypothetical as regards the shapes, properties or absolute magnitudes of the atoms, because we have no facts which it can harmonise in these respects, and no apparent means of gaining them.

In another and more proper sense theory is opposed to practice, just as the general is opposed to the particular. The theory of gravitation means all the more general laws of motion and attraction on which Newton founded his system of the Universe. We may know what those laws are without being able to determine the place of a planet or make any practical use of them; the particular results must be calculated out by skilful astronomers before navigators, travellers or others can make practical use of them in the determination of the latitude or longitude. When we speak of the mathematical theory of sound, the lunar theory, the theory of the tides, the word is employed without any special reference to hypothesis, and is merely equivalent to general knowledge or science, implying the possession of a complete series of general and accurate laws, but in no way distinguishing them from accurate knowledge in general. When a word is really used in an equivocal manner like theory, it is not desirable to attempt to give it an accurate definition which would be imaginary and artificial.

The word **fact** is used very often in this as in most books, and demands a few remarks. It is derived from *factum*, the past participle of *facere*, to do, and would thus mean *something which is done*, an act, or deed; but the meaning is evidently greatly extended by analogy. We usually oppose to each other **fact** and **theory**, but just as theory seems to have two ambiguous meanings, so I believe that fact is ambiguous. Sometimes it means what is certain and known by the evidence of the senses, as opposed to what is known only probably by hypothesis and inference; at other times it is contrasted to a general law, and is equivalent to a particular instance or case. A law of great generality may often be as certain and true especially in mathematics, as the particular facts coming under it, so that the contrast must in this case be that between the general and particular. We often use the word too in common life, as merely equivalent to *truth;* thus we might say, " It is a fact that the primary laws of thought are the foundation of reasoning." In short, as theory means ambiguously what is hypothetical, general, abstract or uncertain, so fact is equally ambiguous, and means confusedly what is intuitively known, particular, concrete or certain.

Mill's *System of Logic,* Book III. Chapters 12, 13 and 14, *Of Explanation, and Hypothesis.*

LESSON XXXII.

CLASSIFICATION, AND ABSTRACTION.

IN an earlier Lesson, upon the subject of the Predicables, we considered the doctrine of classification as it was treated by logicians many centuries ago. The progress of science, however, during the last two centuries has caused great attention to be given to the true principles on which we can arrange a great multitude of diverse objects in order, and we have to consider what are the characteristics of a natural and perfect system of classification.

It may be said, indeed, that the subject we are treating is coextensive with the science of logic. All thought, all reasoning, so far as it deals with general names or general notions, may be said to consist in classification. Every common or general name is the name of a class, and every name of a class is a common name. "Metal" is the name of one class of substances so often used in our syllogistic examples; "Element" of another class, of which the former class is part. Reasoning has been plausibly represented to consist in affirming of the parts of a class whatever may be affirmed of the whole. Every law of nature which we arrive at enables us to classify together a number of facts, and it would hardly be too much to define logic as the theory of classification.

Here we deal, however, with that more conscious and distinct arrangement of objects or notions, which is especially employed in the natural sciences, such as Botany, Zoology, Mineralogy and Palæontology.

The derivation of the word class is somewhat curious. In ancient Rome it was the practice to summon the whole people together at certain periods, and this ceremony was known as a *clāsis*, from the Greek κλάσις, or κλῆσις, derived from καλέω, to call together. Servius Tullius is said to have divided the people into six orders, according to the amount of tribute they could pay, and these orders were not unnaturally called the *classes* of the people. Hence the name came by degrees to be applied to any organized body of people, such as an army; thence it was transferred to a fleet of vessels as marshalled in a fixed order, and was finally extended by analogy to any collection of objects carefully arranged. When, however, we now speak of the lower or higher classes of the people it is curious that we are restoring the word very nearly to its original meaning.

Classification may perhaps be best defined as *the arrangement of things, or our notions of them, according to their resemblances or identities.* Every class should so be constituted as to contain objects exactly resembling each other in certain definite qualities, which are stated in the definition of the class. The more numerous and extensive the resemblances which are thus indicated by any system of classes, the more perfect and useful must that system be considered.

Mr Mill thus describes his view of the meaning—"Classification is a contrivance for the best possible ordering of the ideas of objects in our minds; for causing the ideas to accompany or succeed one another in such a way as shall give us the greatest command over our knowledge already acquired, and lead most directly to the acquisition of more. The general problem of classification, in reference to these purposes may be stated as follows: To provide that things shall be thought of in such groups, and those groups in such an order, as will best conduce to the remembrance, and to the ascertainment of their laws."

A collection of objects may generally be classified in an indefinite number of ways. Any quality which is possessed by some and not by others may be taken as the first difference, and the groups thus distinguished may be subdivided in succession by any other qualities taken at will. Thus a library of books might be arranged, (1) according to their size, (2) according to the language in which they are written, (3) according to the alphabetic order of their authors' names, (4) according to their subjects; and in various other ways. In large libraries and in catalogues such modes of arrangement are adopted and variously combined. Each different arrangement presents some peculiar convenience, and that mode must be selected which best meets the especial purpose of the library or catalogue. The population of a kingdom, again, may be classified in an almost endless number of ways with regard to different purposes or sciences. The population of the United Kingdom may be divided according to their place of birth, as English, Welsh, Scotch, Irish, colonial-born, and aliens. The ethnographer would divide them into Anglo-Saxons, Cymri, Gaels, Picts,

Scandinavians, &c. The statist arranges them according to age; to condition, as married, unmarried, widowed,
&c.; to state of body, as able, incapacitated, blind, im-
becile. The political economist regards the innumerable
trades which are carried on, and classifies them in a
complex manner. The lawyer again treats every one as a
minor, an adult, a feme sole, a feme couverte, a guardian,
ward, trustee, felon, and so on.

In the natural world, again, we may make various
classifications. Plants may be arranged according to the
country from which they are derived; the kind of place
or habitat in which they flourish; the time they live, as
annual, biennial, perennial; their size, as herbs, shrubs,
trees; their properties, as esculents, drugs, or poisons:
all these are distinct from the classifications which the
botanist devises' to represent the natural affinities or
relationships of plants. It is thus evident that in making
a classification we have no one fixed method which can
be ascertained by rule, but that an indefinite number of
choices or alternatives are usually open to us. Logic
cannot in such cases do much; and it is really the work
of the special sciences to investigate the character of the
classification required. All that logic can do is to point
out certain general requirements and principles.

The first requisite of a good classification is, that it
shall be **appropriate to the purpose in hand**; that is to
say, the points of resemblance selected to form the leading
classes shall be those of importance to the practical use
of the classification. All those things must be arranged
together which require to be treated alike, and those
things must be separated which require to be treated
separately. Thus a lawyer has no need to classify persons according to the counties of England they were born
in, because the law is the same independently of counties;
but so far as a Scotchman, a Manx man, or an alien, is

under different laws from the English born man, we shall require to classify them apart. A gardener is quite right in classifying plants as annuals, biennials, perennials; as herbs, shrubs, trees; as evergreen and deciduous; or according to the soil, temperature and other circumstances which affect them, because these are points which must guide him in treating some differently from others.

Another and, in a scientific point of view, the most important requisite of a good classification, is that **it shall enable the greatest possible number of general assertions to be made.** This is the criterion, as stated by Dr Whewell, which distinguishes a natural from an artificial system of classification, and we must carefully dwell upon its meaning. It will be apparent that a good classification is more than a mere orderly arrangement; it involves a process of induction which will bring to light all the more general relations which exist between the things classified. An arrangement of books will generally be artificial; the octavo volumes will not have any common character except being of an octavo size. An alphabetical arrange-ment of names again is exceedingly appropriate and convenient to many purposes, but is artificial because it allows of few or no general assertions. We cannot make any general assertion whatever about persons because their names happen to begin with an A or a B, a P or a W. Even those who agree in bearing the name Smith or Taylor or Robinson might be submitted to the inductive method of agreement without the discovery of any common circumstance which could be stated in a general proposition or law. It is true that if we investigated the antecedents of the Evanses and Joneses we should find them nearly all to be Welsh, and the Campbells to be Scotch, and those who bear a very peculiar name would often be found to descend from common ancestors. So far even an alphabetic arrangement embodies something that is natural in it, and enables general assertions to be made. Hardly any arrangement can be made, in fact, which will not indicate some vestiges of important relations and resemblances ; but what we want is a system which will reveal all the most important general truths.

For this purpose we must select as the ground of union those characters which carry with them most other characters. In Lesson XII. we considered the **proprium** as a quality which belongs to the whole of a class without forming part of the definition of the class. Now we ought to frame the definition of a class that it may contain as few characters as possible, but that as many other characters, properties, or *propria*, as possible, shall be attributable to the things contained in the class. Every one can see, for instance, that animals form one great group of beings, which have many characters in common, and that plants form another group. Animals have sensation, voluntary motion, consume carbonaceous food, and evolve carbonic acid, possess a stomach, and produce fat. Plants are devoid of sensation and voluntary motion, produce carbonaceous tissue, absorb carbonic acid, and evolve oxygen, possess no stomach, and produce starch. At one time it might have been thought that almost any of the characters named was a sufficient mark of the group to which a being belonged. Whatever had a stomach, was an animal ; whatever had not, was a plant ; whatever produced starch or evolved oxygen was called a plant ; whatever absorbed oxygen or produced fat was an animal. To the present day these statements remain generally true, so that we may make assertions in the form of the proposition U, that "all animals are all beings that evolve carbonic acid, and all plants are all beings that absorb carbonic acid." But in reality the exceptions are many, and increasing research makes it continually more apparent that there is no definite line to be drawn between animal and vegetable life. This, of course, is not a failure of logical science, but a fact of great significance concerning the things themselves.

In a classification of plants we meet again with most deep and natural distinctions between the great classes called Exogens, Endogens, and Acrogens. The latter have no true sexual flowers and seeds, are formed almost wholly of cellular tissue, and have an epidermis without cuticular pores. The former two classes have much in common; they have true flowers, woody tissue and cuticular pores, and hence may be united into one wider class, Vasculares. But exogens and endogens are also most strongly distinguished. Exogens have a stem or trunk consisting of distinct bark, pith, and wood in concentric layers, leaves with reticular veins, seeds with two seed-leaves and a naked radicle ; generally speaking, too, the parts of the flower are some multiple of two or five in number. Endogens, on the contrary, have no distinct bark, pith, and wood, no concentric layers, leaves with parallel veins, seeds with one seed-leaf, and a radicle not naked ; they have, too, the parts of the flower generally a multiple of three in number.

These are the very widest classes in what is called the **natural system of botanical arrangement**; but similar principles are observed in all its minor classes. The continual efforts of botanists are directed to bringing the great multitudes of plants together in species, genera, orders, classes, and in various intermediate groups, so that the members of each group shall have the greatest number of points of mutual resemblance and the fewest points of resemblance to members of other groups. Thus is best fulfilled the great purpose of classification, which reduces multiplicity to unity, and enables us **to infer of all the other members of a class what we know of any one member**, provided we distinguish properly between those

qualities which are likely or are known to belong to the
class, and those which are peculiar to the individual. It
is a necessary condition of correct classification, as remarked by Prof. Huxley, that the definition of a group
shall hold exactly true of all members of the group, and
not of the members of any other group. To carry out this
condition in the natural sciences is, however, very difficult,
because kinds of plants or animals are continually discovered which stand in an intermediate position between
classes which would otherwise be well distinguished.
Thus ferns much embarrass the fundamental division of
plants, because though they have no true flowers, and in
this and other respects agree with other acrogens, yet
they have abundance of woody fibre, which would entitle
them to rank with vasculares, the larger group of which
exogens and endogens are the subdivisions.

It may be remarked that the progress of chemistry is
rapidly rendering it a science of classification ; and in fact
the whole theory of chemical combination now depends
on a correct grouping of elements and compounds. Dr
Roscoe in his *Lessons in Elementary Chemistry* enu-
merates no less than eleven classes of metals, each class
having a number of properties in common. Thus the
metals of the alkalies, namely, Potassium, Sodium, Cæsium,
Rubidium, Lithium, form a remarkably natural class.
They are all soft, easily fusible, volatile at high temperatures ; they combine with great force with oxygen, decompose water at all temperatures, forming oxides which are
very soluble in water, and become powerfully caustic and
alkaline bodies from which water cannot be expelled by
heat. Their carbonates are soluble in water, and each
metal forms only one compound with chlorine.

The metals of the alkaline earths, Calcium, Strontium,
and Barium, also form a very natural class, distinguished
by the fact that their carbonates are insoluble in pure

water, but soluble in water containing carbonic acid in solution. The gold class contains the rare or valuable metals Gold, Platinum, Palladium, Rhodium, Ruthenium, Iridium, and Osmium, which are not acted on by nitric acid, and can only be dissolved by chlorine or the mixture of acids called *aqua regia*. The oxides can be reduced or deoxidised by simply heating them.

Natural classifications give us the deepest resemblances and relations, and may lead us ultimately to a knowledge of the way in which the varieties of things are produced. They are, therefore, essential to a true science, and may almost be said to constitute the framework of the science. Yet it does not follow that they are appropriate for all purposes. When our purpose is merely to recognise the name of a chemical element, a plant or an animal, its character as defined in a natural system would give us little or no assistance. The chemist does not detect potassium by getting it into the state of metal, and trying whether it would decompose water. He merely observes which, among all the compounds of potassium, have the best marked and most peculiar characters ; thus a compound of potassium, platinum, and chlorine is most distinctive or characteristic of the metal, and is generally used as a means of recognising it ; but a fine violet colour which potash gives to the flame of a lamp was also used as an indication of its presence long before the spectroscope was introduced to analyse such colours. An artificial classification of the elements is thus necessary to the detection of substances, and accordingly in any book on chemical analysis will be found arrangements of the elements according to characters of very minor importance, but which are selected on account of the ease and certainty with which they can be observed.

In Botany, again, the natural system of classification is far from being well suited for determining the name of a plant, because the classes are often defined by the form of minute parts of the seed, the arrangement of the seed-vessel, and other parts which it is usually difficult or sometimes impossible to examine. Accordingly botanists usually arrange their genera and species in the order of the natural system, but contrive a sort of key or artificial arrangement, in which the most simple and apparent characters, often called characteristics, are employed for the discrimination of the plants. The best arrangement of this kind as regards British plants is to be found in Bentham's *British Flora.* In reality the celebrated Linnæan arrangement of plants was intended by its author to serve in this way. Linnæus was too profound a philosopher to suppose that the numbers of stamens and pistils usually expressed the real relationships of plants. Many of his classes were really natural classes, but the stamens and pistils were selected as the general guide to the classes and orders, as being very plain and evident marks.

Closely connected with the process of classification is that of abstraction. To abstract is to separate the qualities common to all individuals of a group from the peculiarities of each individual. The notion " triangle " is the result of abstraction in so far as we can reason concerning triangles, without any regard to the particular size or shape of any one triangle. All classification implies abstraction, for in framing and defining the class I must separate the common qualities from the peculiarities. When I abstract, too, I form a general conception, or one which, generally speaking, embraces many objects. If, indeed, the quality abstracted is a peculiar property of the class, or one which belongs to the whole and not to any other objects, I may not increase the extent of the notion, so that Mr Herbert Spencer is, perhaps, right in holding that we can abstract without generalizing. We often use this word **generalization**, and the process may be defined as inferring of a whole class what we know only of a part. Whenever we regard the qualities of a thing as not confined to that thing only but as extended to other objects; when, in fact, we consider a thing only as a member of a class, we are said to generalize. If, after studying the properties of the circle, we proceed to those of the ellipse, parabola and hyperbola, it is soon found· that the circle is only one case of a whole class of curves called the conic sections, corresponding to equations of the second degree; and I generalize when I regard certain of the properties of the circle as shared by many other curves.

Dr Whewell added to the superabundance of terms to express the same processes when he introduced the expression **Colligation of facts**. Whenever two things are found to have similar properties so as to be placed in the same class they may be said to be *connected together*. We connect together the places of a planet as it moves round the sun, when we conceive them as points upon a common ellipse. Whenever we thus join together previously disconnected facts, by a suitable general notion or hypothesis, we are said to colligate them. Dr Whewell adds that the general conceptions employed must be (1) clear, and (2) appropriate ; but it may well be questioned whether there is anything really different in these processes from the general process of natural classification which we have considered.

LESSON XXXIII.

REQUISITES OF A PHILOSOPHICAL LANGUAGE.

AMONG the subsidiary processes requisite to the successful prosecution of inductive reasoning must be placed the construction of a suitable language. It is in fact impossible to over-estimate the importance of an accurate and copious language in any science; and the study of things would be almost useless without names to denote those things and record our observations concerning them.

It is easily apparent, indeed, that language serves three distinct and almost independent purposes :—

1. As a means of communication.
2. As a mechanical aid to thought.
3. As an instrument of record and reference.

In its first origin language was used chiefly if not exclusively for the first purpose. Savage tribes exist in great numbers at the present day who seem to accumulate no knowledge. We may even say that the lower animals often possess some means of communication by sounds or natural signs which constitute language in the first sense, though they are incapable of reasoning by general notions.

Some philosophers have held that it is impossible to carry on reasoning without the use of language. The true nominalist went so far as to say that there are no such things as general notions, and that general names therefore constitute all that is general in science and reasoning. Though this is no doubt false (see p. 13), it must nevertheless be allowed that unless general ideas were fixed and represented by words, we could never attain to sustained thought such as we at present enjoy. The use of language in the second purpose is doubtless indispensable in a practical point of view, and reasoning may almost be considered identical with the correct use of words. When language is used solely to assist reasoning there is no need that the meaning of each word should be fixed; we might use names, as the letters x, y, z, a, b, c, &c., are used in algebra to denote any quantity that happens to occur in a problem. All that is requisite is never to confuse the meaning attributed to a word in one argument with the different meaning attributed in another argument. Algebra may, in fact, be said to consist of a language of a very perfect kind adapted to the second purpose only, and capable of leading a person to the solution of a problem in a symbolical or mechanical manner.

Language, as it is furnished to us ready made by the habitual growth of centuries, is capable of fulfilling all three purposes, though by no means in a perfect manner. As words possess a more or less fixed customary meaning we can not only reason by their aid, but communicate our thoughts or record them; and it is in this last respect we have now to treat the subject.

The multitude of facts required for the establishment of a science could not be retained in the memory with sufficient accuracy. Hence an indispensable subsidiary of induction is the means of describing and recording our observations. Thus only can knowledge be accumulated, so that each observer shall start with the advantage of knowing what has been previously recorded and proved. It will be necessary then to consider the mode in which language serves for the registration of facts, and to investigate the requisite qualities of a philosophical language suitable to the needs of science.

As an instrument of record language must evidently possess two principal requisites :

    1. Precision or definiteness of meaning.
    2. Completeness.

A name is worse than useless unless, when used to record a fact, it enables us to ascertain what was the nature of the fact recorded. Accuracy and precision is then a more important quality of language than abundance. The want of an appropriate word will seldom give rise to actual error and fallacy; it will merely oblige us to employ a circumlocutory phrase or else leave the fact unrecorded. But it is a self-evident convenience that whenever a thing, notion, or quality has often to be referred to there should be a name appropriated to the purpose, and there ought only to be one name. Let us consider in succession what must be the character of a precise and complete language.

It may not previously have struck the reader, but it is certainly true, that description is impossible without the assertion of resemblance between the fact described and some other fact. We can only describe a thing by giving it a name; but how can we learn the meaning of that name? If we describe the name by other names we only have more names of which the meanings are required. We must ultimately learn the meanings, not from names but from things which bear those names. If anyone were ignorant of the meaning of *blue* he could not be informed but by reference to something that excited in him the sensation of *blueness*, and had he been blind from birth he could not acquire any notion of what blueness was. There are indeed a number of words so familiar to us from childhood that we cannot tell when or how we learnt their meanings, though it must have been by refer-

ence to things. But when we come to the more precise
use of names we soon have to make fresh reference to
physical objects. Then we should describe the several
kinds of blue colour as sky-blue, azure-blue, indigo-blue,
cobalt-blue; green colour we likewise distinguish as sea-
green, olive-green, emerald-green, grass-green, &c. The
shapes of leaves are described in Botany by such names
as ovate, lanceolate, linear, pinnate, peltate, referring the
mind respectively to an egg, a lance, a line, a feather,
and a shield. In recording dimensions it is equally impossible to avoid comparison with the dimensions of
other things. A yard or a foot has no meaning unless
there be a definite standard yard or foot which fixes its
meaning; and the reader is probably aware that when the
physical standard of a length is once completely lost it
can never be recovered. The word is nothing unless we
somewhere have the thing to which it corresponds.

The first requisite of a philosophical language evidently is that "every general name must have a certain and
knowable meaning." It need hardly be mentioned that
singular or proper names, the names of distinct objects,
must likewise be known; but as such names are merely
marks imposed upon the things they do not need the
same consideration. General names are a more difficult
subject, because, as we have seen in Lesson v., they have a
double meaning in denotation or extension, and connotation or intension. Of these two meanings the connotation
is the one which must be fixed; the other cannot as
a general rule be limited and defined. Had the name
planet been restricted to Jupiter, Saturn, Mars, Venus,
and Mercury, the planets known before the invention of
the telescope, we should have had to find a new name for
those subsequently discovered, and should even then
commit the fault of calling by different names those things
which are closely similar. But if by planet we mean any

round body revolving round the sun in an orbit of slight ellipticity, it will include all such bodies as may be dis covered from time to time, of which more than 100 are already known. Similarly *locomotive engine* is not merely the name of a number of engines now actually existing; for if so a new name must be needed every week as some new engine is made or an old one destroyed. What is fixed in a general name is its connotation, or the qualities implied in the things bearing the name. We ought therefore as far as possible to define the meaning of every general name we use, not by naming the objects which it denotes, but the qualities, which it connotes. Having however considered the subject of definition in previous Lessons (XII. and XIII.), we need only inquire here how far it is desirable to employ words which are in current use in preference to newly invented terms.

The advantage of an old term is that it possesses force of meaning for all persons, and so far saves the necessity of learning the meaning of a strange technical expression. Every one knows what *heat* is, and the expression *science of heat* bears meaning to every person however unlearned. But there is this objection against old terms to be noted, that they are almost always subject to ambiguity; accordingly it will be found that the scientific man really uses the word *heat* differently from other persons. All things are more or less hot in science, whereas in common life we could never say that ice was hot or contained heat. In fact heat means ordinarily the excess of temperature above the ordinary mean, and the notion is purely relative to that of cold. We also apply the word analogously to sensations of taste, as when we say pepper is hot, or even to purely mental phenomena, as in a hot dispute, a hot temper, &c. If to avoid these ambiguities we invent a new term, *Caloric*, we may give it any precision of meaning we like, but we raise one more obstacle to the study of science, because there is one more technical term to be learnt.

This difficulty is especially great in the science of political economy. We there deal with such familiar ideas as wealth, money, value, currency, capital, labour, exchange, but it is the very familiarity of the ideas which occasions the greatest difficulty, because different people attach different meanings to the words, and infinite *logomachy* (Greek λόγος, word; μάχη, battle), or disputes arising on merely verbal questions, is the result. Even if a writer carefully defines the meaning in which he uses those terms he cannot oblige other persons to bear the definitions in mind. The other alternative of inventing wholly new terms is out of the question, as it would undoubtedly render a work intolerable to most readers. The only advice that can be given is to introduce a new term where it is likely to be readily accepted and to displace an old ambiguous term; but otherwise to endeavour to remove the ambiguity of the old term by constantly keeping in view a precise definition of the intended meaning.

A complete philosophical language will be composed of two distinct kinds of terms, which form respectively the descriptive terminology and the nomenclature of the science.

A **descriptive terminology**, as pointed out by Dr Whewell, must include all the terms required to describe exactly what has been observed concerning any object or phenomenon, in order that we may possess a permanent record of the observation. For every quality, shape, circumstance, degree or quantity there must be an appropriate name or mode of expression. Thus in recording the discovery of a new mineral we ought to be able to fix in words its exact crystalline form, its colour, its degree of hardness, its specific gravity, smell and taste if any.

and many other qualities which may possess importance. Modern botany arose from the efforts of Linnæus to create a system of terms by which every part and character of a plant can be accurately described. The language of botany, as since improved, presents the most complete instance of a scientific terminology. Geology suffers much, as I apprehend, from the difficulty of finding accurate terms ; such names as trap, basalt, gneiss, granite, tuff, greenstone, trachyte, porphyry, lava, &c., are exceedingly vague and almost impossible to define, and at the same time to distinguish. Where a quality does not admit of degree or quantity it only requires a single name; otherwise we must find some mode of exact measurement and expression. The invention of any instrument for measuring a quality which has been before unmeasured is always an important step in science, and the construction of the thermometer by Fahrenheit and the pendulum clock by Huyghens were great eras in science.

On the other hand, each science requires a **nomenclature** or collection of names for the distinct objects or classes of objects treated in it. In mineralogy the names of separate minerals, such as hæmatite, topaz, amphibole, epidote, blende, polybasite, form the nomenclature; in chemistry we have all the names of the elements, together with a vast apparatus of names for organic and other compounds, such as ethyl, acetyl, cyanogen, napthalin, benzol, &c. In astronomy the names of the planets, satellites, nebulæ, constellations or individual stars, form a nomenclature of by no means a perfect or convenient kind ; and geology has similarly a nomenclature necessarily of an incomplete character, in the names of the successive formations, silurian, devonian, carboniferous, permian, triassic, eocene, miocene, pliocene, post-pliocene, &c.

It is evident that a **nomenclature** must possess names

of various degrees of generality, including individual
objects if they need separate record, *infimæ species* if
such there be, with wider classes, up to the *summa
genera*, or widest notions embraced in the science. In
astronomy we deal chiefly with the names of individual
objects, and there is as yet but little scope for classification. In such natural sciences as botany or zoology
there is seldom or never any need of names for individuals, as an indefinite multitude of individuals generally
resemble each other very closely in a great number of
properties, so as to constitute what has been called a
natural kind. Mr Mill uses this term to denote " one of
those classes which are distinguished from all others, not
by one or a few definite properties, but by an unknown
multitude of them ; the combination of properties on
which the class is grounded being a mere index to an
indefinite number of other distinctive attributes."

According to Mr Mill's language he seems to include
in a nomenclature only the names of supposed species ;
for he says :—"A nomenclature may be defined, the collection of names of all kinds with which any branch of
knowledge is conversant ; or more properly, of all the
lowest kinds, or *infimæ species*, those which may be subdivided indeed, but not into kinds, and which generally
accord with what in natural history are termed simply
species." But the fact is that naturalists have now aban-
doned the notion that the species is any definite form ;
many species are divided already into subspecies and
varieties, or even varieties of varieties; and according to
the principles of Darwin's theory the subdivision might
go on indefinitely. It is surely most reasonable to regard
the natural kingdoms of vegetables and animals as arranged in an indefinite series of classes and subclasses,
and all the names attaching to any such classes belong
to the nomenclature.

Again, Mr Mill does not include in the nomenclature such general names as denote conceptions artificially formed in the course of induction and investigation. Accordingly, besides a terminology suited for describing with precision the individual facts observed, there is a branch of language containing "a name for every common property of any importance or interest, which we detect by comparing those facts : including (as the concretes corresponding to those abstract terms) names for the classes which we artificially construct in virtue of those properties, or as many of them, at least, as we have frequent occasion to predicate any thing of." As examples of this class of names he mentions Circle, Limit, Momentum, Civilization, Delegation, Representation. While the nomenclature contains the names of natural classes, this third branch of language would apparently contain the names of artificial ideas or classes.

But I feel great difficulty in giving a clear account of Mr Mill's views on this subject, and, as my object in these Lessons does not allow of the discussion of unsettled questions, I must conclude by referring the reader who desires to continue the subject, to the 4th and 6th chapters of the 4th Book of Mr Mill's *System of Logic*, which treat of the *Requisites of a Philosophical Language.*

See Dr Whewell's "Aphorisms concerning the Language of Science," at the end of his *Philosophy of the Inductive Sciences.*

Thomson's *Outline of the Laws of Thought*, contains most interesting remarks on the general nature and use of Language, §§ 17—31.

QUESTIONS AND EXERCISES.

LESSON I.—*Introduction.*

1. What are the meanings of a Law of Nature, and a Law of Thought?
2. Explain the distinction between the Form of Thought, and the Matter of Thought.
3. In what sense may Logic be called the Science of Sciences?
4. What is the derivation of the name Logic?
5. How does a Science differ from an Art, and why is Logic more in the form of a Science than an Art?
6. Can we say that Logic is a necessary aid in correct reasoning, when persons who have never studied logic reason correctly?

LESSON II.—*Three Parts of Logic.*

1. Name the parts of which a syllogism is composed.
2. How far is it correct to say that Logic is concerned with language?
3. What are the three acts of mind considered in Logic? Which of them is more especially the subject of the Science?
4. Can you state exactly what is meant by a general notion, idea, or conception?
5. How do the Nominalists, Realists, and Conceptualists differ in their opinions as to the nature of a general notion?
6 What is the supposed fourth part of Logic?

LESSON III.—*Terms.*

1. Define a name or term.

2. What is a categorematic term?

3. Explain the distinction between a collective and a general term.

4. Distinguish the collective and distributive use of the word *all* in the following :—

> (1) Non omnis moriar (*i.e.* I shall not all die).
>
> (2) " All men find their own in all men's good,
> And all men join in noble brotherhood."
>
> *Tennyson.*
>
> (3) Non omnia possumus omnes (*i.e.* we cannot all do all things).

5. Which of the following are abstract terms?

> Act, ingratitude, home, hourly, homeliness, introduction, individuality, truth, true, trueness, yellow, yellowness, childhood, book, blue, intention, reason, rationality, reasonableness.

6. Define a negative term, and mention the mark by which you may recognise it.

7. Distinguish a privative from a negative term, and find some instances of privative terms.

8. Describe the logical characters of the following terms, with the precautions given at p. 26.

Metropolis	Consciousness	Sect
Book	Lord Chancellor	Nation
Library	Vegetable Kingdom	Institution
Great Britain	Brilliance	Light
Cæsar	Weight	Observation
Void	Sensation	Tongue
Gold	Cæsar	Air
Prime Minister	Cæsarism	Mentor
Indigestibility	Application	Anarchy
Manchester	Individual	Retribution
Recollection	Volume	Solemnity

Insignificant	Language	Understanding
Brilliant	Adornment	Geology
Independence	Agreement	Demeanour
Heaviness	Obliquity	Resemblance
Illustration	Motionless	Departure
Section	Henry VIII.	Nestor
Whiteness	Formal Logic	Alexander

LESSON IV.—*Ambiguity of Terms.*

1. Define univocal terms, and suggest some terms which are perfectly univocal.
2. What are the other names by which equivocal terms are often called?
3. Distinguish the three kinds of ambiguous terms, and find instances of each.
4. Distinguish the three causes by which the third and most important class of ambiguous terms have been produced.
5. Explain the ambiguity of any of the following terms, referring each to its proper cause, and tracing out as far as possible the derivation of each separate meaning from the original meaning.

Bill	Minister	Subject	Letter
Table	Clerk	Object	Star
Term	Order	Earth	Pole
School	Wood	Law	Reason
Air	Bull	Sensation	Bed
Glass	Volume	Art	Bowl
Peer	Scale	Interest	End
Sense	Feeling	Paper	Division
Ball	Kind	Bolt	Class

LESSON V.—*Twofold meaning of Terms.*

1. Distinguish very carefully the meanings in extension and intension of the terms—
   Quadruped, railway, human being, engine, mountain, Member of Parliament.

2 Enumerate the synonyms or other names used instead of extension and intension.

3. According to what law is the quantity of extension connected with the quantity of intension? Show that the law holds true of the following series of terms—

   (1) Iron, metal, element, matter, substance.
   (2) Matter, organized matter, animal, man.
   (3) Ship, steamship, screw-steamship, iron screw-steamship, British iron screw steamship.
   (4) Book, printed book, dictionary, Latin dictionary.

4. Distinguish between the connotation and denotation of a term.

5. Select from the list of terms under Lesson III., Question 8 (p. 297), such terms as are non-connotative according to Mr Mill's views.

6. Arrange the following terms in series as in question 3, placing each term of greater extension before a term of less extension. Point out which are the terms of greatest and least intension in each series. ●

Emperor	Animal	Planet
Teacher	Dissenter	Mammalian
Baptist	Individual	Matter
Timber	Jupiter	Solicitor
Person	Ruler	Quadruped
Horse	Organized substance	Being
Heavenly body	Lawyer	Napoleon III.
Christian	Alexander	Episcopalian

LESSON VI.—*Growth of Language.*

1. Trace out the generalization or specialization which has taken place in any of the following words:—

Kind, genus, class, species, order, rank, Augustus, president, speaker, Utopia, rock, Commons, doctor.

2. Point out metaphors derived from the notions of weight, straightness, rock, wind.

3. Distinguish as accurately as possible the meanings of the following synonyms :—

Sickness, malady; mud, mire ; confutation, refutation; boundary, limit; mind, intellect; recollection, reminiscence; procrastination, dilatoriness ; converse, reverse, obverse, inverse.

4. Form lists of all the words derived from any of the following roots :—

(1) *Tendere,* to stretch, as in intention, attention.

(2) *Ponere,* to place, as in position, supposition.

(3) *Genus,* tribe or kind, as in genus, generation.

(4) *Munus,* gift, as in remuneration, common (Latin, *Communis*).

(5) *Modus,* shape or fashion, as in mood, moderate.

(6) *Scribere,* to write, as in scribe, inscription, describe.

(7) *Capere* to take, as in deception, incipient.

LESSON VII.—*Leibnitz on Knowledge.*

1. What are the characters of perfect knowledge ?

2. Describe the character of the knowledge which we have of the following notions or objects :—

A syllogism.

Electricity.

Motion.

A triangle.

Eternity.

The weight of the earth (5852 trillions of tons)

The colour of the sky.

3. Explain exactly what you mean by *intuitive* know-ledge.

LESSON VIII.—*Propositions.*

1. Define a proposition, and name the parts of which it is composed.
2. How are propositions classified?
3. Name the four kinds of categorical propositions, and their symbols.
4. Under which classes are singular and indefinite propositions placed?
5. Enumerate the most usual signs of the quantity of a proposition.
6. What are modal propositions according to early logicians, and according to Thomson?
7. How far do logicians consider propositions with regard to their truth or falsity?

LESSON IX.—*Opposition of Propositions.*

1. State the quantity of the subject and predicate in each of the propositions A, E, I, O.
2. Select out of the following propositions, pairs of contrary, contradictory, subaltern, and subcontrary propositions :—
   (1) Some elements are known.
   (2) No elements are known.
   (3) All elements are known.
   (4) Not all elements are known.
   (5) Some elements are not known.
   (6) All elements are not known.
3. What propositions are true, false, or doubtful,
   (1) when A is false, (3) when I is false,
   (2) when E is false, (4) when O is false?
4. Prove by means of the contradictory propositions

that subcontrary propositions cannot both be false.

5. Show by means of the subcontrary propositions that contrary propositions may both be false.

6. What quantity would you assign to each of the following propositions?

(1) Knowledge is power.

(2) Nebulæ are material bodies.

(3) Light is the vibration of an ether.

(4) Men are more to be trusted than we think.

(5) The Chinese are industrious.

7. Why is it desirable in controversy to refute a statement by its contradictory and not by its contrary?

LESSON X.—*Conversion and Immediate Inference.*

1. Define inference and conversion.

2. What are converse and convertend propositions?

3. State the rules of valid conversion.

4. Name all the kinds of conversion.

5. By what process do we pass from each of the following propositions to the next?

(1) No knowledge is useless.

(2) No useless thing is knowledge.

(3) All knowledge is not useless.

(4) All knowledge is useful.

(5) What is not useful is not knowledge.

(6) What is useless is not knowledge.

(7) No knowledge is useless.

6. Give the logical opposites of the following proposition, and the converse of its contradictory:—
" He cannot become rich who will not labour."

7. Apply negative conception to the proposition "All men are fallible;" then convert and show that the result is the contrapositive of the original.

8. Classify the propositions subjoined into the four following groups:—

a. Those which can be inferred from (1).

b. Those from which (1) can be inferred.

c. Those which do not contradict (1), but cannot be inferred from it.

d. Those which contradict (1).

(1) All just acts are expedient acts.

(2) No expedient acts are unjust.

(3) No just acts are inexpedient.

(4) All inexpedient acts are unjust.

(5) Some unjust acts are inexpedient.

(6) No expedient acts are just.

(7) Some inexpedient acts are unjust.

(8) All expedient acts are just.

(9) No inexpedient acts are just.

(10) All unjust acts are inexpedient.

(11) Some inexpedient acts are just acts.

(12) Some expedient acts are just.

(13) Some just acts are expedient.

(14) Some unjust acts are expedient.

LESSONS VIII. IX. and X.—*Examples of Propositions.*

The reader is desired to ascertain the logical character of each of the following propositions; he is to state of each whether it is affirmative or negative, universal, particular, singular or indefinite, pure or modal, exclusive or exceptive, &c.; when irregularly stated he is to reduce the proposition to the simple logical order; he is then to convert the proposition, and to draw immediate inferences from it by any process which may be applicable.

(1) All birds are feathered.

(2) No reptiles are feathered.

(3) Fixed stars are self-luminous.

(4) Perfect happiness is impossible.

(5) Life every man holds dear.

(6) Every mistake is not a proof of ignorance.

(7) Some of the most valuable books are seldom read.

(8) He jests at scars who never felt a wound.

(9) Heated metals are softened.

(10) Not one of the Greeks at Thermopylæ escaped.

(11) Few are acquainted with themselves.

(12) Whoso loveth instruction loveth knowledge.

(13) Nothing is harmless that is mistaken for a virtue

(14) Some of our muscles act without volition.

(15) Metals are all good conductors of heat.

(16) Fame is no plant that grows on mortal soil.

(17) Only the brave deserve the fair.

(18) No one is free who doth not command himself.

(19) Nothing is beautiful except truth.

(20) The wicked shall fall by his own wickedness.

(21) Unsafe are all things unbecoming.

(22) There is no excellent beauty that hath not some strangeness in the proportion.

(23) It is a poor centre of a man's actions, himself.

(24) Mercy but murders, pardoning those that kill.

(25) I shall not all die. (*Non omnis moriar.*)

(26) A regiment consists of two battalions.

(27) 'Tis cruelty to load a falling man.

(28) Every mistake is not culpable.

(29) Quadrupeds are vertebrate animals.

(30) Not many of the metals are brittle.

(31) Many are the deserving men who are unfortunate.

(32) **Amalgams** are alloys of mercury.

(33) One kind of metal at least is liquid.

(34) Talents are often misused.

(35) Some parallelograms have their adjoining sides equal.

(36) Britain is an island.

(37) Romulus and Remus were twins.

(38) A man's a man.
(39) Heaven is all mercy.
(40) Every one is a good judge of his own interests.
(41) All parallelograms have their opposite angles equal
(42) Familiarity breeds contempt.
(43) No one is always happy.
(44) Every little makes a mickle.

LESSON XI.—*Logical Analysis of Sentences*

1. How does the grammatical predicate differ from the logical predicate?
2. Distinguish between a compound and a complex sentence ; and between coordinate and subordinate propositions.
3. Enumerate the grammatical expressions which may form

(1) A subject.   (4) An object.
(2) An attribute.   (5) An adverbial.
(3) A predicate.

4. Examine the following sentences, ascertain which are compound or complex, and point out the co-ordinate or subordinate propositions.

(1) Happy is the man that findeth wisdom, and the man that getteth understanding.
(2) Heat, being motion, can be converted into mechanical force.
(3) Ceres, Pallas, Juno, and Vesta are minor planets, or asteroids.
(4) Knowledge comes, but wisdom lingers.
(5) Fortune often sells to the hasty what she gives to those who wait.
(6)   Thousands at His bidding speed,
   And post o'er land and ocean without rest ;
   They also serve who only stand and wait.

20

(7) Pride that dines on vanity, sups on contempt.

(8) Nobody can be healthful without exercise, neithei natural body, nor politic.

(9) Nature is often hidden, sometimes **overcome,** seldom extinguished.

(10) It is impossible to love and be wise.

(11) Though gods they were, as men they died.

(12) He that is not industrious envieth him that is.

(13) Ye are my friends, if ye do whatsoever I command you.—John xv. 14.

(14) The wisdom that is from above is first pure, then peaceable, gentle, and easy to be intreated, full of mercy, and good fruits, without partiality, and without hypocrisy.—James iii. 17.

5. Analyse in the form of a scheme or diagram any of the following sentences :—

(1) The first aphorism of Bacon's *Novum Organum,* on p. 229.

(2) Some judgments are merely explanatory of their subject, having for their predicate, a conception which it fairly implies, to all who know and can define its nature.

(3) There be none of the affections which have been noted to fascinate or bewitch, but love and envy: they both have vehement wishes ; they frame themselves readily into imaginations and suggestions ; and they come easily into the eye, especially upon the presence of the objects, which are the points that conduce to fascination, if any such there be.

Further examples for analysis must be sought in Dalgleish's *Grammatical Analysis, with Progressive Exercises.* (Oliver and Boyd.) Edinburgh, 1866. Price 9*d.*

LESSON XII.—*The Predicables, etc.*

1. Define each of the five predicables.

2. In what sense may we say that the genus is part of the species, and in what sense that the species is part of the genus?

3. Select from the terms in the 6th Question of Lesson v., p. 299, such as are genera, species, highest genera, or lowest species of other terms.

4. Explain the expressions sui generis, homogeneous, heterogeneous, summum genus, infima species, tree of Porphyry.

5. Name a property and accident of each of the following classes :—Circle, Planet, Bird, Member of Parliament, Ruminant Animal.

6. What are the rules of correct logical division.

7. The first name in each of the following series of terms is that of a class which you are to divide and subdivide so as to include all the subjoined minor classes in accordance with the laws of division.

(1) *People.*	(2) *Triangle.*	(3) *Reasoning.*
Laity	Equiangular	Induction (Imperfect)
Aliens	Isosceles	Deduction
Naturalized	Right-angled	Mediate Inference
Subjects	Scalene	Induction
Peers	Obtuse-angled	Hypothetical Syllogism
Natural-born		Disjunctive Syllogism
Subjects		
Clergy		
Baronets		
Commons		

8. Divide any of the following classes :—Governments, Sciences, Logical terms, Propositions.

9. Of what does a logical definition consist?

10. What are the rules of correct definition?

11. What rules do the following definitions break?

(1) Life is the sum of the vital functions.

(2) Genus is the material part of the species.

(3) Illative conversion is that in which the truth of the converse can be inferred from that of the convertend.

(4) Mineral substances are those which have not been produced by the powers of vegetable or animal life.

(5) An equilateral triangle is a triangle whose sides and angles are respectively equal.

(6) An acute-angled triangle is one which has an acute angle.

LESSON XIII.—*Pascal and Descartes on Method.*

(1) What is the use of nominal definitions?

(2) How must we employ definitions in order to avoid confusion?

(3) How far can we be said to be free to use any name for any object?

(4) What according to Pascal is the true method of avoiding error?

(5) How do we learn the meanings of words which cannot be defined?

(6) Give instances of words which can be clearly defined and of others which cannot.

(7) State the five rules of method given in the Port Royal Logic.

(8) Explain Descartes' rules for the attainment of truth.

LESSON XIV.—*Laws of Thought.*

1. State the three Fundamental Laws of Thought, and apply them to the following notions :—

(1) Matter, organic, inorganic.
(2) Undulations, polarized, non-polarized.
(3) Figure, rectilinear, curvilinear.

2. Is it wrong to assert that animal cannot both be vertebrate and invertebrate, seeing that some animals are vertebrate and some are not ?

3. Select from the following such terms as are negatives of the others, and such as are opposites :— Light, plenum, gain, heat, decrease, loss, darkness, cold, increase, vacuum.

4. How is Aristotle's dictum applicable to the following arguments?

(1) Silver is a good conductor of electricity ; for such are all the metals.

(2) Comets cannot be without weight ; for they are composed of matter, which is not without weight.

LESSON XV.—*Syllogism: the Rules.*

1. Distinguish mediate and immediate inference.

2. Define syllogism, and state with what it is synonymous.

3. What are the six principal and two subordinate rules of the syllogism?

4. In the following syllogisms point out in succession the conclusion, the middle term, the major term, the minor term, the major premise and the minor premise, observing this precise order.

(1) All men are fallible ;
    All kings are men ;
Therefore all kings are fallible.

(2) Platinum is a metal ;
    All metals combine with oxygen ;
Therefore Platinum combines with oxygen.

(3) Hottentots are capable of education ; for Hottentots are men, and all men are capable of education.

5. Explain carefully what is meant by non-distribution
of the middle term.

LESSON XVI.—*The Moods and Figures of the
Syllogism.*

1. Name the rules of the syllogism which are broken
by any of the following moods, no regard being
paid to figure :—
A I A, E E I, I E A, I O I, I I A, A E I.
2. Write out all the 64 moods of the syllogism and
strike out the 53 invalid ones.
3. Show in what figures the following premises give a
valid conclusion :—A A, A I, E A, O A.
4. In what figures are I E O and E I O valid ?
5. To what **moods** do the following valid syllogisms
belong?   Arrange them in correct logical order.
   (1) Some Y's are Z's.   (2) All Z's are Y's.
   No X's are Y's.   No Y's are X's.
   Some Z's are not X's.   No Z's are X's.
   (3) No fish suckles its young ;
   The whale suckles its young ;
   Therefore the whale is no fish.
6. Deduce conclusions from the following **premises** ;
and state to what mood the syllogism belongs.
   (1) Some amphibious animals are mammalian.
   All mammalian animals are vertebrate.
   (2) All planets are heavenly bodies.
   No planets are self-luminous.
   (3) Mammalian animals are quadrupeds.
   No birds are quadrupeds.
   (4) Ruminant animals are not predacious.
   The lion is predacious.

7. Invent examples to show that false premises may give true conclusions.
8. Supply premises to the following conclusions :- -
   (1) Some logicians are not good reasoners.
   (2) The rings of Saturn are material bodies.
   (3) Party government exists in every democracy.
   (4) All fixed stars obey the law of gravitation.

LESSON XVII.— *The Syllogism; Reduction.*

1. State and explain the mnemonic lines Barbara, Celarent, &c.
2. Construct syllogisms in each of the following moods, taking X, Y, Z, for the major, middle, and minor terms respectively, and show how to reduce them to the first figure :—
   Cesare, Festino, Darapti, Datisi, Ferison, Camenes, Fesapo.
3. What is the use of Reduction?
4. Prove that the following premises cannot give a universal conclusion—E I, I A, O A, I E.
5. Prove that the third figure must have an affirmative minor premise, and a particular conclusion.
6. Reduce the moods Cesare and Camenes by the Indirect method, or Reductio ad Impossibile.

LESSON XVIII.—*Irregular and Compound Syllogisms.*

1. Describe the meaning of each of the terms—Enthymeme, Prosyllogism, Episyllogism, Epicheirema, Sorites.
2. Make an example of a syllogism in which there are two prosyllogisms.
3. Construct a sorites of four premises and resolve it into distinct syllogisms.
4. What are the rules to which a sorites must conform?

5. The reader is requested to analyse the following arguments, to detect those which are false, and to ascertain the rules of the syllogism which they break ; if the argument appears valid he is to ascertain the figure and mood to which it belongs, to state it in correct logical form, and then if it be in an imperfect figure to prove it by reduction to the first figure. The first six of the examples should be arranged both in the extensive and intensive orders.

1. None but mortals are men.
   Monarchs are men.
   Therefore monarchs are mortals.

2. Personal deformity is an affliction of nature.
   Disgrace is not an affliction of nature.
   Therefore personal deformity is not disgrace.

3. Some statesmen are also authors; for such are Mr Gladstone, Lord Derby, Lord Russell, and Sir G. C. Lewis.

4. This explosion must have been occasioned by gun-powder; for nothing else would have possessed sufficient force.

5. Every man should be moderate; for excess will cause disease.

6. Blessed are the merciful; for they shall obtain mercy.

7. As almost all the organs of the body have a known use, the spleen must have some use.

8. Cogito, ergo sum.   (I think, therefore I exist.)

9. Some speculative men are unworthy of trust; for they are unwise, and no unwise man can be trusted.

10 No idle person can be a successful writer of history; therefore Hume, Macaulay, Hallam and Grote must have been industrious.

11. Who spareth the rod, hateth his child; the parent who loveth his child therefore spareth not the rod.
12. Comets must consist of heavy matter; for otherwise they would not obey the law of gravitation.
13. Lithium is an element; for it is an alkali-producing substance, which is a metal, which is an element.
14. Rational beings are accountable for their actions; brutes not being rational, are therefore exempt from responsibility.
15. A singular proposition is a universal one; for it applies to the whole of its subject.
16. Whatever tends to withdraw the mind from pursuits of a low nature deserves to be promoted; classical learning does this, since it gives us a taste for intellectual enjoyments; therefore it deserves to be promoted.
17. Bacon was a great lawyer and statesman; and as he was also a philosopher, we may infer that any philosopher may be a great lawyer and statesman.
18. Immoral companions should be avoided; but some immoral companions are intelligent persons, so that some intelligent persons should be avoided.
19. Mathematical study undoubtedly improves the reasoning powers; but, as the study of logic is not mathematical study, we may infer that it does not improve the reasoning powers.
20. Every candid man acknowledges merit in a rival; every learned man does not do so; therefore every learned man is not candid.

LESSON XIX.—*Conditional Arguments.*

1. What are the kinds of conditional propositions, and by what signs can you recognise them?

2. What are the rules of the hypothetical syllogism?

3. To what categorical fallacies do breaches of these rules correspond?

4. Select from the following such as are valid arguments, and reduce them to the categorical form; explain the fallacious reasoning in the others.

(1) Rain has fallen if the ground is wet; but the ground is not wet; therefore rain has not fallen.

(2) If rain has fallen, the ground is wet; but rain has not fallen; therefore the ground is not wet.

(3) The ground is wet, if rain has fallen; the ground is wet; therefore rain has fallen.

(4) If the ground is wet, rain has fallen; but rain has fallen; therefore the ground is wet.

N.B. In these as in other logical examples the student must argue only from the premises, and not from any other knowledge of the subject-matter.

5. Show that the canons of syllogism (p. 121) may be stated indifferently in the hypothetical or categorical form.

6. State the following in the form of a Disjunctive or Dilemmatic argument, and name the kind to which it belongs.

If pain is severe it will be brief; and if it last long it will be slight; therefore it is to be patiently borne.

Lessons XX. and XXI—*Fallacies.*

1. Classify fallacies.

2. Explain the following expressions:

A dicto secundum quid ad dictum simpliciter; ignoratio elenchi; argumentum ad hominem; argumentum ad populum; petitio principii; circulus in probando; non sequitur; post hoc ergo propter hoc.

3. What is *arguing in a circle;* and what is a question-begging epithet?
4. What differences of meaning may be produced in
   the following sentence by varying the accent?
"Newton's discovery of gravitation is not generally
   believed to have been at all anticipated by
   several philosophers in England and Holland."
5. Point out the misinterpretations to which the following sentences might be liable.
(1) He went to London and then to Brighton by
   the express train.
(2) Did you make a long speech at the meeting?
(3) How much is five times seven and nine?

MISCELLANEOUS EXAMPLES.

LESSONS IX. to XXI.

(*Continued from p.* 313.)

The following examples consist partly of true and
partly of false arguments. The reader is requested to
treat them as follows :

1. If the example is not in a simple and complete
   logical form, to complete it in the form which
   appears most appropriate.
2. To ascertain whether it is a valid or fallacious
   argument.
3. To assign the exact name of the argument or fallacy as the case may be.
4. If a categorical syllogism, to reduce it to the first
   figure.
5. If a hypothetical syllogism, to state it in the categorical form.
21. Elementary substances alone are metals. Iron is
    a metal; therefore it is an elementary substance.

22. No Athenians could have been Helots; for all the Helots were slaves, and all Athenians were free men.

23. Aristotle must have been a man of extraordinary industry; for only such a man could have produced his works.

24. Nothing is better than wisdom; dry bread is better than nothing; therefore dry bread is better than wisdom.

25. Pitt was not a great and useful minister; for though he would have been so had he carried out Adam Smith's doctrines of Free Trade, he did not carry out those doctrines.

26. Only the virtuous are truly noble; some who are called noble are not virtuous; therefore some who are called noble are not truly noble.

27. Ireland is idle and therefore starves; she starves, and therefore rebels.

28. No designing person ought to be trusted; engravers are by profession designers; therefore they ought not to be trusted.

29. Logic as it was cultivated by the schoolmen proved a fruitless study; therefore Logic as it is cultivated at the present day must be a fruitless study likewise.

30. Is a stone a body? Yes. Then is not an animal a body? Yes. Are you an animal? I think so. Ergo, you are a stone, being a body.—*Lucian.*

31. If ye were Abraham's children, ye would do the works of Abraham.—John viii. 39.

32. He that is of God heareth God's words: ye therefore hear them not, because ye are not of God. —John viii. 47.

33. Mahomet was a wise lawgiver; for he studied the character of his people.

34. Every one desires virtue, because every one desires happiness.

35. His imbecility of character might have been inferred from his proneness to favourites; for all weak princes have this failing.—*De Morgan.*

36. He is brave who conquers his passions; he who resists temptation conquers his passions; so that he who resists temptation is brave.

37. Suicide is not always to be condemned; for it is but voluntary death, and this has been gladly embraced by many of the greatest heroes of antiquity.

38. Since all metals are elements, the most rare of all the metals must be the most rare of all the elements.

39. The express train alone does not stop at this station; and as the last train did not stop it must have been the express train.

40. Peel's remission of taxes was beneficial; the taxes remitted by Peel were indirect; therefore the remission of indirect taxes is beneficial.

41. Books are a source both of instruction and amusement; a table of logarithms is a book; therefore it is a source both of instruction and amusement.

42. All desires are not blameable; all desires are liable to excess; therefore some things liable to excess are not blameable.

43. Whosoever intentionally kills another should suffer death; a soldier, therefore, who kills his enemy should suffer death.

44. Projectors are unfit to be trusted; this man has formed a project; therefore he is unfit to be trusted.

45. Few towns in the United Kingdom have more than

300,000 inhabitants; and as all such towns ought
to be represented by three members in Parliament, it is evident that few towns ought to have
three representatives.

46. All the works of Shakspeare cannot be read in
a day; therefore the play of Hamlet, being one
of the works of Shakspeare, cannot be read in
a day.

47. In moral matters we cannot stand still; therefore
he who does not go forward is sure to fall behind.

48. The people of the country are suffering from famine;
and as you are one of the people of the country
you must be suffering from famine.

49. Those substances which are lighter than water
can float upon it; those metals which can float
upon it are potassium, sodium, lithium, &c.;
therefore potassium, sodium, lithium, &c., are
lighter than water.

50. The laws of nature must be ascertained by Deduction, Traduction or Induction; but the former
two are insufficient for the purpose; therefore
the laws of nature must be ascertained by Induction.

51. A successful author must be either very industrious
or very talented; Gibbon was very industrious,
therefore he was not very talented.

52. You are not what I am; I am a man; therefore
you are not a man.

53. The holder of some shares in a lottery is sure to
gain a prize; and as I am the holder of some
shares in a lottery I am sure to gain a prize.

54. Gold and silver are wealth; and therefore the
diminution of the gold and silver in the country
by exportation is the diminution of the wealth
of the country.

55. Over credulous persons ought never to be believed; and as the Ancient Historians were in many instances over credulous they ought never to be believed.

56. Some mineral compounds are not decomposed by heat; all organic substances are decomposed by heat; therefore no organic substances are mineral compounds.

57. Whatever schools exclude religion are irreligious; Non-sectarian schools do not allow the teaching of religious creeds; therefore they are irreligious.

58. Night must be the cause of day; for it invariably precedes it.

59. The ancient Greeks produced the greatest masterpieces of eloquence and philosophy; the Lacedæmonians were ancient Greeks; therefore they produced the greatest masterpieces of eloquence and philosophy.

60. All presuming men are contemptible; this man, therefore, is contemptible; for he presumes to believe his opinions are correct.

61. If a substance is solid it possesses elasticity, and so also it does if it be liquid or gaseous; but all substances are either solid, liquid or gaseous; therefore all substances possess elasticity.

62. If Parr's life pills are of any value those who take them will improve in health; now my friend who has been taking them has improved in health; therefore they are of value.

63. He who calls you a man speaks truly; he who calls you a fool calls you a man; therefore he who calls you a fool speaks truly.

64. Who is most hungry eats most; who eats least is most hungry; therefore who eats least eats most.

65. What produces intoxication should be prohibited;

the use of spirituous liquors causes intoxication; therefore the use of spirituous liquors should be prohibited.

66. What we eat grew in the fields; loaves of bread are what we eat; therefore loaves of bread grew in the fields.

67. If light consisted of material particles it would possess momentum; it cannot therefore consist of material particles, for it does not possess momentum.

68. Everything is allowed by law which is morally right; indulgence in pleasures is allowed by law; therefore indulgence in pleasures is morally right.

69. All the trees in the park make a thick shade; this is one of them, therefore this tree makes a thick shade.

70. All visible bodies shine by their own or by reflected light. The moon does not shine by its own, therefore it shines by reflected light; but the sun shines by its own light, therefore it cannot shine by reflected light.

71. Honesty deserves reward; and a negro is a fellow-creature; therefore, an honest negro is a fellow-creature deserving of reward.

72. Nearly all the satellites revolve round their planets from west to east; the moon is a satellite; therefore it revolves round its planet from west to east.

73. Italy is a Catholic country and abounds in beggars; France is also a Catholic country, and therefore abounds in beggars.

74. Every law is either useless or it occasions hurt to some person; now a law that is useless ought to be abolished; and so ought every law that occasions hurt; therefore every law ought to be abolished.

75. The end of a thing is its perfection; **death is the** end of life; therefore death is the perfection of life.

76. When we hear that all the righteous people are happy, it is hard to avoid exclaiming, What! are all the unhappy persons we see to be thought unrighteous?

77. I am offered a sum of money to assist this person in gaining the office he desires; to assist a person is to do him good, and no rule of morality forbids the doing of good; therefore no rule of morality forbids me to receive the sum of money for assisting the person.

78. Ruminant animals are those which have cloven feet, and they usually have horns; the extinct animal which left this foot-print had a cloven foot; therefore it was a ruminant animal and had horns. Again, as no beasts of prey are ruminant animals it cannot have been a beast of prey.

79. We must either gratify our vicious propensities, or resist them; the former course will involve us in sin and misery; the latter requires self-denial; therefore we must either fall into sin and misery or practise self-denial.

80. The stonemasons are benefitted by the masons' union; the bricklayers by the bricklayers' union; the hatmakers by the hatmakers' union; in short, every trade by its own union; therefore it is evident that if all workmen had unions all workmen would be benefitted thereby.

81. Every moral aim requires the rational means of attaining it; these means are the establishment of laws; and as happiness **is** the moral aim of man it follows that the attainment **of happiness** requires the establishment **of** laws.

21

82. He that can swim needs not despair to fly; for to swim is to fly in a grosser fluid, and to fly is to swim in a subtler.

83. The Helvetii, if they went through the country of the Sequani, were sure to meet with various difficulties; and if they went through the Roman province, they were exposed to the danger of opposition from Cæsar; but they were obliged to go one way or the other; therefore they were either sure of meeting with various difficulties, or exposed to the danger of opposition from Cæsar.—*De Bello Gallico*, lib. I. 6.

84. Riches are for spending, and spending for honour and good actions; therefore extraordinary expense must be limited by the worth of the occasion.—*Bacon.*

85. If light is not refracted near the surface of the moon, there cannot be any twilight; but if the moon has no atmosphere light is not refracted near its surface; therefore if the moon has no atmosphere there cannot be any twilight.

86. The preservation of society requires exchange; whatever requires exchange requires equitable valuation of property; this requires the adoption of a common measure; hence the preservation of society requires the adoption of a common measure.

87. The several species of brutes being created to prey upon one another proves that the human species were intended to prey upon them.

88. The more correct the logic, the more certainly the conclusion will be wrong if the premises are false. Therefore where the premises are wholly uncertain, the best logician is the least safe guide.

89. If our rulers could be trusted always to look to the best interests of their subjects, monarchy would be the best form of government; but they cannot be trusted; therefore monarchy is not the best form of government.

90. If men were prudent, they would act morally for their own good; if benevolent, for the good of others. But many men will not act morally, either for their own good, or that of others; such men, therefore, are not prudent or benevolent.

91. He who bears arms at the command of the magistrate does what is lawful for a Christian; the Swiss in the French service, and the British in the American service, bore arms at the command of the magistrate; therefore they did what was lawful for a Christian.—*Whately.*

92. A man that hath no virtue in himself ever envieth virtue in others; for men's minds will either feed upon their own good or upon others' evil; and who wanteth the one will prey upon the other.— *Bacon.*

93. The object of war is durable peace; therefore soldiers are the best peace-makers.

94. Confidence in promises is essential to the intercourse of human life; for without it the greatest part of our conduct would proceed upon chance. But there could be no confidence in promises, if men were not obliged to perform them; the obligation, therefore, to perform promises is essential to the same ends and in the same degree.

95. If the majority of those who use public-houses are prepared to close them, legislation is unnecessary; but if they are not prepared for such a measure, then to force it on them by outside pressure is both dangerous and unjust.

96. He who believes himself to be always in the right in his opinion, lays claim to infallibility ; you always believe yourself to be in the right in your opinion; therefore you lay claim to infallibility. —*Whately.*

97. If we never find skins except as the teguments of animals, we may safely conclude that animals cannot exist without skins. If colour cannot exist by itself, it follows that neither can anything that is coloured exist without colour. So, if language without thought is unreal, thought without language must also be so.

98. No soldiers should be brought into the field who are not well qualified to perform their part ; none but veterans are well qualified to perform their part; therefore none but veterans should be brought into the field.—*Whately.*

99. The *minimum visibile* is the least magnitude which can be seen ; no part of it alone is visible, and yet all parts of it must affect the mind in order that it may be visible ; therefore, every part of it must affect the mind without being visible.

100. The scarlet poppy belongs to the genus Papaver, of the natural order Papaveraceæ ; which again is part of the subclass Thalamifloræ, belonging to the great class of Dicotyledons. Hence the scarlet poppy is one of the Dicotyledons.

101. Improbable events happen almost every day ; but what happens almost every day is a very probable event; therefore improbable events are very probable events.—*Whately.*

Lesson XXII.—*Quantification of the Predicate.*

What does the quantification of the predicate mean?

2. Assign to each of the following propositions its proper symbol, and the symbol of its converse ·
(1) Knowledge is power.
(2) Some rectangles are all squares.
(3) Only the honest ultimately prosper.
(4) Princes have but their titles for their glories.
(5) In man there is nothing great but mind.
(6) The end of philosophy is the detection of unity.
3. Draw all the contrapositive propositions and immediate inferences you can from the following propositions:—
(1) London is a great city.
(2) London is the capital of England.
(3) All ruminant animals are all cloven-footed animals.
(4) Some members of parliament are all the ministers.
4. Write out in Hamilton's notation the moods Baroko Darapti, Felapton, Bokardo.

LESSON XXIII.—*Boole's System of Logic.*

1. Apply this system of inference to prove the syllogisms on p. 141, in Cesare, and Camestres.
2. Show that if all A's are not B's, then no B's are A's; and that if all A's are *all* B's, then all **not** A's are *all* not B's.
3. Develope the term *substance*, as regards the terms *vegetable, animal, organic;* then select the combinations which agree with these premises:
    "What is vegetable is not animal but is organic; what is animal is organic."
4. Test the validity of this argument : " Good always triumphs, and vice always fails ; therefore the victor cannot be wrong, nor the vanquished right."

5. It is known of a certain class of things that—

   (1) Where the quality A is, B is not.

   (2) Where B is, and only where B is, C and D are. What can we infer from these premises of the class of things in which A is not present but C is present?

6. If all A's are B's; all B's are C's; all C's are D's; shew that all A's are D's, and that all not D's are not A's.

LESSON XXIV.—*Method.*

1. What is the supposed position of method according to former logical writers, and what are the rules of method?

2. Explain the expressions *nobis notiora*, and *notiora naturæ*.

3. Of what kind is the usual method of instruction?

4. Prove that analysis in extension is synthesis in intension, using some of the series of terms in Question 6, Lesson v. as illustrations.

5. Explain the exact meanings of the expressions *à priori* and *à posteriori* knowledge.

6. To which kind belongs our knowledge of the following facts?

   (1) The light of the stars takes a long time to reach us.

   (2) Vaccination is a preservative against small-pox.

   (3) A meteor becomes heated in passing through the air.

   (4) There must be either some inhabitants or no inhabitants upon Jupiter.

LESSON XXV.—*Perfect Induction.*

1. Define and distinguish Deduction, Induction, and Traduction.

2. Find an instance of reasoning in Traduction.
3. Distinguish Perfect and Imperfect Induction.
4. How does Mr Mill define Induction, and what is his opinion of Imperfect Induction?
5. What is the use of Perfect Induction?
6. Construct some instances of the inductive syllogism, and show that they may be thrown into a disjunctive form.

LESSON XXVI.—*Induction, Analogy and Example.*

1. From what circumstance arises the certainty and generality of reasoning in geometry?
2. Find other instances of certain and general reasoning concerning the properties of numbers.
3. Why are inductive conclusions concerning prime numbers uncertain and not general?
4. Why is a single instance sometimes sufficient to warrant a universal conclusion, while in other cases the greatest possible number of concurring instances, without any exception, is not sufficient to warrant such a conclusion?
5. What are the strict and ordinary meanings of the word analogy?
6. Explain the use of Examples.
7. Explain exactly the difference between analogical argument and ordinary induction.

LESSON XXVII.—*Observation and Experiment.*

1. What is the false method of Science against which Bacon protested?
2. Explain the exact meaning of Bacon's assertions, that man is the Servant and Interpreter of Nature, and that Knowledge is Power.
3. How does experiment differ from observation?

4. Classify the sciences according as they employ passive observation, experiment, or both.
5. Name the chief points in which experiment is superior to mere observation.
6. What is the principal precaution needful in observation?
7. Explain how it is possible to anticipate nature and yet establish all conclusions upon the results of experience.

LESSONS XXVIII. and XXIX.—*Methods of Induction.*

1. Define exactly what is meant by a cause of an event, and distinguish *cause, occasion, antecedent.*
2. Point out all the causes concerned in the following phenomena:
   (1) The burning of a fire.
   (2) The ordinary growth of vegetables.
   (3) The cracking of a glass by hot water.
3. State and explain in your own words Mr Mill's first three Canons of Inductive Method.
4. Point out exactly how the Joint Method differs from the simple Method of Difference.
5. Give some instances of simple experiments fulfilling completely the conditions of the Method of Difference.
6. What can you infer from the following instances?

Antecedents.	Consequents.
ABDE	stqp
BCD	qsr
BFG	vqu
ADE	tsp
HK	xqw
ABFG	pquv
ABE	pqt.

7. (1) Friction alters the temperature of the bodies rubbed together.

(2) The sun is supposed to move through space.

(3) A ray of light passing into or out of a denser medium is deflected.

Point out the successive questions which would have to be decided in the investigation of the above phenomena.

8. Find some simple instances of the homogeneous and heterogeneous intermixture of effects, and of the methods of concomitant variations and residues.

9. Since 1842 there has been a great reform of the British tariff, and a great increase of British trade. Does this coincidence prove that the first circumstance is the cause of the second?

10. Supposing us to be unacquainted with the causes of the following phenomena, by what methods should we investigate each?

(1) The connection between the barometer and the weather.

(2) A person poisoned at a meal.

(3) The connection between the hands of a clock.

(4) The effect of the Gulf-stream upon the climate of Great Britain.

LESSON XXX.—*Empirical and Deductive Methods.*

1. Define Empirical Law, and find a few additional instances of such laws.

2. What are the three steps of the Deductive Method?

3. Trace some of the successive steps in the progress of the theory of gravitation, showing that it was established by this method.

Lesson XXXI.—*Explanation, &c.*

1. What do you mean by the explanation of a fact?
2. State the three ways in which a law of nature may be explained, and suggest some additional instances of each case.
3. Define tendency. Do all causes consist only of tendencies, or can you find examples to the contrary?
4. Give a definition of hypothesis. How may a valid be distinguished from an invalid hypothesis?
5. What place does hypothesis hold in the Deductive Method?
6. Explain the ambiguities of the words *theory* and *fact*.

Lesson XXXII.—*Classification.*

1. Define classification, and give the derivation of the word.
2. What do you mean by important characters in classification?
3. State Dr Whewell's criterion of a good natural arrangement.
4. Distinguish between a natural and artificial system of classification.
5. What do you mean by a characteristic quality? Is it always an important quality?
6. Define abstraction, generalization, and colligation of facts.
7. What are the characters of a notion properly abstracted?

Lesson XXXIII.—*Requisites of a Philosophical Language.*

1. What are the three purposes for which we use language?

2. What are the two chief requisites of a philosophical language?

3. By what considerations should we be guided in choosing between a new and old scientific term?

4. Distinguish a Descriptive Terminology and a Nomenclature; separate the following terms according as they belong to one or the other:— Rose, Rosaceæ, Rose-like, Potassium, Alkaloid, Ruminant Animal, Ruminating, Ruby, Ruby-red.

5. What does Mr Mill mean by the expression **Natural Kind**?

INDEX,

of thought are the same or different in certain points. See *Judgment.*

Compatible terms are those which, though distinct, are not contradictory, and can therefore be affirmed of the same subject ; as "large" and "heavy ;" "bright-coloured" and "nauseous."

Complex conception, inference by, 87

Complex sentence, 91 ; syllogism, 158

Composition of Causes, the principle which is exemplified in all cases in which the joint effect of several causes is identical with the sum of their separate effects. *J. S. Mill.* See pp. 252, 265

Composition, fallacy of, 173

Compound sentence, 90

Comprehension of terms, see *Intension.*

Computation, 127

Concept, that which is conceived, the result of the act of conception ; nearly synonymous with general notion, idea, thought.

Conception (*con,* together ; *capio,* to take). An ambiguous term, meaning properly the action of mind in which it takes several things together, so as to form a general notion ; or again, in which it forms "a mental image of the several attributes given in any word or combination of words." *Mansel.*

Conceptualists, 13

Conclusion of syllogism, 15, 127 ; weakened, 140

Concrete terms, 20

Conditional propositions, 62, 160

Confusion of words, ambiguity from, 31

Conjugate words, those which come from the same root or stock, as *known, knowing, knowingly, knowledge.*

Connotation of terms, 39, 41 ; ought to be exactly fixed, 290

Consciousness, the immediate knowledge which the mind has of its sensations and thoughts, and, in general, of all its present operations. *Reid.*

Consectary = Corollary.

Consequence, the connection be tween antecedent and consequent but often used ambiguously for th latter.

Consequent of a hypothetical pro position, 161

Consequent or effect of a cause 240

Consequent, fallacy of the, 181

Conservation of energy, 263, 269

Consilience of Inductions, th agreement of inductions derive from different and independent serie of facts, as when we learn the mo tion of the earth by entirely differen modes of observation and reasoning *Whewell.*

Consistency of propositions, 78

Consistent terms, see *compatibl* terms.

Contingent, (*contingo,* to touch, that which may or may not happen opposed to the *necessary* and *im possible.*

Contingent matter, 80

Continuity, Law of, the principl that nothing can pass from one ex treme to another without passing through all the intermediate degrees motion, for instance, cannot be instan taneously produced or destroyed.

Contradiction, Law of, 117, 19

Contradictory terms, 24, 119 propositions, 76

Contraposition, conversion by 83, 186

Converse fallacy of accident, 17

Conversion of propositions, 82—85 with quantified predicate, 184

Convertend, 82

Coordinate propositions, 90

Copula, 16

Corollary, a proposition which fol lows immediately from another whic has been proved.

Correction of observations, 253

Correlative terms, 25

Criterion (κριτήριον, from κρίνω, t judge), any fact, rule, knowledge or means requisite to the formatio of a judgment which shall decide doubtful question.

Cross division, 105

Data, (plural of *datum,* that whic

Mill, J. S., on Connotative terms, 41; on Induction, 214; on Analogy and Induction, 227; on Observation, 235; on Terminology and Nomenclature, 294
Minor term, 128; premise, 129
Mnemonic verses, *Barbara,* &c., 144
Modal proposition, 69, 91
Modus, *ponens,* 161; *tollens,* 162
Modus, *ponendo tollens,* 166; *tollendo ponens,* 166
Moods of the syllogism, 136; according to Hamilton, 188

Name, or term, 17
Natural Classification, 280
Natural Kinds, 294
Necessary matter, 80
Necessity (*ne,* not; and *cesso,* to cease), that which always is and cannot but be.
Negation, conversion by, 83
Negative, terms, 22; propositions, 63, 83; premises, fallacy of, 133—4
Newton's experiments, 253, 259
Nomenclature, 293
Nominal definitions, 112
Nominalists, 13
Non causa pro causa, 181
Non sequitur, 181
Notion (*nosco,* to know), the action of apprehending or taking note of the various qualities of an object; or more commonly the result of that action. See *Idea, Concept.*
Notiora naturæ, 204
Novum Organum, first aphorisms of, 229
Numerically definite syllogism, 190

Object of verb, 93
Objective, that which belongs to the object of thought, the *non-ego;* opposed to *Subjective,* which see.
Obscure knowledge, 54
Observation, 231, 235.
Occasion of an event, the proximate cause, or last condition which is requisite to bring other causes into action; 239
Opposite terms, 24, 119
Opposition of propositions, 78
Organon (ὄργανον, Latin *Organum,*

Instrument), a name for Aristo logical treatises, first generally i in the 15th century, implying they may be regarded as an ins ment to assist the mind. The n was adopted by Bacon for his *Nov Organum.*

Paradox (παρά, δόξα, contrary opinion), an assertion contrary common opinion, and which ma may not prove true; often wror used to mean what is self-contra tory and absurd.
Paralogism (παραλογίζομαι, to son wrongly), a purely logical falla or breach of the rules of deduc logic.
Parity of reasoning, an express used to denote that when one c has been demonstrated, other si lar cases can be demonstrated t like course of reasoning.
Paronymous words, see *Con gate* words.
Particular propositions, 63—6,7:
Particular premises, fallacy of, 151
Partition or physical division, 1
Per accidens, conversion, 82
Perfect Figure of the Syllogi 145
Perfect knowledge, charac of, 53
Periodic changes, 250
Peripatetic Philosophy (περιπα to walk about), the name usu given to the doctrines of Arist and his followers, who are said have carried on their studies discussions while walking about halls and promenades of the Lyce
Petitio Principii, 179
Phenomenon, 240
Philosophical language, quisites of, 290
Physical definition assigns parts into which a thing may separated by partition or phys division.
Plurative propositions, 191
Polylemma, an argument of same form as a dilemma, but in wl there are more than two alternati
Porphyry, tree of, 103

MACMILLAN & CO.'S Scientific Class Books and Manuals.

NET PRICES.

THE
PRINCIPLES OF SCIENCE:
A TREATISE ON
LOGIC AND SCIENTIFIC METHOD.

BY

W. STANLEY JEVONS, LL.D., M.A., F.R.S.,

Fellow of and Professor of Political Economy in University College, London.

Reprinting.

ANATOMY.

LESSONS IN ELEMENTARY ANATOMY. By ST. GEORGE MIVART, F.R.S. With upwards of 400 Illustrations. 16mo, $1.75.

" It may be questioned whether any other work on anatomy contains in like compass so proportionately great a mass of information."—LANCET.

ASTRONOMY.

ELEMENTARY LESSONS IN ASTRONOMY. By J. NORMAN LOCKYER, F.R.S. With numerous illustrations. New Edition. 18mo, $1.25. Questions on, 40 cents.

" This book is full, clear, sound, and worthy of attention, not only as a popular exposition, but as a scientific 'Index.'"—ATHENÆUM.
"The most fascinating of elementary books on the sciences."—
NONCONFORMIST.

POPULAR ASTRONOMY. With Illustrations. By G. B. AIRY, Astronomer Royal. Seventh Edition. 16mo, cloth, $1.10.

HANDBOOK OF DESCRIPTIVE ASTRONOMY. By GEORGE F. CHAMBERS, F.R.A.S. Third Edition, enlarged, with numerous Illustrations. 8vo, $7.00.

"There is much in this Handbook to interest the general reader, while the practical worker will find an invaluable mass of information on celestial subjects, besides ample references to astronomical authorities."—PALL MALL GAZETTE.

BIOLOGY.

A COURSE OF PRACTICAL INSTRUCTION IN ELE-
MENTARY BIOLOGY. By T. H. HUXLEY, LL.D. Assisted
by H. N. MARTIN, B.A., M.B., D.Sc., Professor of Biology in
Johns Hopkins University, Baltimore. Revised Edition. 12mo,
cloth, $2.60.

*" The work is entirely practical, and should be one of the first books
read by the student of natural history, and by the student of medicine
who desires to rest his later physiological studies upon a sound elementary basis."*—MEDICAL RECORD.

*"It is impossible for an intelligent youth, with this book in his hand,
placing himself before any one of the organisms described, and carefully
following the directions given, to fail to verify each point to which his
attention is directed."*—ATHENÆUM.

BOTANY.

LESSONS IN ELEMENTARY BOTANY. By D. OLIVER,
F.R.S. With Illustrations. New Edition. 18mo, cloth, $1.10.

*This book is designed to teach the elements of Botany on Professor
Henslow's plan of selected Types and by the use of Schedules. The
earlier chapters, embracing the elements of Structural and Physiological
Botany, introduce us to the methodical study of the Ordinal Types.
The concluding chapters are entitled "How to Dry Plants" and
"How to Describe Plants."*

LECTURES ON THE PHYSIOLOGY OF PLANTS. By
JULIUS VON SACHS. Translated by H. MARSHALL WARD,
M.A., F.L.S., Fellow of Christ College, Cambridge, and Pro-
fessor of Botany in the Forestry School, R. I. E. College,
Cooper's Hill. With 455 Woodcuts. Royal 8vo, half morocco,
$8.00.

*This, with the works of " Goebel on the Classification and Mor-
phology of Plants" and "De Bary on the Vegetative Organs of the
Phanerogams and Ferns" are intended by Professor J. von Sachs to
supersede his Text-Book of Botany, the second edition of the authorized
English translation of which was published in 1882, and which it is
not proposed to reprint.*

*"One of the most lucidly and forcibly written treatises to be found
in botanical literature. . . . There is no book which may be more
unhesitatingly recommended to all who desire a thorough knowledge of
the physiology of plants. It is the work not only of the greatest living
authority on the subject, but of one who is at the same time an un-
rivaled master in the exposition of it."*—ACADEMY.

HEMISTRY.

LESSONS IN ELEMENTARY CHEMISTRY, INOR. GANIC AND ORGANIC. By HENRY E. ROSCOE, F.R.S., Professor of Chemistry in Owens College, Manchester. With numerous Illustrations. New Edition. 16mo, cloth, $1.10.

"As a standard general text-book it deserves to take a leading place." SPECTATOR.

" We unhesitatingly pronounce it the best of all our elementary :atises on Chemistry."—MEDICAL TIMES.

HE OWENS COLLEGE JUNIOR COURSE OF PRACTICAL CHEMISTRY. By FRANCIS JONES, Chemical Master in the Grammar School, Manchester. With Preface by Professor ROSCOE. 18mo, cloth, 70 cents.

SERIES OF CHEMICAL PROBLEMS. For Use in Colleges and Schools. Adapted for the Preparation of Students for the Government, Science, and Society of Arts Examinations. With a Preface by Professor ROSCOE. With Key, 18mo, cloth, 50 cents.

In the Preface Professor Roscoe says : "My experience has led me feel more and more strongly that by no method can accuracy in a iowledge of chemistry be more surely secured than by attention to the orking of well-selected problems, and Dr. Thorpe's thorough ac- iaintance with the wants of the student is a sufficient guarantee that is selection has been carefully made. I intend largely to use these iestions in my own classes, and I can confidently recommend them to l teachers and students of the science."

HEMISTRY FOR STUDENTS. By A. W. WILLIAMSON, Phil. Doc., F. R. S., Professor of Chemistry, University College London. Second Edition, with Solutions. 16mo, cloth, $2.10.

XERCISES IN PRACTICAL CHEMISTRY. By A. G. VERNON HARCOURT, M. A., F. R. S., and H. G. MADAN, M. A., Fellow of Queen's College, Oxford. Qualitative Exercises. 12mo, cloth, $2.60.

"An invaluable work for those who are beginning to learn practi- lly the beautiful science of Chemistry."—MEDICAL PRESS AND CIR- JLAR.

HEAT.

AN ELEMENTARY TREATISE ON HEAT. By BAL- FOUR STEWART, LL.D., F.R.S. Professor of Natural Philosophy at Owens College. Third Edition, enlarged. 16mo.

HEAT.—*continued.*

To this edition have been added notices of such discoveries connectea with "Heat" which have taken place since the second edition was published, and also articles on " The Molecular Theory of Gases," "The Connection between the Two Elasticities and the Two Specifu Heats," "The Velocity of Sound," and "Graphical Representations oj Physical Laws."

·LOGIC.

ELEMENTARY LESSONS IN LOGIC ; Deductive and In-ductive, with copious Questions and Examples, and a Vocabu-lary of Logical Terms.   By W. STANLEY JEVONS, M.A., Pro-fessor of Logic in Owens College, Manchester.   New Edition, 16mo, 40 cents.

"A Manual alike simple, interesting, and Scientific."—ATHENÆUM.

"It brings before the reader in a concise and very intelligible mannei the whole body of recognized logical doctrines.   Refers them to the greai principles or so-called laws of thought from which they appear to be derived, furnishes the student with a variety of examples, and indicates the sources where he may find a full discussion of the subjeci treated."—SPECTATOR.

THE ELEMENTS OF DEDUCTIVE LOGIC, designed mainly for the use of Junior Students in the Universities.   By T. FOWLER, M.A., Fellow and Tutor of Lincoln College, Ox-ford.   Sixth Edition, corrected and revised, with a Collection o: Examples.   16mo, cloth, 90 cents.

"Mr. Fowler appears to us to have cccomplished his task skillfull; and usefully.   His book contains all the essential details of its subject, is clearly expressed, and embodies the result of much accuratt thought."—GUARDIAN.

THE ELEMENTS OF INDUCTIVE LOGIC, designed mainl; for the use of Students in the Universities.   By the same Author.   Third Edition, corrected and revised.   16mo, 387 pp.; cloth, $1.50.

"A most useful hand-book, mainly intended for University students, but which will be a convenient book, also, for those whose student day. are over, but who wish to keep up with more recent methods."—LITER-ARY CHURCHMAN.

MORAL PHILOSOPHY.

HAND-BOOK OF MORAL PHILOSOPHY.   By the Rev HENRY CALDERWOOD, LL.D., Professor of Moral Philosophy University of Edinburgh.   Third Edition.   12mo, $1.50.

IORAL PHILOSOPHY.—*continued.*

"A compact and useful work. . . . will be an assistant to many udents outside the author's own University."—GUARDIAN.

" It is, we feel convinced, the best hand-book on the subject, intellectially and morally, and does infinite credit to its author."—STANDARD.

HYSICS.

LESSONS IN ELEMENTARY PHYSICS. By BALFOUR STEWART, F.R.S. With numerous Illustrations. New Edition. 16mo, $1.10.

Questions on the same, by Prof. THOMAS H. CORE. 40 cents.

RACTICAL PHYSICS. For Schools and the Junior Students of Colleges. By BALFOUR STEWART, M.A., LL.D., F.R.S., and W. W. HALDANE GEE, B.Sc.

> Vol. 1. Electricity and Magnetism. Illustrated. 16mo, 60 cents.
>
> Vol. 2. In preparation.
>
> Vol. 3. In preparation.

ESSONS IN ELEMENTARY PRACTICAL PHYSICS. By the same authors.

> Vol. 1. General Physical Processes. 12mo, $1.50.

" In this, the first volume of what will evidently be an elaborate work i practical physics, the authors have treated of general physical prosses only, i.e., *of the methods employed in the laboratory for the exact 'termination or measurement of the geometrical and mechanical prortions of bodies. It is impossible to overestimate the importance of iese fundamental measures, for upon them depends the accuracy of 'most all physical work."*—NATURE.

> Vol. 2. Electricity and Magnetism. 12mo, 2.25.

" The second volume of this admirable work—succinctly and admirably iscribed by its brief title—fully bears out the promise of the first. An lmirable and most useful work."—INDUSTRIES.

> Vol. 3. Optics, Heat, and Sound. *In Press.*

PHYSICAL GEOGRAPHY.

ELEMENTARY LESSONS IN PHYSICAL GEOGRAPHY. By ARCHIBALD GEIKIE, F.R.S., Professor of Geology, etc., Edinburgh. With numerous Illustrations and Colored Maps. New Edition. 16mo, $1.10. Questions on, 40 cents.

"Anything more different from and more superior to the ordinary school-book it is impossible to imagine. Were text-books adopted on their merits we should expect to see this one supplant all others on Physical Geography."—CHRISTIAN UNION.

" We heartily commend this little volume to all teachers and students of Physical Geography."—NATIONAL JOURNAL OF EDUCATION.

"The subject is treated in such a manner as to engage the interest of the young student, and to excite him to observations and investigations for himself."—HARTFORD COURANT.

PHYSIOLOGY.

LESSONS IN ELEMENTARY PHYSIOLOGY. By T. H. HUXLEY, F.R.S. With numerous Illustrations. New Edition. 16mo, cloth, $1.10. Questions on, 40 cents.

This book describes and explains, in a series of graduated lessons, the principles of Human Physiology, or the Structure and Functions of the Human Body.

"Pure gold throughout."—GUARDIAN.

"Unquestionably the clearest and most complete elementary treatise on this subject that we possess in any language."—WESTMINSTER REVIEW.

A COURSE OF ELEMENTARY PRACTICAL PHYSIOLOGY. By M. FOSTER, M.D., F.R.S. Assisted by J. M. LANGLEY, B.A. New Edition. 12mo, cloth, $2.00.

"This work will prove of great value to the teacher of physiology, as an aid to the preparation of an eminently practical course of lectures and demonstrations of elementary experimental physiology. Its chief utility, however, will be to the intelligent student, who, armed with a dissecting case, a microscope, and the book, will be enabled to pass his summer vacation in a manner at once interesting and profitable."—MEDICAL RECORD.

A TEXT-BOOK OF PHYSIOLOGY. By M. FOSTER, M.A. M.D., F.R.S. Fourth Edition, revised. 12mo, cloth, $5.50.

"After a careful perusal of the entire work we can cordially recommend it, both to the student and to the practitioner, as being one of the best text-books of Physiology extant, the facts recorded being as reliable

SCIENTIFIC CLASS BOOKS. 7

PHYSIOLOGY.—*continued.*

as the reasonings are sound, while the arrangement and style are alike excellent."—LONDON LANCET.

"I recommend it to my students as the latest, and in some respects the best, Physiology in the English Language."—From a Letter from Professor BURT G. WILDER.

POLITICAL ECONOMY.

MANUAL OF POLITICAL ECONOMY. By HENRY FAWCETT, M.P., University of Cambridge. Fifth Edition, revised and enlarged. 12mo, cloth, 663 pp, $2.65.

" It forms one of the best introductions to the principles of the science, and its practical applications."—DAILY NEWS.

" The book is written throughout with admirable force, clearness and brevity, every important part of the subject being duly considered."—EXAMINER.

POLITICAL ECONOMY FOR BEGINNERS. By MILLICENT G. FAWCETT. New Edition. 18mo, 75 cents.

" We cannot conceive a book more fitted for popularizing this science than the clear, compact and comprehensive treatise, for which we are indebted to Mrs. Fawcett."—DAILY NEWS.

" The relations of capital and labor have never been more simply or more clearly expounded."—CONTEMPORARY REVIEW.

A MANUAL OF POLITICAL ECONOMY. By J. E. THOROLD ROGERS, M.A., formerly Professor of Political Economy, Oxford. Second Edition, with Index. 16mo, cloth, $1.10.

" Political economy is not a subject of which, in these days, sensible men can afford to be ignorant. Much of the ignorance which prevails respecting it will be cut at the root, if the able manual of Mr. Rogers is used extensively in our schools and colleges."—GUARDIAN.

STEAM.

AN ELEMENTARY TREATISE OF STEAM. By JOHN PERRY, B.E.; Whitworth Scholar, etc., late Lecturer in Physics at Clifton College. With numerous Woodcuts, Numerical Examples and Exercises. 18mo, $1.10.

"Mr. Perry has, in this compact little volume, brought together an immense amount of information, new told, regarding steam and its application, not the least of its merits being that it is suited to the capacities alike of the tyro in engineering science or the better grade of artisan."—IRON.

MATHEMATICAL WORKS,

BY

I. TODHUNTER, M.A.F.R.S.,

OF ST. JOHN'S COLLEGE, CAMBRIDGE.

"Mr. Todhunter is chiefly known to students of Mathematics ‹ the author of a series of admirable Mathematical text-books, whie possess the rare qualities of being clear in style, and absolutely fr from mistakes, typographical or other."—SATURDAY REVIEW.

THE ELEMENTS OF EUCLID. For the use of Colleges an Schools. 18mo, 90 cents. Key, $1.75.

ALGEBRA FOR BEGINNERS. With numerous Example 16mo, 75 cents. Key, 12mo, $1.75.

MENSURATION FOR BEGINNERS. With numerous E: amples. 18mo, 75 cents. Key, $1.90.

MECHANICS FOR BEGINNERS. With numerous example 18mo, $1.10. Key, $1.75.

TRIGONOMETRY FOR BEGINNERS. With numerous exar ples. 18mo, 75 cents. Key, 12mo, $2.25.

ALGEBRA. For the use of Colleges and Schools. Seventh Editio with new Chapters. 12mo, $1.80. Key, $2.60.

PLANE TRIGONOMETRY. For the use of Colleges and Schoo! 12mo, $1.30. Key, $2.60.

A TREATISE ON SPHERICAL TRIGONOMETRY. 12m $1.25.

AN ELEMENTARY TREATISE ON THE THEORY C EQUATIONS. Third Edition. 12mo, $1.80.

PLANE COÖRDINATE GEOMETRY, as applied to the Straig Line and the Conic Sections. 12mo, $1.80. Key, $2.60.

A TREATISE ON THE DIFFERENTIAL CALCULUS. Wi numerous examples. 12mo, $2.60. Key, $2.60.

A TREATISE ON THE INTEGRAL CALCULUS AND I1 APPLICATIONS. Fourth Edition. 12mo, $2.60.

MACMILLAN & CO., 112 FOURTH AVENUE, N.Y